Your Complete Forecast 2017 Horoscope

Your Complete Forecast
2017
Horoscope

BEJAN DARUWALLA
With
NASTUR DARUWALLA

RB Ranvir Books

HARPER
element

First published in India in 2016 by Harper Element
An imprint of HarperCollins *Publishers*

Copyright © Bejan Daruwalla 2016

P-ISBN: 978-93-5264-199-4
E-ISBN: 978-93-5264-200-7

2 4 6 8 10 9 7 5 3 1

Bejan Daruwalla asserts the moral right
to be identified as the author of this work.

The views and opinions expressed in this book are the author's own and the facts are
as reported by him, and the publishers are not in any way liable for the same.

All rights reserved. No part of this publication may be reproduced,
stored in a retrieval system, or transmitted, in any form or by any means,
electronic, mechanical, photocopying, recording or otherwise,
without the prior permission of the publishers.

HarperCollins *Publishers*
A-75, Sector 57, Noida, Uttar Pradesh 201301, India
1 London Bridge Street, London, SE1 9GF, United Kingdom
Hazelton Lanes, 55 Avenue Road, Suite 2900, Toronto, Ontario M5R 3L2
and 1995 Markham Road, Scarborough, Ontario M1B 5M8, Canada
25 Ryde Road, Pymble, Sydney, NSW 2073, Australia
195 Broadway, New York, NY 10007, USA

Typeset in 10.5/13.7 Sabon
By Saanvi Graphics Noida

Printed and bound at
MicroPrints (India), New Delhi

Contents

Aries (21 March–20 April)	1
Taurus (21 April–21 May)	31
Gemini (22 May–22 June)	59
Cancer (23 June–22 July)	90
Leo (23 July–22 August)	122
Virgo (23 August–22 September)	155
Libra (23 September–22 October)	188
Scorpio (23 October–22 November)	221
Sagittarius (23 November–22 December)	256
Capricorn (23 December–22 January)	289
Aquarius (23 January–22 February)	322
Pisces (23 February–22 March)	356

Achievements	393
World Horoscope 2017	397
Key Dates For 2017	406
Your Birth Time Reveals You	413
The Aquarian Age	416
Jupiter in Virgo	417
Important Announcement	418

ARIES

21 March–20 April

Ganesha's Master Key: Work and willpower

'O Lord, make my life full of divine inspiration, that it may become productive only of good. Free me from all pettiness and narrowness. Help me to keep my thoughts fixed on that which is vast and majestic. Expand my heart and enlarge my mind that I may be able to contain Thee and give myself up wholly to Thee.'

– SWAMI PARAMANANDA

This is the real spiritual message for all born under this sign. The important traits are: Enthusiastic, energetic, active; Planning, leading, mentally polarized; Assertive, purely being; Exemplifying an intangible quality; Having the courage of convictions; Being true to the self, forming new ideas; Pioneering new inspired ways of thought; Directing spiritual power into concrete form; Asserting the will of the soul.

By Western astrology it is your personality which will have an effect and influence on your destiny. Therefore, it is very clear that if you know who you are, and what you can do, success will be easier and even more enjoyable. This is my own personal point of view. This is what I really specialize in. This is what I want to emphasize with all my power and observation. These traits in the given order apply very specially to everyone born under this sign. Read them again and again.

Your Beauty-scope: It won't pay to hide your light under a bushel to play a coy, modest, look-but-touch-me-not type. Better put on royal purple or red, with shoes to match, and step out in style. For everyone born under this sign, any sort of headgear would be eye-catching. Normally, the movements of one typically belonging to this sign are rapid but not graceful and flowing. Perhaps dancing could help here. As you are large-boned types and rather hairy, a bit of covering up will certainly help. Since diet and beauty are bedfellows these days, the food favoured for all those born under this sign are lettuce, walnuts, apples, radishes, beans, fish more than meat, spinach, onions, cabbage. Besides red, a mix of red and white will show you off to a supreme advantage! Lucky herbs and flowers are geranium, honeysuckle, peppermint, crowfoot and mustard.

CENTRAL IDEA

Marriage, Foreign affairs, Alliances, Journeys, Collaborations, Ties

Ganesha says that my son Nastur comes straight to the point. This is what he has to say: The year 2017 will be about matters regarding sex partner, marriage, adultery, lust or passion, nature and character of spouse, sexual union, secret love affairs, journeys, deviation from one's path, partnership in business, overt enemies, quarrels, theft, loss of memory, recovery of lost wealth, progress, attainment of status, the grandfather, the brother's son and death.

Other significant points to note: Connections, contacts, reaching out to people and places; Journeys, ceremonies, legal matters; Public relations and competition, change of surroundings; Collaborations and cooperations, wedding/engagement; Blowing hot and cold in relationships; Change of locale; Contests; Sales and public relations; Marketing and distribution; Opening of new branches; Expansion at all levels, thanks to Jupiter in the seventh angle; Being flexible, accommodating, more accepting of views other than your own will help.

The year 2017 will be wonderful for your inspiration, growth, knowledge, wisdom, pilgrimages, immigration, spirituality, yoga, meditation, publicity, image building and active preparations for big new projects, ventures, collaborations, joint efforts and so on. I am predicting for you mighty new achievements and a stepping stone for the future provided you work hard and wisely. This applies very specially to you because by Western astrology Saturn is in Sagittarius. I will not go into the technicalities of it.

Mars, your main planet, will be in your own sign from 28 January to 9 March. It means achievement and progress. Venus, planet of love, luxury and marriage, will be in your sign from 4 February to 2 April and again from 28 April to 5 September. Enjoy and be happy. Live and laugh. Mercury, the planet of messages and travel, will be in your sign from 14 to 31 March. This will help you plan about travelling. The other months are December, April and June.

My father gives great importance to the outer planets – Neptune, Pluto and Uranus. I do not give them great importance because I feel they have a greater impact and meaning for countries and not individuals. Therefore, I am not taking them into consideration.

September to November, a little health care will be needed. I will give you a very broad and important hint which I shall elucidate in the 2018 yearly forecast. The year will be very important for finance, investment, business and commerce.

I agree totally with my father that the monthly round-up is very important. Here it is.

MONTHLY ROUND-UP

January: Parents, in-laws, work, rewards, family, the effort you put in. **February**: Contacts and group activities, gains and joys. **March**: Expenses, health, but God's grace and success in ventures, fine connections and collaborations. **April**: Confidence, success, charm. **May**: Finances, family, food, fortune, the four Fs. **June**: Communications and contacts at all levels. **July**: House, home, family. **August**: Romance, children, creativity. **September**: Work and health improvement measures. **October**: Marriage, relationships, contacts, trips, ties and opposition. **November**: Loans, funds, health, taxes, accidents, legal matters. **December**: Publicity, publishing, fame, religious rites, matters to do with parents and in-laws; in short, being in the public eye.

Money: I am the face of modern India which is ambitious, enterprising, willing to take a few calculated risks and certainly in for a good, honest, comfortable lifestyle. Therefore, money is mighty important. You will have a better chance to make money from April to June and from December to February next year. The months of May and February will be the most important. I am not God; I may go wrong. But I do believe money and good times will be yours during these months.

Happiness Quota: I have great respect for my father. My father gives me the right to be free and independent, and to think as I like. He does not force me into anything. But I agree with my father that happiness is most important in life. I personally give you 87 per cent.

Uranus will be in Aries till 14 May 2018: I don't normally write about planets like Uranus impacting personal charts; they impact countries more. But since Uranus is in Aries till mid-2018, let me say a few words. Uranus brings change, and change can be upsetting, even exhilarating and exciting. Uranus plays an important role as the provocateur, the bringer of the cosmic wake-up call for both individuals and the collective as a whole. Uranus is called the 'Divine Awakener' and the influence of Uranus on a generation is revealed through innovations, breakthroughs, shifts in perception, etc.

MONTH BY MONTH

January: You begin the new year with a bang that can be heard light years away. Ego drives run high. Mid-month sees you on a roller coaster of entangled emotions. It could be a love affair that has gone awry or a family dispute or even an altercation with friends that has upset you. Your emotions are in ferment. You are pushed to the wall with domestic demands. You are gripped with intensity as the month ends. This could well be an explosive phase. You are all fire and fury. There could be experimentation of all kinds, from the sublime to the bizarre.

February: There is stability and you roll up your sleeves and get down to the hard task of making a living. You make wise investments and ensure that your family is well taken care of. *This* is the time for consolidation and preparation for the great leap forward. Mid-month sees you full of love, passion and intensity. There are ego drives, arrogance, angry outbursts, altercations and disputes. Use your free will to detach from explosive situations. As the month ends, there is travel and undue risk taking. Money also flows out of your fingers. Luckily, the softer side of your personality makes its presence felt and saves the day. If you are already in a spiritual group, you bond deeper with fellow seekers.

March: Social outreach is the new mantra and you are doing just that in fast-forward mode. You are filled with new ideas, hopes, dreams and aspirations and want to share it with the cosmos. This is a time for ideating. Mid-month sees a period of high achievement. You make for the home run in a dash of bravado, splendour and swashbuckling brilliance. There are stability, balance and rich rewards. You are blessed. As the month ends, you propel ahead with an unseen energy. You win the approval of your peer group, accolades and applause, rewards and awards. You are unstoppable.

April: There are maudlin times. You drive down memory lane and cry over spilt milk. The energies are powerful mid-month and you opt for new adventures. There is love in the air and fun times. As the month ends, you set your sights high. Superlative performances are yours for the asking. There are holidays, parties, travel, alumni meetings, engagements, marriages, possibly even an addition to the family.

May: You are pushing ahead on all cylinders. No distraction can deter you. There is new-found passion and intensity in your life. Mid-month sees headway at work, but your mind is like a monkey on a stick. It needs to be tethered. As the month ends, you are dredged by pessimism and negativity. You want to be delivered from this moment and look for answers. You network with frenzy. Family life can be scattered like your energies.

June: There is hard work ahead. There are domestic calls and a health issue that needs attention. There are bonds, wills, inheritances, and other fiscal instruments to deal with. Mid-month is a good period. There are love, travel, expenses and many fancy purchases. The month-end sees a highly creative phase. Writers and painters excel. You could be in line for some sort of recognition. There are powerful psychological energies at play. You are filled with joy and happiness and look at spiritual growth.

July: Your life has many possibilities. You deliberate over them and look at all options before making a move. Yoga, natural healing and a stint at a health spa may be on the cards. Mid-month you are filled with the power of a thousand horses. You strike hard and true. You go for the jugular and make life happen. As the month ends, it is a good time for business expansion. There is also the possibility of international travel. There are windfalls as money fills your coffers from unexpected quarters. There could even be crazed love.

August: You start the month looking for answers to life situations which are not so rosy right now. There is stability mid-month and your monkey mind is tethered. You roll up your sleeves and get to work. There are innumerable domestic calls too which take your time. As the month ends, many frontiers open up dramatically. There are unpredictable changes in the way you define your individuality. You initiate changes that allow you new freedom and fresh experience.

September: Your emotions are softened. You are hailed as a valuable team player. The married bask in contentment and courting couples feel that they have met their soulmate. Mid-month sees you bask in a strong sense of well-being. You are in harmony and look at rejuvenation and restoration. You may enlist in a yoga centre or a health spa. As the month ends, the mood is quiet and mellow. You radiate warmth and love. Your mind is also sharp and alive. You are honest and forthright and win kudos for your position on several contentious issues. Your ambitions are also aroused.

October: This is a good period. Make the most of it. There could be business expansion and foreign travel. Children could be leaving the nest and you could also have an addition to the family. Mid-month sees some domestic disruptions. There are emotional issues and possibly petty squabbles. In the midst of it all, you make valuable investments, plan ahead and ensure a nest egg. As the month ends, you are filled with dreams and fantasies and let your mind fly like a kite. You live in fantasies and illusions. You network with all and sundry. There is powerful intensity but it is all scattered.

November: You are back on terra firma and in balance. There is material success. You make miracles happen. There is new love too. Mid-month sees many purchases and money runs through your fingers. You are propelled by determination, stamina and perseverance. As the month ends, you are in creative mode and make new associations. You are also extravagant and self-indulgent. There are ego drives and altercations.

December: You are in communication mode. The year is fast ending and you want to be in touch with all your buddies and loved ones. Family life has unexpected twists and turns. There could be rifts at the workplace too. Mid-month sees stability and balance. You have set targets for yourself and work towards achieving them. Family life is stable and children bring joy. As the month ends, there could be work-related travel. There are new associations as new vistas open up. This period is propitious for new beginnings. Ego drives are high and you are powered by an unseen force. There is success in all your undertakings.

WEEKLY REVIEW (BY PHASES OF THE MOON)

5 January: First Quarter in Aries

The first quarter is in your sign and you begin the new year with a bang that can be heard light years away. 'Elegance over ego,' says Danielle LaPorte, the life coach. That should be the motto now as ego drives run high. You want to be everywhere at the same time and do everything all at once. This will be a tough task. Passions rule you. You play the field and if you have recently broken up, you look hard for a replacement. It is a busy time with work and play; there is no let-up. Ganesha blesses you as you start the year with sound and fury, quite different from the emotional start of last year. Now, a bit about Aries. This adds to the reading and I shall repeat what is written in stone. Aries is symbolized by the ram. A ram's horn is part of a cornucopia, the 'horn of plenty', symbolizing abundance. Those born under this sign are said to be leaders and pioneers. Aries is the first sign of the zodiac. It is an active, energetic sign. Generally, people born under this sign are direct, straightforward, and uncomplicated. Famous people under this sign include Edgar Wallace, Ayrton Senna, Al Gore, Rene Descartes, Arnold Toynbee, Bob Woodward, Sir Charles Chaplin, David Lean, Eddie Murphy, Wilbur Wright, Jackie Chan, Leonardo Da Vinci and Lady Gaga, among others. You sure do keep great company!

12 January: Full Moon in Cancer

The year starts with a bang but you are soon on a roller coaster of entangled emotions. It could be a love affair that has gone awry or a family dispute or even an altercation with friends that has upset you no end. Your emotions are in ferment. It is easy to pass the buck, but remember that you attract what you need and are the centre of *your* universe. The buck starts and stops with you, and endless complaining won't help. Be a winner and not a whiner. Ganesha agrees with me. You are pushed to the wall with domestic demands, ill health of loved ones and even the little challenges of life, like waiting endlessly in a queue for a child's admission to school or to pay a bill or meet the authorities. All this is a part of the game of life and you will have to play it hard. Good luck!

19 January: Last Quarter in Scorpio

You are gripped with intensity. You are fed up with the status quo and want to take a break from it. It is a make-or-break situation and you want to go all out to achieve your ends. There is trouble at the work front and you could be the victim of treachery and deceit. Politics rears its ugly head and you are caught in the crossfire. There could also be a visit to the doctor. All the unease could take a toll on your health. Find 'me' time, meditate or do yoga. Ganesha holds your hand.

28 January: New Moon in Aquarius

Mars is in Aries from 28 January to 9 March and this could well be an explosive phase. You are all fire and fury. The new moon is in Aquarius, and you are filled with zany ideas and look at life with unusual glasses. You may elope or start a new political campaign or even take a trek to an offbeat location. There could be experimentation of all kinds, from the sublime to the bizarre. I quote from the world's oldest spiritual text, the Bhagavadgita: 'The mind acts as an enemy for those who do not learn to control it.' While it is exciting to chart a new course and dodge the norm, ensure that you don't cut the branch that you are sitting on. Mars is like the volcano of vitality inside you and influences endurance, persistence and discipline. Mars was named for the Roman god of war, and is also known as 'the bright and burning one'. Red is the colour of Mars, and it stimulates the dynamic, potent and fertile drives that power our lives. Mars rules physical energy and action and governs energy, strength, courage, life force and expansion. Well-placed Mars endows powerful energy and an indomitable will to succeed. Mars propels us like an ignited rocket. It is an important energy since it determines how we pursue what we want to achieve in life. In short, Mars represents energy, force, violence, aggression, sports, combat, wars, battles, accidents, operations. Mars in your own sign gives energy, courage and a very positive attitude. Ganesha watches over you and that helps.

4 February: First Quarter in Taurus

You are blessed with the stabilizing influence of Taurus. You roll up your sleeves and get down to the hard task of making a living. This is a wonderful time for those playing the market; you strike pay dirt. You make wise investments and ensure that your family is well taken care of. Ganesha is happy for you. Soon, you will be scorching the tarmac like a runaway race car. But this is the time for consolidation and preparation for the great leap forward. Passion follows you and you play the field. Life is calling you for the dance and you readily accept.

11 February: Full Moon in Leo

You are full of love, passion and intensity. There are ego drives, arrogance, angry outbursts, altercations, disputes, police and court cases. Love affairs and the inevitable break-up may also happen. I am not God and these are just gentle proddings. I do not have your personal chart and astrology never compels. I hope I am wrong. Use your free will to detach from explosive situations. You could lose out on very valuable associations if you doggedly stick to your position. Look at the other person's point of view and do not take every remark as a personal affront. Learn to be a team player. That is my message to you. Ganesha agrees. 'Nature does not hurry, yet everything is accomplished,' said Lao-tzu. When the time is ripe, it will all happen. There is no point in rushing things, getting impatient, and bruised.

18 February: Last Quarter in Sagittarius

You are moving ahead fast and determined. You want to make up for lost time. There is travel and undue risk taking. Money also flows out of your fingers. You shop till you drop in a gigantic display of careless and ceaseless extravagance. 'There are no fixtures in nature. The universe is fluid,' said Ralph Waldo Emerson. You may need to be grounded lest it all get out of hand. You are hungry for power and pelf and in this phase do not know how to use it. Apply the brakes, advises Ganesha. Or take a step back from the adrenaline rush and be mindful of your actions.

26 February: New Moon in Pisces

Luckily, the softer side of your personality makes its presence felt. You make time for the mellow aspects of life. You attend concerts, poetry readings and film festivals, and just hang out with friends. You realize that you need a handle on your overbearing emotions. You may go looking for a guru and take to esoteric reading, yantra, tantra and mantra. If you are already in a spiritual group, you bond deeper with the teacher and fellow seekers. Ganesha blesses you.

5 March: First Quarter in Gemini

You are making contact with the whole wide world with the latest marvels of technology. Social outreach is the new mantra and you are doing just that in fast-forward mode. You are filled with new ideas, hopes, dreams and aspirations and want to share it all with the cosmos. This is not a time for concrete results or disciplined hard work; it is a time for ideating and thinking things out and aloud. You take a step back, survey the field, and then decide on your course of action. Ganesha holds your hand as you navigate tricky, but certainly not treacherous, waters.

12 March: Full Moon in Virgo

As you approach your birth period, beneficial Mercury goads you on. It is in your sign from 14 to 31 March. This can be a fortnight of high achievement. Don't spare the horse as you make for the home run in a dash of bravado, splendour and swashbuckling brilliance. There are stability, balance and rich rewards. You are blessed, says Ganesha. Mercury, the mighty, all-powerful planet is in your sign now. It favours travels, meetings, conferences, interviews, trips, more brainpower, contacts, communication, correspondence and contracts. Mercury has a special connection with the circuits of the brain. Chess, crossword and other such games belong to Mercury. Also, short-distance runners and spin bowlers are controlled by Mercury. Mercury, in short, is the ambassador and salesman of the zodiac. Mercury is the symbol of news, views, messages, interviews, contacts, communications, travel and transport. Mercury gives an impetus to all of the above in the sun sign where it is located. Messages and trips are the special characteristics of Mercury.

20 March: Last Quarter in Capricorn

The last quarter is in Capricorn and you are propelling ahead with an unseen energy. It is all magical as you achieve all that you dream of. You win the approval of your peer group, accolades and applause, rewards and awards. Those working with the less privileged earn special mention from the government. You ride high and surf the waters like a champion surfer navigating the Pacific Ocean in a tornado on one leg. You are unstoppable. There is little time for family life. It is not that you have discarded your loved ones; it is just that you have other distractions that line your pocket and ego well. Ganesha is delighted.

28 March: New Moon in Aries

You propel away without a pause. Good times continue and you are on a roll. The new moon is in your sign and you can do no wrong in this phase. You are on a bull run. Cash in. 'The measure of a man is what he does with power,' said Plato. Yes, wisely said. I repeat, let not ego drives mar the beauty of the moment. Use the energies well and you will be remembered for posterity. There are love and longing too, and your heart strings are pulled. Ganesha watches with interest and some amusement.

3 April: First Quarter in Cancer

You play a maudlin tune. You drive down memory lane and cry over spilt milk. *If* and *but* are potent words but you have to live in the present. Your mind is your world; tune into the right vibrations. We are all subject to mood swings and changes in biorhythms and perspectives. Depression is a part of human existence but ensure that it doesn't ensnare you. Domestic life also comes calling and you take a break from the hectic upward mobility of your life. 'The real enemy of happiness is the mind's fixations and delusions. Look at the situation differently; see the truth, and the suffering is less. If you have the right mind, you can overcome anything – you can be happy, no matter what,' said the Dalai Lama. Ganesha agrees wholeheartedly.

11 April: Full Moon in Libra

The full moon is in Libra and this is also your birth period. The cumulative energies are powerful in an esoteric way. You step aside from the beaten path and opt for new adventures. You weigh the pros and cons of every move and then decide that it is party time and let your hair down. The bubbly flows, there is love in the air, and fun times follow. Friends, loved ones, old and new paramours drop by. Life is calling you to the dance and you cannot refuse. Of course you don't. The subcontinent is sizzling and so are you. Ganesha is happy.

19 April: Last Quarter in Capricorn

'Seek not to follow in the footsteps of men of old; seek what they sought,' said Matsuo Basho, the poet. Mercury is once again in your sign from 21 April to 15 May. The good times just never seem to cease. Use the beneficial influence of the planets well. You have it going for you for over a month and with the influence of Capricorn this week your sights are set high. You are determined to achieve a lot, and you will. Superlative performances are yours for the asking; also, there are money and honey, rewards and awards, applause and accolades. Ganesha is delighted for you. Family life has nothing to croon about, but that doesn't mean it is ruffled.

26 April: New Moon in Taurus

The going gets even better with Venus in your sign from 28 April to 5 June. The gods are being kind. You have the luck of the draw. There are holidays, parties, travel, alumni meetings, engagements, marriages, possibly even an addition to the family. You make expensive purchases and love lures you into several indiscreet alliances. Ganesha watches as you slaughter the bowling on the front foot in demonic fashion. This is a metaphor for the good life that has unassumingly latched on to you for better or for worse. With the new moon in Taurus the only direction you are headed is forward.

3 May: First Quarter in Leo

You are pushing ahead on all cylinders and nothing can come in the way. You are like an avalanche in the Andes, like a migratory bird or like salmon making the long journey home across thousands of kilometres. Like them, your sight is fixed and you allow no distraction to deter you. Along with the heat and dust of the subcontinent (that is if you live here as I do) is new-found passion with intensity as you plough new furrows. Money flows in and out of your account. Good times roll and you put on unwanted lard. Discipline is most certainly not your handmaiden. You break all the rules and could even land in a soup. These are mere indications. Astrology never compels. Ganesha watches.

10 May: Full Moon in Scorpio

'It isn't what you have, or who you are, or where you are, or what you are doing that makes you happy or unhappy; it is what you think about,' said Dale Carnegie. You are filled with the intensity of Scorpio and there are love and longing which cannot be concealed. There is headway at work, but your mind is like a monkey on a stick. It needs to be tethered. You want to be everywhere and interfere in people's lives as though you own them and their minds. You live in a glass house too, so you cannot afford to cast stones. Ganesha wishes you well.

19 May: Last Quarter in Aquarius

Your soul is being dredged by pessimism and negativity. You feel like a loser and could get into severe depression. Of course, I do not have your personal chart and could be wrong. But these are the tendencies of the period. You are sending these signals to the cosmos. 'Believe in an abundant universe,' says Danielle LaPorte. Yes, do that, I say too. You look for yantra and mantra and go looking for a guru. You want to be delivered from this moment and look for answers. You are in torment, and it hurts. It is not your normal style and you will return to the bounty of creation soon. Until then, you wrestle with your demons. Ganesha holds your hand and steers you to safety.

25 May: New Moon in Gemini

The new moon is in Gemini and you are networking with frenzy. You have been in a rut and you want to break out. What better way than reaching out to all and sundry and unburdening yourself. You are filled with new ideas, and a chance acquaintance will have a significant impact on you. This person could be from another culture and be much older and could hold your hand metaphorically and lead you out of the woods. Family life can also be scattered like your energies. Ganesha blesses you.

1 June: First Quarter in Virgo

The first quarter is in Virgo and there you have balance and stability. You roll up your sleeves and get down to the hard task of making a living. There are domestic calls and a health issue that needs attention. If you have been off the rails for some time you need to get back on track and find discipline. There are bonds, wills, inheritances, and other fiscal instruments to deal with. You go through the fine print with a magnifying glass. Nothing escapes your eagle eye. The week is soft and mellow, with time spent at home and with the family. Nothing exceptional or out of the ordinary. Enjoy, says Ganesha.

9 June: Full Moon in Sagittarius

You have had your rest and now you propel through life like a gazelle in the Serengeti National Park. This is a good period; make the most of it. This is marked by love, travel, expenses and many fancy purchases. Ganesha journeys with you and you couldn't ask for a better travel companion. Money creeps into your pocket and flows out. Your passions and energies are at a high point. Use your free will to steer your life in the direction that you want it to take.

17 June: Last Quarter in Pisces

This is another mellow but highly creative phase. Writers and painters excel. You could be in line for some sort of recognition from the government. According to Deepak Chopra, 'If we want peace we become that peace; if we want love, we become the love within us; if we want abundance or health, we contact and become that part of our Self, which is always content, happy and healthy. At that core level of your life those statements are not false. By gently allowing our intentions to drop into that state of silence and joy, we put ourselves in the best position for those intentions to manifest.' You have a wonderful opportunity to do just that. Manifest the right intention and, like a genie, it will appear and take hold of you. There are powerful psychological energies at play. You could also wallow down memory lane and play a maudlin tune. Like I always say, it is most unnecessary, but is, at the same time, a part of human existence. We all have to suffer our moods and biorhythms. Ganesha holds your hand as family life could run into some turbulence.

24 June: New Moon in Cancer

This is time for friends and loved ones. You are filled with joy and happiness, and look at spiritual growth. You are seriously working towards a higher consciousness. You are amiable and well mannered. People flock to you and you top the popularity charts. You delve into the deeper aspects of life as you gaze intently at the mysteries of the universe. Lovers walk in and out of your life and you sample all the offerings. Ganesha is bewildered. Evidently, a lot is happening in your life!

1 July: First Quarter in Libra

Your life has many possibilities. You deliberate over them and look at all options before making a move. You spend too much time working the pros and cons and could miss out on gilt-edged chances. After all, it is being the right person in the right place at the right time that matters. If there has been a chronic health problem, it may reappear after a prolonged remission. Yoga, natural healing and a stint at a health spa will help. Ganesha watches over you.

9 July: Full Moon in Capricorn

The full moon is in Capricorn and you are filled with the power of a thousand horses. You strike hard and true. I am a published poet and also a former professor of English. So I make it a point to pepper my predictions with quotes to give you added value for your buck. I call it 'Predictions Plus'. According to Tom Stoppard, the British playwright, 'A healthy attitude is contagious. But don't wait to catch it from others; be a carrier.' You don't need any prodding in the phase you are in. You go for the jugular and make life happen. You are like Sehwag in his heyday, blasting the boundary even when he is on the verge of a historic milestone. You take risks and make miracles happen. Domestic life rumbles along on a full belly. Ganesha blesses you.

16 July: Last Quarter in Aries

The last quarter is in your sign and you are all over the place making your presence felt in no uncertain terms.

This is a good time for business expansion. Freelancers bag lucrative contracts and life looks up. Those in the corporate world and those playing the markets strike pay dirt. There is also the possibility of international travel and a home away from home. Life is humming happily for you. Ganesha is happy.

23 July: New Moon in Leo

'If you don't make mistakes, you're not working on hard enough problems. And that's a big mistake,' said F. Wikzek. You are powered by Leo and will not accept being second best in what you do. There are fire and intensity, new assignments and foreign travel. There are also ego issues, altercations, brushes with the law, indiscretions and risk taking. You break the boundaries and frontiers of your existence in quest of the holy grail. The energies are powerful; tweak them well. Ganesha blesses you.

30 July: First Quarter in Scorpio

Scorpio prods you into secret deals. There are windfalls as money fills your coffers from unexpected quarters. There could even be crazed lust, or love, if you want to call it that. They are often confused. Ask me. I have seen the caprices of both over the decades. You could feel trapped by it and may even take the object of your affections to the altar. Youngsters are difficult to handle in this phase. The health of elders may be a cause of concern. This is a mixed period. Ganesha holds your hand.

7 August: Full Moon in Aquarius

'You've got to do your own growing, no matter how tall your grandfather was,' says an Irish proverb. There is a restlessness that is ailing you no end. Your soul is in pieces.

You look hard for answers and go in search of a guru. You look at tantra, yantra and mantra and enlist in several spiritual courses. You may even embark on a pilgrimage. You have to find answers to your peculiar life situation and go through the rough and tumble of life. Only empirical evidence will help. Till then, all the theory you can get hold of can only assuage you somewhat. Ganesha is with you and that is the greatest blessing. You have little time for family life. Those in matrimony may find the going difficult as you are pulled in many directions and have little time to devote to domestic demands.

15 August: Last Quarter in Taurus

There is a semblance of stability now. Your monkey mind is tethered. I quote the Buddha here: 'Though one man conquers a thousand men, a thousand times in battle, he who conquers himself is the greatest warrior.' Swami Vivekananda rightly called the mind a drunken monkey. Your mind has been playing games with you but now you realize that you cannot fritter away energy in mind games. The real world is calling and you have to dress up for the dance. There are secret liaisons, jealousy, anger, hate, negativity and possessiveness. You wrestle with it all like Sushil Kumar, the powerful Olympic medallist, and emerge victorious. Ganesha watches. You roll up your sleeves finally and get to work. There are innumerable domestic calls too, and you cannot be lost in indulgent pursuits.

21 August: New Moon in Leo

There is hard work as many frontiers open up. You sizzle with passion. Expenses mount. There could be international travel as new vistas open dramatically. There are unpredictable changes in the way you define your individuality. You could look at a complete break from your profession and your social standing. You initiate changes that allow you new freedom and fresh experience. Every change is upsetting, but with it is also a broadening of horizons and you grow as a person. There could be tensions in public and private life, but that is how it is. Ganesha journeys with you.

29 August: First Quarter in Sagittarius

There is a lot of movement, and this can be a rather tense time. There is stimulation of all kinds to keep you on your twinkletoes. If you have been bottling up domestic and work pressures they may just blow up in your face. There could be a battle between your emotions and your conscious will. You are at a crossroads and don't know which direction to take. 'We crucify ourselves between two thieves: regret for yesterday and fear of tomorrow,' said Fulton Oursler. Ganesha is with you as you seek solutions. On the plus side, there is a lot of excitement which could do you a world of good and lead you to greener pastures.

6 September: Full Moon in Pisces

Your emotions are softened by the full moon in Pisces. You are shorn of any kind of anger or resentment. Additionally, you could feel protective, vulnerable and nurturing. This endears you to others and you are hailed as a valuable team player. You spend time socializing and meeting people you care for. You could make a wonderful host as you are relaxed and chilled out, as they say these days. The married bask in contentment, and courting couples feel they have met their soulmate. Ganesha is happy too.

13 September: Last Quarter in Gemini

You bask in a strong sense of well-being. You are in harmony and enjoy the fellowship of loved ones. You want to be surrounded by familiar objects and people. This is not a time for adventures and challenges. You look instead at rejuvenation and restoration. You may enlist in a yoga centre or a health spa. 'The secret of health for both mind and body is not to mourn for the past, not to worry about the future, or not to anticipate troubles, but to live in the present moment wisely and earnestly,' said the Buddha. You do just that. After periods of intense disquiet you are now in your comfort zone and loving it. Way to go, says Ganesha.

20 September: New Moon in Virgo

The pastel shades follow you. The mood is quiet and mellow. You are in total harmony with the inner self. This is a soft and sober influence. You enjoy the fellowship of people and make room for new social contacts. You radiate warmth and love. You could also feel overtly sentimental and possessive and could get indulgent with food and drink. Discipline is not a strong point now. The Dalai Lama said, 'If you want others to be happy, practise compassion. If you want to be happy, practise compassion.' You are doing just that. Ganesha blesses you.

28 September: First Quarter in Capricorn

'First you should know who is inside you, then the same god will show you who is inside others,' said Ramana Maharshi. The first quarter is in Capricorn and your mind is sharp, alive and ready for all kinds of experiences. You look for new knowledge and understanding and find it even in the ordinariness of the mundane world. You are in contact mode and people want to be in touch with you from all over the globe. You use the marvels of modern technology with profit. You speak your mind and make it clear where you stand on every issue. There is no pulling punches. You stand your ground and are honest and forthright and win kudos for your position on several contentious issues. Your ambitions are aroused and you want to step out of ordinariness. You want renown at all costs. Ganesha watches closely lest you take the unethical route.

5 October: Full Moon in Aries

The full moon is in your sign and you are pushing hard to achieve your goals. You are like Roger Federer, the tennis ace. Your serves and slices are adroit and deceptive as you slaughter the opposition to win another Grand Slam title. You have the consistency of Sardar Singh, India's hockey captain, and the ball play and cunning of Dhanraj Pillay, the hockey legend. I am old and corpulent now but I must remind readers that I was a sprinter and hockey goalkeeper in my youth; hockey remains my first love. Time flies and we change. You will too, I dare say. This is a good period. Make the most of it. There could be business expansion and foreign travel. Children could be leaving the nest and you could also have an addition to the family. The health of elders causes concern. Ganesha is with you and that is all that matters.

12 October: Last Quarter in Cancer

You are preoccupied with domestic disruptions. You may also be working your way through an inheritance. There are emotional issues and possibly squabbles over petty and unrealistic demands. Elders may need urgent medical care and children could also be a cause for concern. You are in a spot, as no one wants to listen to you. Ganesha will; don't worry. In the midst of it all, you make valuable investments, plan ahead and ensure a nest egg. There are expenses as money runs out of your pocket without a break. This is certainly not a boring period.

19 October: New Moon in Libra

You are in an indulgent mode. You live large, almost seven-star. You are filled with dreams and fantasies and let your mind fly like a kite above the Alps. You are totally out of touch with reality and live in fantasies and illusions. You are simply unable to roll up your sleeves and slog it out. You have been there and done that. Now you want to coast along without a thought in the world. You just want to hang out and watch the birds build their nests and the squirrels scurry for food. Ganesha watches.

27 October: First Quarter in Aquarius

Your mind is everywhere, like a drunken monkey. It has no beginning or end as it slithers through the undergrowth like an aimless boa constrictor. Mahatma Gandhi said, 'The only devils in this world are those running around inside our own hearts, and that is where all our battles should be fought.' You are furiously networking with all and sundry and if you have broken up recently you look for another partner on the rebound. There is powerful intensity but it is all scattered like confetti falling from the sky. Your energies are not being garnered in a single powerful stream. Luckily, you spend time and energy on philanthropy and that dilutes the uselessness of the moment. Ganesha holds your hand.

4 November: Full Moon in Taurus

Socrates said, 'Contentment is natural wealth, luxury is artificial poverty.' The full moon is in Taurus and the tide has changed. You have sighted terra firma and are back to rolling up your sleeves and slogging away. There is material success. You see the greenbacks checking into your bank account and you are thrilled. Money does make the world go round, and there is no free lunch. This goads you into greater effort. You make miracles happen. There is new love too. You are like Greg Louganis at the Olympics, springing from the board to immortality. Like my friend, the former India captain Sourav Ganguly, you are batting with elan on the front foot, smashing the ball over the boundary line. Ganesha is thrilled.

10 November: Last Quarter in Leo

You live large and take risks. You live like there is no tomorrow. There are many purchases and money runs through your fingers like grains of sand. William Shakespeare said, 'Our doubts are traitors, and make us lose the good we oft might win, by fearing to attempt.' The Bard is right and you know it. You are like a new T20 striker playing every shot in the book and outside. You are like a wild Arabian colt running through the desert without a pause. You are propelled by determination, stamina and perseverance. You play the field and invite jealousy and offensive barbs. But who cares? You don't, Ganesha doesn't, and I don't. So continue walking the talk and talking the walk!

18 November: New Moon in Scorpio

The year began well and it seems to be ending well too. You are in creative mode and make new associations. You are also extravagant and self-indulgent, and ready to take on any and every challenge. There are ego drives and altercations which you may do well to contain. Mark Twain said, 'Our opinions do not really blossom into fruition until we have expressed them to someone else.' Right on! You network without a pause and meet with people from all over the globe. Life is charming at the moment and showering you with goodies. Keep a tab on your indulgences lest they boomerang. You could buy extravagant gifts for the significant other and possibly take the family for an exotic cruise. The omens are good and Ganesha is thrilled.

26 November: First Quarter in Pisces

According to psychologist Carl Jung, 'We are in this world but not of it. We are now able to observe ourselves from a different perspective. We are now capable to step out of our own mind, out of our own body and understand who we really are, to see things the way they are. We become the observer of our lives.' You have been in overdrive for a while now and step back a bit to understand what you really need. You realize that mere materialism will take you thus far and no further. You look at gurus and spirituality, yantra, tantra and mantra, pilgrimages and higher consciousness. You want to plug the hole that is embedded in your soul. Ganesha helps.

3 December: Full Moon in Gemini

The full moon is in Gemini and you are in communication mode. The year is fast ending and you want to be in touch with all your buddies and loved ones. 'In this world, you must be a bit too kind to be kind enough,' said Pierre Carlet de Chamblain de Marivaux, dramatist and novelist. Family life has unexpected twists and turns as the spouse and children will articulate viewpoints totally divergent from yours. There could be rifts at the workplace too. Nothing too serious, but you will have to swim through dark, shark-infested waters. You do what it takes and reach the banks high and dry. Ganesha lends a helping hand.

10 December: Last Quarter in Virgo

You are blessed with stability and balance. Last year at this time you were facing innumerable challenges. But time flies, and life changes dramatically. You roll up your sleeves and slog hard. The year is ending and life calls out to you to put on your dancing shoes and partake of the bubbly. But you have other plans. You have set targets for yourself and work towards achieving them, come what may. You may also be signing important documents and run through them with a magnifying glass. Family life is stable and children bring joy. Ganesha smiles.

18 December: New Moon in Sagittarius

There could be work-related travel. You could be moving solo or in a group, possibly even eyeing emigration. There are new associations as new vistas open up. Henry Ford said, 'Wealth, like happiness, is never attained when sought after directly. It comes as a by-product of providing a useful service.' Those in business look to massive expansion. This period is propitious for new beginnings. Love smiles, and your world is in the lap of bliss. Ganesha is thrilled.

26 December: First Quarter in Aries

I quote the great sage Ramana Maharshi. He said, 'Your duty is to *be*, and not be this or that.' The year ends well.

The first quarter of the moon is in your sign. Your energies are at a high point and no stone is unturned in your quest for money, fame and more freedom. Ego drives are high and you are powered by an unseen force. There is success in all your undertakings. Family life is exciting and singles play the field. You have come into your own after a lot of struggle, and it shows. Ganesha blesses you as you embark on another adventure and another year.

Taurus

21 April–21 May

Ganesha's Master Key: Possessions and benefits

'He who plants a tree, plants a hope.'
— LUCY LARCOM

This is the special message for you Taureans. You are essentially builders, be it a house, a garden, or even character. In other words, you specialize in growing life. Cooking and the arts certainly come under this wide definition.

The important traits are: Greedy, materialistic; Sensual, controlled by material desire; Stubborn, thick-headed, inflexible; Earthbound, single-minded; Determined, persistent; Firm, developing intellectual values; Attuning to true inner values; Becoming detached from materialism and astral glamour; Controlling emotional desires; Seeing possession as a means to an end instead of an end to a means; Helping to lift the world into light; Right use of possessions, talents and material goods.

Your Beauty-scope: Blue is the colour for Taurus. Make lavish use of it. It goes well with a soft skin such as yours. If you can afford it, wear a big sapphire, only around the neck. The neckline should have a V-shape. You see, your neck as a rule is short and thick. Body line is powerful, the height average, but you can move fast, pleasingly so. Practise that naturally pleasing walk. As you have small, shapely feet, wear open slippers or sandals. Nail polish should preferably be bright. Yes, the palms are soft, the hands well shaped with slightly conical fingers. So wear a ring to go with it, a showy one. Thin bracelets too. As stated above, the face is full and fleshy, the lips sensual. Personally, I prefer a vivid lipstick, the hair done at the back as in a bun.

CENTRAL IDEA

Health, Services, Servants, Pets, Food

My father and I have decided that the central idea will be best expressed in informing you, dear readers, about the Indian way of life. As we are now on the sixth angle of work, let me quote Michael Useem. Michael says, 'The Indian way revolves around the holistic engagement with employees … the Indian business ethos views companies as "one big family".'

Special Note: The 'Indian way' is of 'one big family' and this holds true for all the signs. When we talk and write about India, we will mention it as a plus point.

Here are other the important features this year: Loans, debts; Work, be it service (job) or profession or freelancing; New ventures and projects; Community service, social welfare; All matters pertaining to health and hygiene; Servants, colleagues, subordinates, pets, stepmother and maternal uncles and aunts.

The minor planets are also very important in astrology. Venus is definitely your main planet. This year Venus will be in your own sign from 6 June to 4 July. Venus will give you comforts and luxuries, and help you in all matters about money, health and services. I will go one step further for you and say that this lucky period will continue till the end of July. This does not mean that the other months will be bad.

Mercury represents not only travel and communication but also creativity, children, hobbies, entertainment and speculation for you. Mercury will be in your own sign from 1 to 20 April and 18 August to 6 June next year. For business, negotiation, communication and travel, this span of time will be pivotal; that is, very important.

Mars is the planet of energy and courage. For you, Mars could mean travel, secret affairs, romance, sex, marriage, union and ties. The period of it will be 10 March to 20 April and possibly 9 December 2017 to 26 January 2018. But law cases, bad health, and accidents are the pitfalls or downtrends. My father always says that in life you cannot have everything. I agree with him.

My father has given me the freedom to live the way I like and to think independently. He does not bind me. I am not under his shadow. Therefore, I repeat, I do not take into consideration Uranus, Neptune and Pluto for individual charts. I use them in determining the future of nations.

Like the last year, Saturn remains in the same sign, Sagittarius, by Western astrology. But this year Saturn is in a good formation with Jupiter. Therefore, your health should improve and so should your finances. This should give you hope, joy and courage.

MONTHLY ROUND-UP

January: You leapfrog to fame, publicity, spirituality, fulfilment, journey, education, future plans, relations. **February:** Tough decisions, health of elders, parents, in-laws, work premises; absolutely tremendous issues of prestige and status are possible. **March:** Friendship, the social whirl, romance, material gains, hopes, desires, ambition, happy days are here again. **April:** Expenses, losses, contacts, love, secret deals, journeys, spirituality; therefore, April will be a paradox, a big contradiction. **May:** Confidence, power, gains, happiness, right timings, the realization of wishes. **June:** Finances, food, family, buying/selling/shopping, property, functions and meets; you will be a crowd-puller! That's great. **July:** The three Cs: contacts, communication, computers. **August:** Home, house, parents, in-laws, property, requirements for the elderly, foundations for new projects. **September:** Entertainment, love, engagement, hobbies, sports, games of chance – in a word, creativity. **October:** Health, employment, pets, subordinates, colleagues, debts and funds. **November:** Marriage, legal issues, friends and enemies, trips and ties, collaborations, competition, it is a mixed bag. **December:** Money, passion, joint finance, buying/selling/shopping, taxes, real estate, insurance, focusing on health, and strain and drain (on the purse).

Money: Ganesha says that by Western astrology the money signs are the fixed signs, namely Taurus, Aquarius, Scorpio and Leo. Astrology is not perfect. The other eight signs can also be very great in finance. For Taureans, 2017 will be vital for funds, loans, investments, joint finance, collaborations. This very major trend will continue right up to the end of

December. In 2018 the complete culmination or result of it will be recognized. Therefore, plan accordingly this year. Even if there is a big money squeeze you will come out of it. I, Nastur, am a Scorpio. My nature and tendency are to really investigate and only then come to a definite conclusion. Therefore, I am giving you this hope by astrology. Like my father, I also agree that astrology is not perfect. But I have tried my best.

Happiness Quota: I give you 85 per cent.

MONTH BY MONTH

January: You start the year with a bang, full of hope and optimism. You have prioritized your life very clearly and don't hold back in getting what you want. You are filled with energy and are zipping away at a frantic pace. Mid-month sees you wrestle with emotional issues. There could be celebrations and even an addition to the family. As the month ends, there is passion and extra energy in whatever you undertake. Creative energy oozes out of you. Writers and artistes do exceptionally well. You could sign new deals, and new vistas open.

February: You check out finances and then sort out your moves. You are fiery, ambitious, aggressive and hard-working. You reach for the stars and are determined to get there. There is powerful intensity goading you on. There are expenses and affairs of the heart. Mid-month sees you filled with the spirit of adventure. This is not a period of stability; it is a period of growth. As the month ends, there are money and honey.

March: Nothing much is achieved though you are brimming with ideas. Mid-month, it all changes. There is hectic activity. You will be moving at supersonic speed and achieving the impossible. Importantly, you will be suitably earthed and will not fly off the handle. This is an achievement phase packed with excitement, enthusiasm and zeal. As the month ends, you are ambitious, determined and hard-working, and nothing can or will hold you back.

April: This is a fantastic phase. All I can say sagely is: Make the most of it! You are propelled by an irresistible force. You are possessed and make things happen. Your world is multi-splendoured and shines bright like a cluster of chandeliers. Mid-month sees you wining and dining in style. You could be feted for your achievements. You articulate your talent and drive in eloquent terms and there are rewards and awards. As the month ends, you are propelled by ambition. You have the Midas touch. There is also new love that takes you by storm.

May: The trends are propitious. Use your discretion. There are infinite possibilities facing you and it all depends on how you exercise your free will. Mid-month sees an extension of your lucky streak. You seek out knowledge and are attracted to the vast reservoirs of deep learning like a moth to a flame. As the month ends, you are growing in consciousness and want to reach the highest echelons of evolution. You achieve a lot but your energies are scattered. There is also great creativity surging within you.

June: The stars have generated great euphoria in your life. You are in full flow now. There could be travel and new associations. There could be new love too. Family life may see rocky times but it is nothing that you cannot salvage.

Expenses also mount. Mid-month is a powerful creative phase and you come up with masterpieces. There are several profitable social interactions too. As the month ends, you spend quality time with family.

July: Your mind is in several places. You weigh the pros and cons before embarking on a venture. Time and energy are wasted but you want to do the groundwork with precision before rushing ahead. Mid-month sees you push ahead with zeal and determination. If you have come into wealth through an inheritance or some windfall, this is a good time to invest and multiply your money. As the month ends, there is love and longing. There are expenses that tear into your savings. Your passions are also on overdrive. On the work front there is suitable expansion. There could also be exotic holidays and pleasurable times spent with friends and loved ones.

August: You indulge in maudlin moments. You are also filled with empathy for the downtrodden. You are also filled with zany ideas, and this could be a vibrantly creative phase. There are many influences at play. Mid-month sees you more balanced. You look at business expansion. You swing into action and sign important deals. The self-employed spread their wings. As the month ends, you are pulsating with new energy. Your sixth sense guides you to new horizons and discoveries.

September: This is a creative phase and you could churn out a best-seller or even make a go for the Oscars. You win applause. You could also spend some quality time with family and visit amusement parks and the theatre. Love life is on fire. Mid-month sees you in communication mode.

There are powerful transformative and regenerative energies at work. As the month ends, you get down to hard work. If you use this period well, miracles will be achieved.

October: You reach for the stars and achieve your dreams. There is time for family life too but there are many expenses. Mid-month may see you on the brink of a new cycle of growth and progress. As the month ends, there are multiple associations. Singles may find a partner. It may also be a time to explore new modalities of healing. New vistas open dramatically. You are brimming with new ideas and creativity and think out of the box. Those in media and entertainment win kudos.

November: You are on a bull run. Your dreams come to fruition. There are ecstatic moments of love when you and your partner touch ethereal heights. There are family celebrations and fun times. This is a powerful phase. Mid-month sees powerful ego drives and passions at work. It is a good idea not to take undue risks. Avoid people and situations that can get out of hand. You are on a brilliant run but ensure that you are grounded. As the month ends, you fire on all cylinders. There are moments of magic as you ride the crest of sheer genius. You are ideating and will blossom like a beautiful flower when the time is ripe.

December: Nothing deters you from reaching out to the world at large. You use technology to leverage your ideas and they meet with applause. You are laying the seeds for the future. Mid-month sees more stability. There are domestic issues to attend to. The health of a parent may need attention. On the upside are festivities and travel. You are on the move. As the year ends, you realize that life is multidimensional. You waltz into the new year serenaded by love, luck and the goodies of life.

WEEKLY REVIEW (BY PHASES OF THE MOON)

5 January: First Quarter in Aries

I shall start with a quote from Dr Deepak Chopra, 'The highest levels of performance come to people who are centred, intuitive, centred and reflective – people who know to see a problem as an opportunity.' You start the new year with a bang, full of hope and optimism. You have prioritized your life very clearly and don't hold back in getting what you want. You are filled with energy and are zipping away at a frantic pace, getting things done. This is indeed a great start to the year, quite different from how the new year began last year. As I always do, I must underscore the fact that Taureans are generally lucky, and good with money. They are practical and have a strong materialistic streak. They are also prone to philanthropy and can be deeply spiritual. But finer considerations and nuances depend on the personal chart. Audrey Hepburn, George Clooney, Andre Agassi, Billy Joel, Al Pacino, Barbara Streisand, Jay Leno, Pierce Brosnan and several other celebrities in all walks of life are Taureans; even the late dictator Saddam Hussein! Ganesha gives you the necessary push to get on with your dreams. Use this period well.

12 January: Full Moon in Cancer

The full moon is in Cancer and you wrestle with emotional issues. The family, friends, loved ones and close associates come into play. You are the charmer and can soothe ruffled feathers with ease. There could be celebrations and even an addition to the family. The fun times continue though moods will vacillate. Ganesha holds your hand.

19 January: Last Quarter in Scorpio

You are juggling many things at the same time. Love could sneak into your life and catch you unawares. There is passion and extra energy in whatever you undertake. If you have been dealing with a chronic medical problem, it will be a good idea to see a specialist. Skin problems and the throat could be a cause of concern. However, Ganesha ensures that you emerge unscathed.

28 January: New Moon in Aquarius

You are filled with zany ideas and could win the Oscar in the mood you are in. 'Words are loaded pistols,' said Jean Paul Sartre, the writer and philosopher. Keep away from altercations of any kind and focus on your creative energy which is oozing out of you at this moment. Writers and artistes do exceptionally well. You win applause and are the toast of your peer group. You could sign new deals, and new vistas open. You could also surprise loved ones with crazy ideas that are bubbling in your mind like a volcano about to erupt. Ganesha watches over you and that should suffice.

4 February: First Quarter in Taurus

There is balance and you are on terra firma. You know where you are headed and what to do to get there. You check out finances first and then sort out your moves accordingly. Businessmen dig their heels in and strike quick deals. Taureans are very good with money and are streetwise. If they don't get too greedy they can find a fine balance in life. But in the mood you are in the fragrance of greenbacks is simply all too alluring. Ganesha smiles.

11 February: Full Moon in Leo

You are powering ahead like a new monorail. You are fiery, ambitious, aggressive and hard-working. You reach for the stars and are determined to get there. There is powerful intensity goading you on. There are expenses and affairs of the heart. Your plate is full and overflowing. You mow down the opposition like a bull in the rutting season. You play the field like there is no tomorrow but also manage to ensure that your career goals are met and money floods your account. Ganesha is happy for you.

18 February: Last Quarter in Sagittarius

There could be group or solo travel. You are filled with the spirit of adventure. You may try out new recipes or even a new healing technique. You could fall under the spell of a person you meet on the road. There could be love and longing as you fall under the spell of amour. There are immense possibilities in this phase. This is not a period of stability, but it is a period of growth. Ganesha, I dare say, winks naughtily.

26 February: New Moon in Pisces

The new moon is in Pisces. There are maudlin moments and you think of lost love and what could have been if you had acted differently in the past. This is also a creative phase and those in the arts showcase their skills. There are money and honey, rewards and awards. In addition to Taurus being a builder in the material sense, I must add here that they are extremely creative and often deeply spiritual. Only your personal chart can tell which type of Taurean you are. This is merely a general reading and I am not God. I am your favourite astrologer and I do my best, as you know only too well. Ganesha agrees.

5 March: First Quarter in Gemini

Your mind is all over the place, bouncing around like a rubber ball. You want to do too many things at the same time and don't know where and how to start. Nothing much is achieved though you are brimming with ideas. But they are like inflated balloons soaring across the sky till they are deflated or lose their way. Einstein said, 'There are only two ways to live your life: one as though nothing is a miracle, the other as though everything is a miracle.' Which way will you choose? This is a passing phase and you will soon get down to terra firma. Often, the trends of one week coalesce into another; sometimes they last long. Ganesha holds your hand and that is more than enough.

12 March: Full Moon in Virgo

Mars is in Taurus from 10 March to 20 April. This makes for an entire month of hectic activity. You will be moving at supersonic speed and achieving the impossible. The full moon is also in Virgo and this is an interesting combination. You will be suitably earthed and will not fly off the handle. You will also examine details closely with a magnifying glass before reaching a conclusion. This is an achievement phase and you will not spare the horses as you gear up for the home run with excitement, enthusiasm and zeal. Mars in your own sign gives energy, courage and a very positive attitude. Mars is like the volcano of vitality inside you and influences endurance, persistence and discipline. Mars was named for the Roman god of war, and is also known as 'the bright and burning one'. Red is the colour of Mars and it stimulates the dynamic, potent and fertile drives that power our lives. Mars rules physical energy and action, and governs energy, strength, courage, life force and expansion. Well-placed Mars endows powerful energy and an indomitable will to succeed. Mars propels us like an ignited rocket. It is an important energy since it determines how we pursue what we want to achieve in life. In short, Mars represents energy, force, violence, aggression, sports, combat, wars, battles, accidents and operations. Ganesha ensures that you don't fall off the rails.

20 March: Last Quarter in Capricorn

You are powering away with reckless abandon. You are like a stallion that has bolted from the stables. You are ambitious, determined and hard-working and nothing can or will hold you back. Freelancers find new avenues to market their skills and those in jobs get promoted. Businessmen and those playing the markets hit pay dirt. It is going your way. Of course, I don't have your personal chart but, most certainly, this is a good period. Go for it, says Ganesha.

28 March: New Moon in Aries

You are moving ahead at supersonic speed. Avoid altercations and get a grip on your temper. You could be judged and criticized but it is better to sidestep it all. Success breeds enemies, and it is wise not to retaliate. You are brimming with ambition and as you get closer to your birthday you are sending the right signals to the universe. Success is yours if you want it badly. Do you? Ganesha knows the answer.

3 April: First Quarter in Cancer

Osho said, 'When your creativity comes to a climax, when your whole life becomes creative, you live in God ... Love what you do. Be meditative while you are doing it – whatsoever it is!' Mercury is in Taurus from 1 to 20 April. This is a fantastic phase. All I can say sagely is: Make the most of it! You are propelled by an irresistible force. You are possessed and make things happen. Your world is multi-splendoured and shines bright like a cluster of chandeliers. There are domestic issues to solve, and that you will. There could also be an addition to the family. Apart from happy domestic tidings, there are great moves on the career front. It is all happening for you. Ganesha is delighted for you. Messages and trips are the special characteristics of Mercury. Mercury, the mighty, all-powerful planet is in your sign now. It favours travels, meetings, conferences, interviews, trips, more brainpower, contacts, communication, correspondence and contracts. Mercury has a special connection with the circuits of the brain. Chess, crossword and other such games belong to Mercury. Also, short-distance runners and spin bowlers are controlled by Mercury. Mercury, in short, is the ambassador and salesman of the zodiac. Mercury is the symbol of news, views, messages, interviews, contacts, communications, travel and transport. Mercury gives an impetus to all of the above in the sun sign where it is located. Ganesha is delighted for you.

11 April: Full Moon in Libra

The full moon is in Libra and you are wining and dining in style. You are a winner and you could be feted for your skills and achievements. You articulate your talent and drive in eloquent terms and there are rewards and awards. 'I never lose sight of the fact that just being is fun,' said Katherine Hepburn, the actress. You live your passion out and it is not a chore. The results are for all to see. You also look at the fine print with great diligence and leave no stone unturned in making your mark in life. Ganesha is thrilled.

19 April: Last Quarter in Capricorn

You are propelled by the ambition of Capricorn. You want to reach the very acme of your work. You could be bulldozing your way through life and treading on corns. Get a hold of your temper and ego. 'Ego is hard to conquer and arises from seven factors – wealth, physical prowess, birth, scholarship, beauty, power and penance. As long as *ahamkara* is predominant, it is impossible to recognize the divinity within,' said Sai Baba. Pride comes before a fall. Watch your step lest you fall into a manhole while reaching for the stars. You are on a dream run. Don't break it. Ganesha is with you all the way and that helps.

26 April: New Moon in Taurus

It is your birth month and the signs are propitious. The new moon is in Taurus. You have the Midas touch. Do I have to prod you on? You are not one to miss the signs! There is also new love that takes you by storm. Family life, for those in steady relationships, is alive and well. There could be foreign travel and an array of celebrations. Ganesha smiles.

3 May: First Quarter in Leo

There are many expenses as you spend without a care in the world. You also play the field. Love eyeballs you, and you stare back. The trends are propitious. Use your discretion and let wiser counsel prevail. There are infinite possibilities facing you and it all depends on how you exercise your free will. You can pull a rabbit out of the hat even on a busy Mumbai thoroughfare. You can do miracles. What will you choose? Ganesha watches in anticipation.

10 May: Full Moon in Scorpio

The full moon is in Scorpio, and Mercury is in Taurus from 16 May to 6 June. Your lucky streak continues. The gods are smiling on you. I am not God. I am just a humble astrologer who tries his best. With all modesty I admit I am extremely popular because I am also reasonably accurate. Your investigative skills are aroused. You want to know more and more of the world you inhabit. You delve into the esoteric sciences and wander into many new areas of research. You are seeking out knowledge and are attracted to the vast reservoirs of deep learning like a moth to a flame. Ganesha holds your hand.

19 May: Last Quarter in Aquarius

You are travelling in many directions. There could be physical movement too, though the focus will be on inner journeys. You are growing in consciousness and want to reach the highest echelons of evolution. You turn the powerful energies of this period inward. The three Ps – power, pelf and privileges – are yours for the asking, but you take a step beyond it all. You tap into the many mysteries of the universe. You want to study the journey of the soul, not only on this planet but in the Milky Way too. Ganesha is amazed.

25 May: New Moon in Gemini

Your mind is in a million different places. You achieve a lot but your energies are scattered. There is great creativity surging within you too. This could be a good time for personal R&D before you decide which direction to embark on. Domestic issues take backstage as you press the throttle on personal evolution. But, like I always say, I am not God. This is a general reading and I do not have your personal chart. 'If you are depressed, you are living in the past. If you are anxious, you are living in the future. If you are at peace, you are living in the moment,' said Lao-tzu, the legendary philosopher. You are now living in several time zones. You will emerge wiser and stronger, affirms Ganesha.

1 June: First Quarter in Virgo

Venus is in Taurus from 6 June to 4 July, and do I add that the bubbly flows even more? You are in balance and well rooted to terra firma and do not get carried away by all the euphoria the stars have generated in your life. You look at the balance sheet dispassionately and chart out your immediate goals and go for the jugular. The simple rule is that when Venus is in your own sign you will get comforts and luxuries, ornaments and money. Venus is another important planet and is of great significance. This is an important phase. As often discussed, Venus is the planet for love, romance, sex, beauty and good life. This is the planet of attraction, love, wealth, knowledge and prosperity. The compatibility of partners and also the type of life the individual will lead is also judged from the placement of Venus in the horoscope. As a planet, Venus is considered to be beneficial, feminine and gentle. Venus symbolizes the force of attraction in the universe. In human beings, this attractive force manifests as love and beauty. When Venus is well placed in the chart, there is love, art, beauty and all the goodies of life that make life worth living. Venus rules Libra and Taurus, though its role in every sign is important. Like other planets, it also has its transits. In Libra, Venus is aesthetic and cultured. In Taurus it is more earthy, materialistic and sensual. Venus rules the venous system, kidneys, urinary tract, throat and larynx, and is responsible for good looks. In short, Venus, in Western astrology, stands for comforts, arts, wealth, relationships, sex, decorations, luxuries and wealth. Ganesha is with you and that is an added bonus.

9 June: Full Moon in Sagittarius

You are in full flow now. You are like Chris Gayle on song. You have the determination of Tendulkar and the style of Brian Lara; incidentally, both are Taureans. You also check out new vistas and are keen on growing as a person. There could be travel and new associations. There could be new love too. Youngsters, in particular, are filled with bravado and may be difficult to rein in. 'A closed mind is like a closed book, just a block of wood,' says a Chinese proverb. Well, in this phase you are anything but that. Family life may see rocky times but it is nothing that you cannot salvage. Expenses also mount. Ganesha isn't worried.

17 June: Last Quarter in Pisces

Your sensitivities are aroused. You look at higher learning and may spend time at poetry readings and film festivals. You want to be surrounded by beauty and may take nature walks or check out new healing modalities. This is a powerful creative phase and you come up with masterpieces that win peer group approval. There are several profitable social interactions too. Ganesha is happy for you.

24 June: New Moon in Cancer

The new moon is in Cancer, and you find quality time with family to share golden moments. You want to be surrounded by love and spend time with friends and relatives and those you call your own. Elders are in the lap of comfort. They feel cherished and are filled with a new sense of belonging. There is love in the air. I must add here that it always hovers around Taureans. They are, without a doubt, one of the greatest lovers of the zodiac! Ganesha winks. He knows you better than your shadow.

1 July: First Quarter in Libra

Your mind is in several places. You weigh the pros and cons before embarking on a venture. Time and energy are wasted but you want to do the groundwork with precision before rushing ahead. 'The secret of the greatest fruitfulness and the greatest enjoyment of existence is to live dangerously,' said Nietzsche. You may not be doing that in the phase you are in now. You are moving at a snail's pace, but like Rommel, the great general, your calculations are exact. I insist though, like I always do, that astrology impels and never compels. A lot depends on your personal horoscope. There is free will too, and a set of circumstances which differ in everyone's life. The stars prod and push and influence you of course, but the final decision making is dependent on a sea of factors. Ganesha nods sagely.

9 July: Full Moon in Capricorn

You are pushing ahead with zeal and determination. You are like a kite soaring high with manja in place. You are the master of jugaad. If you have come into wealth through an inheritance or some windfall, this is a good time to invest and multiply your money. I have worked with Taureans and know that they also understand the practical aspects of life and know when, where and how to invest. They are empire builders. It is change that upsets them. In this phase you are surging ahead on well-defined lines. Ganesha agrees that nothing and no one can stop you from achieving your goals.

16 July: Last Quarter in Aries

You are propelled by the power of Aries. There is love and longing as you play the field. There are powerful ego drives and you can get unusually stubborn. Learn to cede ground and retreat to victory! It is an old gambit used in every theatre of war. Do not squander energy in petty squabbles. There are expenses that tear into your savings but you are in that kind of mood now. There is also that extra bit of bingeing as you party away like there is no tomorrow. Ganesha watches over you.

23 July: New Moon in Leo

The new moon is in Leo and you are unstoppable. This is a free world and I am not advocating a multi-partner existence but you are most certainly playing the field. Your passions are on overdrive and you are ready to mingle and tumble in the hay and what have you! Those in committed relationships take intimacy to new heights. On the work front there is suitable expansion. You could be investing in property or heavy machinery. Businesspeople take risks and the employed pamper their savings accounts. Ganesha is with you and that is what matters in the end.

30 July: First Quarter in Scorpio

You could be eyeing a home away from home. There could be exotic holidays and pleasurable times spent with friends and loved ones. There could also be secret deals and negotiations of all kinds. A Spanish proverb says, 'If you do not dare, you do not live.' You dare big time and live large. There are maudlin moments too, but they help you appreciate the good times. Life has many shades, nuances and undercurrents. They coalesce all the time like the tributaries of a great river.

Since human beings live in the mind I suggest you harness the mind for profit. Ganesha holds your hand.

7 August: Full Moon in Aquarius

You get sidetracked and indulge in maudlin moments and voices from the past. There is no point crying over spilt milk. It is done and dusted. You are also filled with empathy for the downtrodden and may loosen your purse strings for charitable causes. You are also filled with zany ideas, and this could be a vibrantly creative phase. There are many influences and it all depends how you steer the period depending on your requirements of the moment. Family life may undergo a rough patch. Ganesha watches.

15 August: Last Quarter in Taurus

You find steady ground and are balanced. You look at major business expansion. You are not one to drown yourself in sorrows and abstractions. You need tangible evidence of growth. You need the fragrance of new currency notes. You need to laugh all the way to the bank. You are certainly not one to flourish on an empty stomach. You need ideas that work, to hold on to something that is real. You swing into action and sign important deals. The self-employed spread their wings and bag lucrative contracts. The home front is steady, and you sleep with a smile on your lips. All is well with your world. Ganesha is happy.

21 August: New Moon in Leo

You are pulsating with new energy. The new moon is in Leo, and you stop at nothing to get where you want to go. 'The three grand essentials to happiness in this life are something to do, something to love, and something to hope for,' said Joseph Addison, the writer. In this phase you have all three.

You go for the jugular and reap rich rewards. There is little time for the family as you are in expansion mode. You suffocate them with goodies and so the complaints, if any, are muffled. Your sixth sense guides you to new horizons and discoveries. Ganesha is impressed.

29 August: First Quarter in Sagittarius

There is a lot of movement now. You could be moving in many ways: geographically, emotionally, spiritually. Ganesha holds your hand as you navigate turbulent waters. You take undue risks, which is quite unlike your natural disposition. You look at adventure sport and exotic travel. In business you invest where you haven't before; you tread new territory without checking the waters. You have that extra liquidity and want to take the chance. Nothing ventured, nothing gained. You strike a hard bargain as you erupt on the home run in brilliant fashion. The stars are with you and you seem to be backing the right horse! Whew!

6 September: Full Moon in Pisces

The full moon is in Pisces and your sensitivities are heightened. This is a creative phase and you could churn out a best-seller or even make a go for the Oscars. You win applause for sure. Even those playing the market or in hard-core business look at creative angles in their daily, otherwise possibly dull and mundane, routines. You could also spend some quality time with family and visit amusement parks and the theatre. Love life is on fire. There could be an addition to the family, or you could take your partner up the aisle. Anything can happen. It is a period of many surprises; all pleasant I dare say. Ganesha agrees.

13 September: Last Quarter in Gemini

Your mind is all over the place. You are in communication mode. You are in constant contact with the world through the marvels of technology. You use Facebook, Twitter and WhatsApp the most. You look at social transformation through the Net and are smart enough to use it to advantage. There are powerful transformative and regenerative energies at work. You may have embarked on a new course in life and there are new challenges. You may have reached your destination, but then another journey begins. It is an endless process. Family life takes backstage as you look for an enhancement in consciousness. Ganesha is impressed.

20 September: New Moon in Virgo

There is more stability now. Quite often, influences from one week spill over into another and this may continue for weeks on end. But you are now faced with the stabilizing influence of Virgo. You get down to the hard task of making a living and nothing can take you away from the practicalities of life. This period works in your favour. Ganesha asks you to go for the kill. You have sighted the quarry like a lion in the Serengeti National Park and you make no bones about getting it for supper. These are general indications. Astrology never compels. Use your free will to advantage, especially when the stars are in your favour.

28 September: First Quarter in Capricorn

You are moving ahead with great speed. Nothing can stop you now as you run over the opposition like a breakaway race car on a crowded Mumbai street. You are galloping ahead like a horse that has bolted from the stables before the big Derby. Nothing can hold you back. If you use this period well, miracles will be achieved. 'The miner does not sit at the top of the shaft waiting for the coal to come bubbling up to the surface. One must go deep down, and work out every vein carefully,' said Arthur Sullivan, the composer. You are charged, and raring to go. You also have a sense of purpose and that lights the direction you take. Ganesha says success is yours. There are money and power. Use these well, I say.

5 October: Full Moon in Aries

The full moon is in Aries and the energies are heightened. You want to accomplish a great deal. You reach for the stars. The best part is that you achieve your dreams. There is time for family life too, and you could be planning an exotic holiday. Singles play the field and those in committed relationships take ecstasy to new heights. There are many expenses as you loosen your purse strings. But it is money well spent. You are not prone to wasting. Ganesha blesses you.

12 October: Last Quarter in Cancer

This is family time. You feel blessed to be around kids and grandkids, if any. Friends, loved ones and even distant cousins come together for fun times around the fireplace. You have worked hard and long, and as another year edges to a close you look back and savour the golden moments with people who mean the world to you. One eye is clearly on the workstation, but that is your wont; it is the way you are made. It comes with Taurean territory. But it doesn't dilute the festivities. On the contrary, with all the wining and dining you could put on a few unwanted pounds! You could well be on the brink of a new cycle of growth and progress. The foundation has been well and truly laid. Ganesha is happy for you.

19 October: New Moon in Libra

This is a period of multiple associations. Singles may find a partner and those looking for work-related connections may see lady luck smiling on them. It may also be a time to explore new modalities of healing. You check out tantra and mantra and go looking for a guru. You may even check into a health spa for detoxifying the ills of urban living. New vistas open dramatically. People enter your life and you profit from the association. A person from a different culture may exert a powerful influence on you. Ganesha watches.

27 October: First Quarter in Aquarius

You are brimming with new ideas and creativity and think out of the box in almost all areas of your life. Your dour Taurean self is changed dramatically. Taureans are also excitingly creative and this aspect of yours superimposes itself on everything else. You allow change to happen. Like in Zen, you empty the glass for fresh water to flow in. Those in media and entertainment win kudos. Money and honey are yours. Your philanthropic urges are also highlighted as you give generously to charities. Ganesha is impressed. So am I. One should always give to the less fortunate. What you give returns manifold. Charity also begins at home!

4 November: Full Moon in Taurus

The full moon is in your sign and nothing can stop you in its tracks. You are on a bull run. You have had many dreams and they all come to fruition. There are ecstatic moments of love when you and your partner touch ethereal heights. You seem to have found your mojo as the year ends, and like the great Messi you manage to score goals from acute angles. There are family celebrations and fun times. You could also make expensive purchases. The possibilities are endless. This is a powerful phase and you can tweak it in your favour with ease. Ganesha smiles.

10 November: Last Quarter in Leo

There are powerful ego drives at work. Control your tongue and desist from altercations of any kind. There are good tidings all around but there is an element of danger lurking around, and it is a good idea not to take undue risks. Avoid people and situations that can get out of hand. I am not God, but these are gentle prods. You feel invincible, almost superhuman, and therein lies the danger. Pride comes before a fall. You are on a brilliant run but ensure that you are grounded. Ganesha watches over you. Family life could also be in disarray as you play the field without a care.

18 November: New Moon in Scorpio

The new moon is in Scorpio and there is powerful energy goading you on. You fire on all cylinders. There are moments of magic as you ride the crest of sheer genius. 'The creative experience is one of heightened consciousness,' said Rollo May, a mid-twentieth-century psychologist who wrote *The Courage to Create*. You are also in investigative mode and delve deep into mysteries and secrets. You could well be seeking exotic and extinct marine life for the Discovery Channel. This is a great time for scientists, counsellors and analysts. You showcase your creative genius with flamboyance. Love hangs on to you like bees to honey; there is no respite, and that could be a problem of concern as a lot of energy and time and, I dare say, money is wasted on feminine foibles. I have lived long enough to know the dangers and distractions of amour. In this case, you court the affections of more than one partner, and that could be deadly. You are in a magical whirl, but read with caution. Ganesha watches with concern.

26 November: First Quarter in Pisces

Johannes Brahms, the great composer said, 'Straightaway the ideas flow in upon me, directly from God.' You are in the throes of creative genius. This is not a time for sustained work. It may appear to others that you are not working at all. But not working, just consolidating, is also a form of action. You don't have to enter the arena like Genghis Khan brandishing a scimitar. You are ideating and will blossom like a beautiful flower when the time is ripe. You are in the bud stage. Your eccentricities stun others. Your prodigious output, when it does happen, will shatter the status quo. Ganesha is impressed.

3 December: Full Moon in Gemini

The full moon is in Gemini and you are all over the place. The winter chill assaults your bones but nothing will deter you from reaching out to the world at large. You have a lot to say and you will say it with style and substance. Your echoes will reverberate across continents. You use technology to leverage your ideas and they meet with applause. You are not building an empire now. But you are laying the seeds for the future. Ganesha applauds from the sidelines.

10 December: Last Quarter in Virgo

There is stability now. Practicality and Taureans can never be divorced. Even the most creative and spiritual ones understand money and its place in the scheme of things. You spend quality time with family. Children may be leaving home for greener pastures or there may be a homecoming of the prodigal. There could be an addition to the family too. You are busy with outings and celebrations, maybe even with an alumni meet. You look back at the year with gratitude and yet silently plan for the future. Ganesha watches you.

18 December: New Moon in Sagittarius

The new moon is in Sagittarius, and the year is ending well. There are domestic issues to attend to. The health of a parent may need attention. You don't normally wear your emotions on your sleeve but there are times when you do break down. Ganesha holds your hand as you navigate troubled waters. On the upside are festivities and travel. You are on the move. There is no quiet moment that stagnates you as you seek out answers from the universe for the pressing concerns of your soul.

26 December: First Quarter in Aries

I shall end this year's forecast for Taurus with a quote from Andrea Dykstra from *Shortcuts to Spirituality*, 'In order to love who you are, you cannot hate the experiences that shaped you.' This has been a magnificent year by any account. The gods have been kind, and if you tweaked your free will to advantage miracles would have been achieved. Life is multidimensional and one person's priorities may not be those of others. This has been an all-encompassing and fruitful twelve months. You are now propelled by Aries as you waltz into the new year. Love, luck and the goodies of life serenade you as you enter 2018 with a spring in your step and a song in your heart. Ganesha applauds.

GEMINI

22 May–22 June

Ganesha's Master Key: Curiosity and sharp intelligence

'Intelligence without ambition is a bird without wings.'
— Salvador Dali

I am writing this on 12 October 2015. You Geminis are so intelligent and curious that the Nobel Prize in chemistry for work on DNA repair has gone to Geminis Tomas Lindahl and Paul Modrich in 2015. This should give you a great booster dose and thrust.

The important traits are: Overly rational and logical; Sensing only the immediate environment; Perceiving the world through the physical plane manifestation only; Prejudiced due to lack of higher mind understanding; Being unable to connect everyday life with spiritual philosophy; Unstable, shifting viewpoints constantly; Fluid in thought and speech; Recognizing the duality of soul and form; Beginning to recognize that through love all people are linked; Blending logic with abstract thought; Transmuting knowledge into wisdom; Recognizing that we are all united, but separate; Speaking and writing in order to express love wisdom; Spreading love wisdom through teaching.

Your Beauty-scope: Beauty for you is directly and very intimately connected with sleep. And don't nibble at food either. Eat it regularly and well. It can generally be said that you have a short trunk, not much body hair and a very alert look. Emphasize it by mascara and cultivate the trick of noticing one and all in a very personal manner. As the complexion is pale, use bright colours. The skin is fine, clear, hairless; so, for you, miniskirts, sleeveless dresses, housecoats, blouses are in. You have slim hands; therefore, as far as possible, heavy jewellery please!

CENTRAL IDEA

Love, Entertainment, Children, Hobbies, Gambling

Love, romance, hobbies, children (starting at conception or actual delivery of the child); exceptional creative pursuits requiring imagination and organization (Geminis use the two superbly); the use of tantra and mantra, a possible recall of your past life or lives (you are most welcome to have your personal opinion about past lives and reincarnation); success in property, affairs, buying and selling or just developing new and vast outlets of entertainment and amusement, or, it could be a different way or style of entertainment (for example, a different film story, a terrific directorial venture); speculation and indulgence in games of chance (such as horse racing) are foretold. A word of warning, please. This is only a solar-scopic reading, not a real horoscopic one. Results and predictions are, therefore, not guaranteed to come correct. Or, you have the choice of new music, which means that new music can be influenced by the full range of musical styles, both past and present. This includes classical Indian music, as well as traditional Western classical music or more popular styles such as rock, New Age music, improvisation and more. The music performed is the result of collaborative efforts with living composers. So the music is usually inspired by our everyday lives.

There are also other uses and events connected with Jupiter in your fifth angle, namely, children and childbirth; creativity at all levels, be it poetry or carpentry or film direction or acting and so on; entertainment and amusements; sports, hobbies and pastimes; luck in games of chance, such as football pools, lotteries, at the casino. Tantra and mantra, prayers and hymns, very surprisingly, also fall under the domain of Jupiter in your fifth angle; so pray with a will, and possibly your wishes will be granted. Your avenues and sources of self-expression will multiply and that, in simple English, means many opportunities. You will be excellent at capitalizing on this.

Saturn will be in your opposition angle throughout the year. You Geminis are intelligent and grasp things very quickly. As Saturn is in your opposition angle, expect opposition and difficulties. But this year, 2017, the difficulties will be much less. The reason is that Saturn, the tough and difficult planet, will be in happy relationship with Jupiter, the biggest and the best and the luckiest planet. Therefore, the bad effects of Saturn will be controlled and subdued.

Mercury is your main planet. It helps you in terms of confidence, intelligence, communication, good health, research, studies, contacts, consciousness. Mercury will be in your sign by Western astrology from 7 to 20 June. Therefore, important decisions could be taken then. Mercury will also be favourable from 6 to 25 July; 2 to 8 September; 30 September to 16 October; 14 to 31 March; 7 to 25 February. In other words, you have a wide choice. We all know that Mars represents energy, adventure and courage. But for you Geminis, Mars specially represents jobs, friendship, entertainment, love, happiness. Mars will help you from 21 April to 4 June; 20 July to 4 September; 23 October to 8 December; and 28 January to 9 March. Once you know this you can use it to your advantage.

We all know that Venus symbolizes wealth, all the arts, luxuries and everything that is beautiful. For you very specially, Venus symbolizes children, hobbies, arts, prayers and most certainly foreign countries and collaborations. Venus will be in your sign from 5 to 31 July; 28 April to 5 June; 4 February to 2 April; 14 October to 6 November; 28 August to 19 September; and possibly 1 to 24 December. Give your best shot then.

MONTHLY ROUND-UP

January: Joint finances, funds, loans, legacy, family issues are problems. **February**: Sweet and sour relationships, publicity, conferences and meets, inspirational and intuitive moves and manoeuvres. **March**: Prestige, status, power, struggle, perks, new ventures and means of communication. **April**: Socializing, group activities, marriage, love affairs, happiness, laughter, the goodies of life. **May**: Secret activities, health, expenses, visits to hospitals, welfare centres, medical check-ups. **June**: Fulfilment, happiness, money, marriage, confidence. **July**: Money, honey, riches, beautification, augmentation of income, good food, jewellery. **August**: Research, contacts, communication, correspondence, brothers, sisters, relatives. **September**: Home, house, property, renovation, decoration, alteration. **October**: Love, romance, children, relationships, hobbies. **November**: Health, pets, servants, jobs, hygiene, colleagues; **December**: Love, marriage, divorce, journeys, reaching out to people, also separations.

Happiness Quota: I give you 85 per cent.

MONTH BY MONTH

January: You look for fame and money and will do everything in your power to achieve both. There are parties and entertaining and you could be the toast of the peer group. This could also be a wonderful time for creative folk. Mid-month sees you take stock of your life and work. You are busy poring over bank statements and working your way through other fiscal instruments. There are domestic issues to contend with too. As the month ends, there are powerful energies at play; adversaries try to trip you. You wrestle with demons and emerge triumphant.

February: You are back on track. You roll up your sleeves and get down to earning a livelihood. Those in creative fields earn kudos. Mid-month sees you powering away on all cylinders. Nothing can stop you. Success crowns you. There are affairs of the heart and many expenses. An independent, exuberant, extravagant and rebellious streak finds eloquent expression. As the month ends, you open your life to new vistas. There is magic in newness, and your sparkling mind leads the way. You indulge in the good things of life and want to be surrounded by love and beauty.

March: You tango with self-created demons. Courting couples go through a harrowing time. These are indulgent times with separations and breakdowns, bingeing and irrational behaviour. A health crisis may also rear its ugly head. Mid-month sees more balance. Family life is more settled and you sight your goals and work towards them. You make sensible purchases, get disciplined and organized. You are looking ahead with hope and attitude, intensity and purpose. Singles find new love and committed ones take ecstasy to ethereal heights.

April: You are filled with compassion for the less fortunate. You indulge in philanthropy. The family is content and you are filled with gratitude for the way life is shaping up for you. These are happy days. You spread bonhomie. The month sees you in an expansive mood. There is business expansion calling for heavy investments. As the month ends, you leave no stone unturned till you achieve your goals. This is a period of achievement. Your task is clear-cut, and so are your efforts. Success garlands you.

May: There is business expansion and many expenses. The grand times continue. Mid-month sees you filled with intensity, passion, love and longing. You are also on a spiritual quest. As the month ends, you bask in fantasy, magic and illusion. There are indulgences and hallucinations. Avoid altercations and take to yoga or meditation. The month-end sees a propitious time for creative folk. Those in the media and entertainment worlds do exceptionally well. There is travel, money, new friends and vital associations.

June: Your attention, energy and focus are powered and well directed and the results are nothing short of miraculous.

There is also a lot of social networking as you gear up to get your message out to as many people as possible. You want to experience every vista of life and grow as a person. Mid-month sees you reach for the stars and touch them. Miracles are in your grasp. There is movement, travel, investments, love, spiritual urges, new discoveries and vistas that reveal life's hidden treasures. This is a powerful phase. As the month ends, you are at a creative peak. This is also the time for love.

July: This is a period of love and expensive and exquisite purchases. You want to be surrounded by beautiful objects. You want to live in the lap of comfort. Family life returns to harmony. Mid-month sees you dazzle with your expertise and craftsmanship and win kudos. Fresh greenbacks swarm into your kitty. Your world is on song. As the month ends, you mow down the opposition in a brazen display of showmanship. You love the limelight and bask in its glory. There are rewards and awards and overseas travel. There are indulgences and risk taking.

August: You are charged emotionally and easily angered. You are ego-driven, intolerant and irritable. Your contentious mood could derail your plans. Relationships go for a toss and you remain sullen and morbid. Those with escapist tendencies open various windows of indulgence. Mid-month sees more balance. You roll up your sleeves and get down to the hard slog. As the month ends, you power ahead. Ego drives and passions are strong. You enter a new era of love, beauty, compassion and sacrifice.

September: This is a powerfully creative phase. You articulate your zeal with flamboyance and attract a niche as well as widespread audience. There are profitable associations and collaborations. Mid-month sees you move ahead at rapid speed. You are optimistic, energetic, joyous, happy and affirmative. Luck is on your side too. There are new expansion plans on the anvil. Family life is stable though a minor health problem may recur.

October: You are filled with energy and work miracles. You seize the moment and success beckons. Married life is happy and children bring joy. There could be an addition to the family. Mid-month sees maudlin times. Friends drop by and there are family gatherings. Creative folk do exceedingly well. As the month ends, you are spoilt for choice. You try to reinvent yourself. There could be new love.

November: You tweak all the rules and invent new ones. You leave the opposition behind. There are rich dividends. Mid-month sees you gripped by powerful intensity. You excel in group discussions, contractual negotiations and conferences. There are expenses and indulgences of all kinds. As the month ends, you are at your creative best. You take a step back from all the excitement and take to music, poetry and the arts. You surround yourself with love and longing. There is a joyous hum to life.

December: You are in the throes of communication and use every technological tool in the world. You move fast and sign deals. There is success. This is a profoundly creative phase. Mid-month sees stability and energy that powers you. You strike pay dirt and win the approval of your peer group. As the month ends, you are on the highway of success and travel. You spend money without a thought in the world. This is a great time for group activities. You began 2017 on a cracking note and you end it with thunder. You are at the centre of action and love every moment of the limelight.

WEEKLY REVIEW (BY PHASES OF THE MOON)

5 January: First Quarter in Aries

Jung said that the greatest desire of the unconscious is to become known; and it will use everything as vehicles for that. With the first quarter of the moon in Aries, this is the exact feeling that you are going through. The last year began on a soft and mellow note. This year begins quite the opposite. You look for fame and money and will do everything in your power to achieve both. There are money and honey and you are tempted to take short cuts and use unethical means to achieve your goals. I am of the old school – I still maintain that honesty is the best policy. There are parties and entertaining and you could be the toast of the peer group. This could also be a wonderful time for creative folk, who strike pay dirt. Ganesha journeys with you all the way. Now, a bit about you, as I always do, as I have many new readers every year. Gemini is an air sign and could be inconsistent, impatient, changeable, creative and restless. Gemini's world is one of duality. Geminis are curious, talkative, versatile and mentally active. They are born communicators. Every sign has its list of celebrities, and this one is no exception. You share your birth sign with Angelina Jolie, Anna Kournikova, Anne Frank, Ben Johnson, Marilyn Monroe, Johnny Depp, Bob Dylan, Brooke Shields, Che Guevara, Donald Trump, Jackie Stewart, John F. Kennedy, Frank Lampard, Salman Rushdie, Paul McCartney, Steve Waugh, Venus Williams and Gaugin, among others.

12 January: Full Moon in Cancer

'Many people know so little what is beyond their short range of experience. They look within themselves and find nothing! Therefore, they conclude that there is nothing outside themselves either,' said Helen Keller. The mood is mellow. The new-year rush is over. After the thrills of a breathtaking start to the year you take stock of your life and work. You are busy poring over bank statements and working your way through other fiscal instruments. There are domestic issues to contend with, including the illness of a child or parent; your health too may come under the scanner. These are all part of the ebb and flow of life and we all have to go through the wringer. Ganesha holds your hand and that is consolation indeed.

19 January: Last Quarter in Scorpio

There is a new intensity that takes hold of your life. There is love and lust and we often confuse one for the other; ask me, as I have been there several times, over and over again. You play the field and there is intrigue and deception. Your life resembles a Bollywood potboiler. There are many players and the coil of love gets murkier, thicker and even deadly. You play with the serpent in the Garden of Eden and it can strike anytime. There are powerful energies at play at work too, as adversaries try their best to trip you. You are at your wit's end. But Ganesha assists you across murky waters.

28 January: New Moon in Aquarius

You wrestle with demons like the great grapplers Sushil Kumar and Yogeshwar. Like them, you too will emerge triumphant in the end. Your mind is everywhere, drunken and besotted by trivia. You go looking for a guru and look at tantra, mantra and yantra with new eyes. You may take to yoga, natural healing and meditation. You may even join a Vipassana course or enrol in a spa. There are several possibilities. But most certainly, your mind is not tethered to work. There are several unfinished projects but they can wait. We live in our minds and right now your mind is a complex maze of infinite possibilities with the entrances and exits in doubt. Ganesha watches.

4 February: First Quarter in Taurus

You now have the stability of Taurus. You have been away from the scene of action thanks to the machinations of an unruly mind. But you are now back on track. You roll up your sleeves and get down to earning a livelihood. Life is calling and you are ready for the dance. Those in creative fields earn kudos. Marital life is stable and children bring joy. Ganesha wishes you well.

11 February: Full Moon in Leo

'It is only when the mind is completely quiet, free of conflict – it is only then that the mind can go very far into the realms that are beyond time, thought and feeling,' said J. Krishnamurti. You are powering away on all cylinders. Nothing can stop you now. There was a lull in your affairs for a while but you are back on track and will not spare the horses on the home run. You are possessed by the power of Babe Ruth, the artistry of Roger Federer, the grim determination of Miruts Yifter the Shifter, the genius of Gary Sobers and the staying power of Dhanraj Pillay. You are a showman like Vijender Singh in the ring. Of course, success crowns you; there can be no other option in the mood you are in. As you can see, I know my sport, having been a sportsman myself! There are affairs of the heart and many expenses. You are on overdrive, take risks and ascend the loftiest peaks. An independent, exuberant, extravagant and rebellious streak finds eloquent expression. You buck the status quo and emerge triumphant. There is no time for the mundane dullness of life which occupies most of mankind. Ganesha is impressed.

18 February: Last Quarter in Sagittarius

You are moving with the speed of light. You criss-cross continents. If you are a mountaineer or lover of adventure sport, this is a wonderful phase. You are like Marco Polo or even Genghis Khan minus the atrocities. You open your life to new vistas and territories. There is magic in newness, and your sparkling mind leads the way. There are expenses, risks and every type of challenge thrown your way. But you sidestep them all with the deftness of Nureyev and the guile of Muhammad Ali. 'Made of Great', says the Tata Motors slogan; they could be talking about you in the same breath as Messi. Ganesha is amazed.

26 February: New Moon in Pisces

Thankfully, there is a let-up in your movement. You take a step back and watch the world from the sidelines. In a way, you have to catch your breath; it is a much needed timeout. You spend refreshing moments in amusement parks, art galleries, music concerts, art exhibitions and at cafes, lolling away or serenading your love. You indulge in the good things of life and want to be surrounded by love and beauty. You look at the world with the innocent eyes of a gurgling baby. Ganesha smiles.

5 March: First Quarter in Gemini

Your monkey mind is up to tricks again. You feel lonely, unloved and uncared for as you tango with self-created demons. Courting couples go through a harrowing time as you are unable to come to any conclusion. To be or not to be is the question that rears its head in every area of your life. These are indulgent times with separations and breakdowns, bingeing and irrational behaviour. A health crisis may also rear its ugly head. Of course, astrology never compels and this is a general reading. On the plus side there are powerful bursts of creativity. Writers and actors win applause. You can pass off your eccentricities as creative genius. Ganesha is with you.

12 March: Full Moon in Virgo

There is more balance now. Sometimes influences of one period coalesce into another, sometimes they don't. Thankfully, you are more tethered now due to the influence of Virgo. Family life is more settled and you sight your goals and work towards them. You make sensible purchases, get disciplined and organized, and realize that life has no real estate or freebies for losers. It is the survival of the fittest, and only shrinks love whiners; it is their vote bank. Ganesha walks with you as you get back into the groove and take life by the scruff of its neck and give it a good shake, like a golden retriever after its weekly bath. You are looking ahead with hope and attitude.

20 March: Last Quarter in Capricorn

You roll up your sleeves and plunder everything in sight. You are merciless. You excel. There are money and honey, rewards and awards, applause and accolades. 'Loving ourselves works miracles in our lives,' said Louise Hay. You get a new wardrobe, engage an image consultant and get a complete makeover. You spend time at spas, and preen. There is a new you in the making. There are love, energy, hope, strength, joy and passion in whatever you do. You sight money like the great whalers sighting Moby Dick. Nothing can stop you now. Money is also power, and you know that only too well. Ganesha watches.

28 March: New Moon in Aries

You are moving ahead with intensity and purpose. The winter is gone and the subcontinent is heating up slowly but surely. Your life is heating up too. Steve Jobs said, 'I think death is the most wonderful invention of life. It purges the system of those models that are obsolete.' You have found wings and are reinvented. You are not the same person who wallowed in self-pity a few weeks ago. You look at the blue yonder, take deep breaths, wear your armour and get ready for battle. You are a mix of Don Quixote and Genghis Khan. Ganesha is awestruck. Singles find new love and committed ones take ecstasy to ethereal heights. Need I say more?

3 April: First Quarter in Cancer

'The best portion of a good man's life is his little, nameless, unremembered acts of kindness and of love,' said William Wordsworth, the poet. You are filled with compassion for the less fortunate. You indulge in philanthropy and make time and resources available for charity. The family is content and you are filled with gratitude for the way life is shaping up for you. You want to give back to society. You feel that it is your karma and dharma. That is the mood you are in. These are happy days. You spread bonhomie and it returns to your bosom manifold. Youngsters do well at examinations and interviews, and the elderly feel loved and cared for. Your world is at peace. Ganesha is also at peace.

11 April: Full Moon in Libra

The full moon is in Libra and you surround yourself with all the goodies of life. You are in an expansive mood and shopping away like there is no tomorrow. You court new lovers and play the field. Singles have a merry time. There is business expansion calling for heavy investments and you don't back off. There are loans to be paid off and you take risks; you gamble big. But nothing ventured, nothing gained. You venture, stick your neck out, take risks and reap the whirlwind. Ganesha is thrilled.

19 April: Last Quarter in Capricorn

Mars is in your sign from 21 April to 4 June. This is indeed a long time and you are roused to action. You will not take anything lying down now, and this could be a cause for concern. Avoid altercations and any intercourse with the law. You could run into trouble if you do not control your fiery temperament, although generally Geminis are of a calm disposition. You are also influenced by Capricorn and will leave no stone unturned till you achieve your goals. This is a period of achievement. Ganesha watches from the sidelines; he is the coach and is always ready to pick you up when it matters. Mars is like the volcano of vitality inside you and influences endurance, persistence and discipline. Mars was named for the Roman god of war, and is also known as 'the bright and burning one'. Red is the colour of Mars and stimulates the dynamic, potent and fertile drives that power our lives. Mars rules physical energy and action and governs energy, strength, courage, life force and expansion. Well-placed Mars endows powerful energy and an indomitable will to succeed. Mars propels us like an ignited rocket. It is an important energy since it determines how we pursue what we want to achieve in life. In short, Mars represents energy, force, violence, aggression, sports, combat, wars, battles, accidents, operations.

26 April: New Moon in Taurus

You are on terra firma and in balance. Your task is clear-cut, and so are your efforts. You know where to go and how to get there. You are in achievement mode and are a classic combination of Messi, Neymar and Ronaldo, the contemporary soccer greats. In other words, you are invincible. There are indulgences, magic and fantasy. You are awed by the greenbacks stealing into your account. You sense that it is time to go for the kill, like the American eagle, high up, swirling the blue firmament, sighting a rodent with its third eye, thousands of metres away, and zooming in for the kill. Your timing too is perfect. You are at the right place at the right time. Ganesha is also amazed.

3 May: First Quarter in Leo

You are propelled by a fierce energy like a Red Indian scouting scalps. There is business expansion and many expenses. You are headed in the right direction. This is a good period. Use your free will to tweak it to advantage. The grand times continue. An Irish proverb says that a good laugh and a good sleep are the best cures in the doctor's book. In this phase you may not have a lot of sleep as you are prospecting new growth areas and will be burning the midnight oil. Those in the areas of pharmaceuticals do exceptionally well. You also play the markets and hit pay dirt. Success crowns you, but ensure that it doesn't go to your head. Married life may be tricky but you are beyond caring. Ganesha watches.

10 May: Full Moon in Scorpio

The full moon is in Scorpio and you are filled with intensity, passion, love and longing. You are also on a spiritual quest and look with great intent for a guru. You go on pilgrimages and explore yantra, tantra and mantra. You want to uncover secrets of yourself, as well as the secrets of the universe. You are thirsting for knowledge and pore over all available material in your specific areas of interest. You are far removed from domestic calls as you examine the larger issues of life. This is a wonderful period for scientists, counsellors, teachers and analysts. Ganesha blesses you.

19 May: Last Quarter in Aquarius

You live in the mind. Your eccentric behaviour surprises your friends. You bask in fantasy, magic and illusion. You live in an unreal world of your own making. There are indulgences and hallucinations. If you are prone to excessive drinking, promiscuity and other such habits you could get into trouble. There could be brushes with the law. Avoid altercations and take to yoga or meditation. This period shall also pass like everything else. Ganesha journeys with you and that helps.

25 May: New Moon in Gemini

The new moon is in your sign and the tide changes in your favour. This is a propitious time for creative folk. Those in the media and entertainment worlds do exceptionally well. There are money and honey, rewards and awards, accolades and applause. This is not a great period for crunching numbers as you are in the mood to give life to your fantasies. Film-makers and writers will win peer group and box-office approval. There are travel, money, new friends and vital associations that pitchfork you into the realm of stardom. Ganesha is impressed.

1 June: First Quarter in Virgo

There are balance and direction in all your moves. You are buoyed by a sense of purpose. There are many accomplishments in this period. Your attention, energy and focus are powered in one direction and the results are nothing short of miraculous. You are strong-willed and do not suffer fools gladly. There is also a lot of social networking as you gear up to get your message out to as many people as possible. Advertising and marketing is the name of the game and you know how important it is. You do not want to be left out. In fact, you want fame at all costs. You want to experience every vista of life and grow as a person. There are many possibilities. Use your free will to advantage. Astrology never compels. Ganesha watches.

9 June: Full Moon in Sagittarius

'Fill the brain with the highest ideals, place them day and night before you, and out of that will come great work,' said Swami Vivekananda. Mercury is in Gemini from 7 to 20 June. The full moon is also in Sagittarius and your world is heavenly. You reach for the stars and touch them. Miracles are in your grasp. There are movement, travel, investments, love, spiritual urges, new discoveries and vistas that reveal life's hidden treasures. This is a powerful phase. Make the most of it. The gods are blessing you, and now the direction you give life is literally in your hands, as astrology never compels. This is also a general reading as I do not have your personal chart. But, according to the stars, the period is excellent. Optimize it. Ganesha wishes you well. Mercury, the mighty, all-powerful planet, favours travels, meetings, conferences, interviews, trips, more brainpower, contacts, communication, correspondence, contracts. Mercury has a special connection with the circuits of the brain. Chess, crossword and other such games belong to Mercury. Also, short-distance runners and spin bowlers are controlled by Mercury. Mercury, in short, is the ambassador and salesman of the zodiac. Mercury is the symbol of news, views, messages, interviews, contacts, communications, travel and transport. Mercury gives an impetus to all of the above in the sun sign where it is located.

17 June: Last Quarter in Pisces

You are at your creative peak. Playwrights, actors, singers and others in the media strike pay dirt. This is also the time for love. You are in the arms of amour. You feel that you have met your soulmate, and in your paramour's arms nothing else seems to make sense. You bask in the unreal; it is a dream come true. I am not a cynic. In fact, I am a lover in the true sense of the word. But I know what happens when love crashes, which it must, at some point in time. All love has an expiry date. Until then, hang on to it, hold on to the ethereal nanoseconds and stretch them to eternity. True love happens rarely and when it does one is blessed. You are blessed now. There are also celebrations, festivities, fun times and parties. You are the toast of the ballroom and you love your moment in the sun. Enjoy, says Ganesha.

24 June: New Moon in Cancer

You are waylaid by domestic concerns. If you have strayed from a committed relationship, which I suspect you may have, there is a price to pay, and it may be quite heavy. There is turbulence on the home front and you are hard-pressed to quell the fires. The health of elders could also be a cause of concern. All these distractions take you away from work. Ganesha is with you all the way and you manage to stub it all and get back on track. You have learnt your lessons and are in no mood to repeat your mistakes.

1 July: First Quarter in Libra

Clearly, the gods are on your side. Venus is in Gemini from 5 to 31 July. I don't have to say much more. You also have the influence of Libra working on you and this is a period of love and expensive and exquisite purchases. You want to be surrounded by beautiful objects. You want to live in the lap of comfort. Family life returns to harmony, and children bring joy as they excel in examinations and interviews. Your life is humming a soft tune. Venus is another important planet and is of great significance. This is an important phase. As often discussed, Venus is the planet for love, romance, sex, beauty and good life. This is the planet of attraction, love, wealth, knowledge and prosperity. The compatibility of partners and the type of life the individual will lead are also judged from the placement of Venus in the horoscope. As a planet, Venus is considered to be beneficial, feminine and gentle. Venus symbolizes the force of attraction in the universe. In human beings, this attractive force manifests as love and beauty. When Venus is well placed in the chart, there are love, art, beauty and all the goodies of life that make life worth living. Venus rules Libra and Taurus, though its role in every sign is important. Like other planets, it also has its transits. In Libra, Venus is aesthetic and cultured. In Taurus it is more earthy, materialistic and sensual. Venus rules the venous system, kidneys, urinary tract, throat, larynx, and is responsible for good looks. In short, Venus in Western astrology stands for comforts, arts, wealth, relationships, sex, decorations, luxuries and wealth. Ganesha blesses you.

9 July: Full Moon in Capricorn

You are moving fast and ferocious like a cheetah in the Serengeti National Park. Your sights are on quarry and you cannot miss. You are like Messi taking a penalty kick in a World Cup final, and you don't miss. You dazzle with your expertise and craftsmanship and win kudos. Fresh greenbacks swarm into your kitty. You just love the fragrance and feel of it. Money is honey. It makes the world go round. You make shrewd investments and prepare a nest egg. Your world is on song. Ganesha loves it.

16 July: Last Quarter in Aries

You mow down the opposition in a brazen display of showmanship. You are like Ranbir Singh at the film awards. You hog the limelight with your skills as you dazzle all and sundry. You love the limelight and bask in its glory. There are rewards and awards and overseas travel. Those in business look seriously at expansion. Freelancers get gilt-edged chances. Life is a bouquet of red roses. Love calls from the rooftops and you are spoilt for choice. The singles play the field without a care. Ganesha watches in awe.

23 July: New Moon in Leo

'Everyone can be great because everyone can serve,' said Martin Luther King. You long for greatness and immortality. You want to be a legend like Dilip Kumar. You put your heart and soul into achievement because we all know that genius is hard work. It is about perspiration and not mere inspiration. How do you think one churns out book after book every year for decades? Just sheer hard work, burning the midnight oil. You do just that and achieve miracles. You emerge as a leading player in your field. The cosmos has blessed your efforts. Ganesha is thrilled.

30 July: First Quarter in Scorpio

'Be selfish, be generous,' said the Dalai Lama. You are both, as a powerful intensity grips you. Your soul is in a whirl. To be or not to be is the question. You want to be everywhere at all times but that, I must add, is the sole privilege of Ganesha. There are indulgences and risk taking. Your shadow side takes hold of your life. Your underbelly is exposed and you are vulnerable. Love walks in and walks out like the morning breeze. You wonder what to do. Ganesha holds your hand.

7 August: Full Moon in Aquarius

'Show me a sane man and I will cure him,' said Jung, triumphantly. He may have been talking about you in the phase that you are in. You are charged emotionally and easily angered. You are ego-driven, intolerant and irritable. Your contentious mood could derail your plans. But you are as helpless as a mouse in the belly of an anaconda. Relationships go for a toss and you remain sullen and morbid. Those with escapist tendencies open various windows of indulgence. Family life is a casualty. Work also suffers. Of course, I am not God and this is a mere astrological reading. Astrology never compels. These are just general indications as I do not have your personal chart. Ganesha journeys with you and that is a huge consolation.

15 August: Last Quarter in Taurus

'Truly it is in the darkness that one finds the light, so when we are in sorrow, then this light is nearest of all to us,' said

Meister Eckhart. Your boat is righted. Probably, Ganesha has saved you. You are back on terra firma and have found balance. You roll up your sleeves and get down to the hard slog. You earn and spend. Money used well is no cause for regret. You also spend on the less fortunate and that helps. Whatever you give away also returns manifold. I have seen this in my life, dear readers, and I fully encourage philanthropy. We are all a part of the cosmos and are one big human chain. Nothing goes unnoticed. You shower your loved ones with gifts, and even that doesn't go unnoticed.

21 August: New Moon in Leo

'I don't know what your destiny will be, but one thing I do know: The only ones among you who will be really happy are those who have sought and found how to serve,' said Nobel laureate Albert Schweitzer. The new moon is in Leo and you are powering ahead. You are charged like a new cycle dynamo in the interiors of India. Ego drives and passions are strong but you have learnt your lessons well and do not allow your base instincts to take over. You display naked power play and emerge trumps at brinkmanship. The family is well taken care of and that is a consolation. Love smiles at singles. Ganesha watches nonplussed.

29 August: First Quarter in Sagittarius

You are using the marvels of modern technology to communicate with the world at large. You meet new people and open picturesque vistas. Someone from another culture will play an important role in your life. He or she may don a guru's role and lead you by the hand into a new era of love, beauty, compassion and sacrifice. Despite the distractions, you sign big deals and do well at the negotiating table. You are knocking on the doors of spirituality too. Wealth and a higher consciousness are a great combination. Ganesha watches with interest.

6 September: Full Moon in Pisces

The one and only Osho said, 'When your creativity comes to a climax, when your whole life becomes creative, you live in God ... Love what you do. Be meditative while you are doing it: whatsoever it is!' You are in the throes of a hard slog and you love what you do. That is the key. You dazzle and razzle because work is your worship. This is a powerfully creative phase. You articulate your zeal with flamboyance and attract a niche as well as widespread audience. There are profitable associations and collaborations. Love comes knocking and health is good. Ganesha sees it all.

13 September: Last Quarter in Gemini

Bob Marley said, 'I have no education. I have inspiration. If I was educated, I would be a damn fool.' You are moving ahead at rapid speed. The monkey mind assails you. You want to do everything at once and realize that it simply cannot happen. But you are not upset. Despite the limitations of the moment, you are optimistic, energetic, joyous, happy and affirmative. Luck is on your side and, if you are one of the players being bid for in the IPL, Lady Luck smiles happily; you are in for big money. The moon is in your sign and you are in an infectious mood and the cynosure of all eyes at all festivities. This is not a time when you dirty your elbows at the workplace but it is certainly a time to have fun. Your heart is pure and open and you want to croon like the nightingale. Ganesha is impressed.

20 September: New Moon in Virgo

There are stability and balance and you are back on track setting your papers right. 'The ability to concentrate and to use your time well is everything if you want to succeed in business: or almost anywhere else for that matter,' said Lee Iacocca. You realize that time wasted is money lost. There are new expansion plans on the anvil and you leave no stone unturned to get where you want to be. Family life is stable though a minor health problem may recur. Children bring joy, and as the winter chill gathers around you there is no cause for complaint. Ganesha is happy.

28 September: First Quarter in Capricorn

There is hard work ahead. If you have started on new projects, they have to be completed well and on time. You have been on an expansion spree and the nuts and bolts of the new deals you have signed have to be tightened. 'Gratitude is like love or fresh air: you cannot get too much of it,' says life coach Danielle LaPorte. You are indeed filled with gratitude for all the good tidings that have fallen on your head from heaven like manna. You have little time for emotions now as money and honey beckon and you have to move every nerve and sinew to get where you want to be. Children could also be leaving home for further studies. You may also look at migrating for better prospects. Ganesha blesses you.

5 October: Full Moon in Aries

The full moon is in Aries and you are on a roll. You are filled with energy and work miracles. 'Those who cannot remember the past are condemned to repeat it,' said George Santayana. His words resound in your soul and you rejoice in the present. You have learnt your lessons well and there is no chance in heaven or hell for a repetition of mistakes. You do not want to live in regret and have ensured that you will seize the moment. This works well for you and success beckons. At the least, it makes you happy and content. You are a better human being now and are more amiable and amenable to reason. Married life is happy and children bring joy. There could be an addition to the family. Ganesha is delighted.

12 October: Last Quarter in Cancer

'Fiction gives us a second chance that life denies us,' said Paul Theroux, the novelist. There are maudlin times ahead; nothing to disturb or disrupt your life, but it adds sauce to the dream run. The focus is on the family. You may take them for a holiday or tend to elders and others who haven't seen much of you lately. Friends drop by, and there are family gatherings. Creative folk do exceedingly well and you are in line for rewards and awards. You use the time well and hang out in amusement parks and go on picnics. Life is a dream and you love every moment of it. You may also take to helping the less fortunate, be it humans or animals. Ganesha is impressed. So am I.

19 October: New Moon in Libra

The new moon is in Libra and you are spoilt for choice. You weigh the pros and cons of every move and possibly don't take an inch forward or backward. 'On the mountains of truth you can never climb in vain: either you will reach a point higher up today, or you will be training your powers so that you will be climbing higher tomorrow,' said Friedrich Nietzsche. You are looking hard to cleanse your soul and go in searching of a guru. You try to reinvent yourself and do things that you haven't done in aeons. From a change in wardrobe to new hobbies and interests your life undergoes a metamorphosis. Your soul is seeking out a higher consciousness and Ganesha will not let you down in the pursuit. He knows your call and the answer.

27 October: First Quarter in Aquarius

You withdraw from the world and enter the shadows. You take a step back and, like the great generals, retreat to win in the future – Rommel would be proud of you as you strategize your moves far from the scene of action. You will come back rejuvenated and strike where it hurts the enemy. In this case, if you are in the corporate world, you will checkmate the opposition and sell your ideas to management. They will be suitably impressed and you are in line for more perks and a promotion. There could be new love and domestic disruptions, but that comes with the territory called life. Ganesha watches without concern as he knows it all.

4 November: Full Moon in Taurus

You are hacking away to global stardom. If you are a cricketer in the IPL you don't know what to do with all the money that has landed on your lap. Sadguru Jaggi Vasudev, today's popular mystic says, 'There is security in repetitive life patterns, but there are no possibilities, no growth.' He couldn't be more spot on. You tweak all the rules and invent new ones. You leave the opposition behind like a cunning hyena with the strength and stamina of a cheetah. You break all rules and listen to a distant drummer. There are rich dividends. You know what you are doing and the beaten path is not your chosen avenue. Ganesha says hurrah.

10 November: Last Quarter in Leo

'An ant on the move does more than a dozing ox,' said Lao-tzu. You are on the move for sure. You are gripped by powerful intensity and work wonders. You trump the opposition in group discussions, contractual negotiations and conferences. Students excel, parents are thrilled and there is happiness at home, which is half the battle won. There could be international travel too, along with ego drives and uncontrolled passions. The singles play the field and committed partners take love to ethereal heights. There are expenses and indulgences of all kinds. But Ganesha says that is par for the course, and he is the last word on life and its caprices.

18 November: New Moon in Scorpio

You are looking hard at unusual achievement. You want to get into the *Guinness Book of Records* or, at the very least, into the *Limca Book of Records*. You want renown and will go the whole hog for it. You are like the trapeze artist seeking the thrill of walking across the Niagara Falls and back with eyes closed; you are the lion tamer with your head in the lion's mouth, hoping he has barely noticed; you want to make love to the king cobra at the Bangkok snake park in front of a startled audience; you want to eat tube lights and the entire marine plywood furniture at Walmart; you want to tattoo your eyeballs in fluorescent shades; you want to eat your liver and regurgitate it for the great medical minds at Johns Hopkins. You want to freak out every possible way, break the status quo and carve a niche for yourself for posterity. You are at your creative best. Of course, this is a general reading and I do not have your personal chart. Astrology also never compels. But in the mood you are in, you are in a league of your own and that is such a sorry understatement. I will not mention family life and other domestic concerns here. If you cannot figure that one out, Ganesha will.

26 November: First Quarter in Pisces

There is a softness in your step. 'When you do things from your soul, you feel a river moving in you, a joy,' said Rumi. Ganesha and I agree. You take a step back from all the excitement and take to music, poetry and the arts. You surround yourself with love and longing and get indulgent. You plead for the goodies of life to embalm you. There is a joyous hum to life and you not only want to partake of it but also share it with all and sundry. Love is in the air and you pluck it out. Is it a dream? Who knows? You trade everyday life for a spell of gossamer dreams woven in the womb of your imagination and desires. There is an element of truth there as you move into ethereal realms of existence like a dream sequence in a Hindi film that has suddenly turned real from surreal or should I say sur-'reel'. As you may know I take pride in giving my readers much more than mere astrology which is never absolute.

3 December: Full Moon in Gemini

The full moon is in your sign and you hum like a new locomotive in the hills of Darjeeling. You are in the throes of communication and use every technological tool in the world, and I dare say there are many, and more are growing by the nanosecond. 'Faith is the bird that feels the light and sings when the dawn is still dark,' said Rabindranath Tagore. You move fast and sign deals. There is success without much hard work. It all comes too easy. You marvel at your luck. This is a profoundly creative phase and you can make a zebra appreciate your creations. Even if you step on a landmine in Cambodia it won't explode. Seize the moment, said the Bard. 'There is a tide in the affairs of man. When taken at the flood it leads to fortune.' Ganesha agrees.

10 December: Last Quarter in Virgo

There are stability and energy that power you ahead in the right direction. This is not party time though the dance floor is calling. You are ideating with the speed of a cement churning machine trying to lay a road in Mumbai hours before the rains liquidate every brick. But your ideas are worth their weight in gold. You strike pay dirt and win the approval of your peer group. Life is calling and you are ready for the waltz. Home life is steady. Children bring joy. There may be an addition to the family. You may even take an exotic pet home. Ganesha smiles.

18 December: New Moon in Sagittarius

'A scholar who cherishes the love of comfort is not deemed to be a scholar,' said Lao-tzu. The new moon is in Sagittarius and you are on the highway of success and travel. You spend money without a thought in the world and gather lovers like it is going out of fashion. The singles have a field day and the married are tempted to stray. I will not say any more as this is a mere general reading and astrology never compels. This is a great time for group activities; even solo journeys are possible. Your mind is fixated at several places and you are in a hurry to get to some place or other; it is the journey that matters and not the destination. Family life is fine but the health of elders may cause concern. Ganesha holds your hand.

26 December: First Quarter in Aries

This is a great end to the year; you began 2017 on a cracking note and you end it with thunder. If last year came to a close on an emotional note, this year's end wears as much plumage as a junglefowl. You are at the centre of action and love every moment of the limelight, though it gets sweaty at times. Ganesha has been with you right through every ebb and flow and guided you when you needed it most, and you are grateful for that. You could be taking the family for a long holiday now or making expensive purchases to embellish a new home. These are good tidings. Money slips through your fingers, but then what is money for? You live once, so party hard and true. I leave you with Bob Marley's wisdom as you embrace 2018: 'Emancipate yourselves from mental slavery, none but ourselves can free our minds.'

CANCER

23 June–22 July

Ganesha's Master Key: Sensitive and sympathetic.

'For as long as space endures, and for as long as living beings remain, until then may I, too, abide, to dispel misery in this world.'
— THE DALAI LAMA, A CANCERIAN, QUOTING FROM THE *SHANTIDEVA*

The important traits are: Blending logic with abstract thought; Transmuting knowledge into wisdom; Recognizing that we are all brothers and sisters; Loving universally; Expressing love wisdom; Recognizing that we are all united, but separate; Speaking and writing in order to express love wisdom; Spreading love wisdom through teaching; Overly sensitive, emotionally insecure; Automatic and unthinking; Instinctual, unfocused; Wanting to mother and be mothered; 'Smothering' instead of mothering; Emotionally clinging, needing a protective shell; clannish, tenacious; Excessively holding on to people and things; Holding on to the past; Being a victim of the mass consciousness; Needing to belong to a biological family;

Sympathetic, compassionate; Nurturing others with a higher love; Differentiating solar plexus love from heart love; Being able to still the emotions; Directing and controlling the emotions; Needing to belong to a group; Controlling instincts by means of the mind; Recognizing mass consciousness; Working to dissolve biological and man-made boundaries; Turning into the consciousness of the masses in order to help them; Awareness of belonging to the family of humanity; Working within mass consciousness, yet being above it; Uplifting the masses through intuitive guidance; Relating and identifying with the common, everyday person with the knowledge that we all have the same roots; Identifying with the need to build the form needed for New Age living; Being aware of the illusionary nature of life.

My father is also a Cancerian. My father has the highest regards for the Dalai Lama. The Dalai Lama is *goodness* personified and exemplified. On 7 December 2013, my father met the Dalai Lama at the India International Centre in Delhi. The Dalai Lama took the hand of my father and put it on his (Dalai Lama's) head. My father was completely overwhelmed. My father knew very well that the Dalai Lama was far greater and superior to him in every way. My father was knocked out by the humanity of the mighty Dalai Lama. It was certainly the most memorable experience in the entire life of my eighty-five-year-old father. The article on Cancer is not done by me. It is done by my father. My father says health + hope + home = happiness. Every word begins with an 'H'.

Your Beauty-scope: Unless you are very, very careful your stomach will protrude. Here, mere dieting, however strict, will not help. Exercise (especially bends and swimming) is the right answer. You will have a round or, at least, a slightly dreamy appearance. Quite a few men fall for it, not knowing your great persistence and tenacity. But you can play it up by wearing a string of pearls (lucky for you) around the neck. Your arms and limbs are long in comparison to the rest of the body. But the hands are usually very expressive and should be given free play. Maxis suit you.

CENTRAL IDEA

Intuitive, Easily hurt, Family, Kind, Remembers the past

Robert Hand is my favourite astrologer. Therefore, I quote Robert Hand: 'The fourth house is more than the home. Many relationships have nothing that could be called a home, and yet the fourth house remains important. First of all, it is one of the angular houses, which gives it an added significance. But, more fundamentally, the fourth house indicates the basic roots of a relationship, both literally, in geographical terms, and figuratively, in terms of mental and emotional background. The fourth house signifies the innermost depths of a relationship, which may be so far within as to be invisible on the surface. The fourth house should be checked to see if there is an underlying compatibility between two people. Do they have compatible backgrounds in the senses just described, and are their basic emotional and psychological characteristics compatible? On top of this, the fourth house does not mean a collective "home" if such a notion is appropriate. The home is where a couple's deepest emotional and psychological attitudes have their strongest impact. The home is in many ways the physical embodiment of one's innermost being, and is therefore influenced by anything that affects inner life.

Afflictions to the fourth house have a negative effect upon the home, if there is one, and upon the deepest levels of compatibility. A composite chart with a strong fourth house usually indicates that the two people share their innermost lives and that they probably share their actual place of residence.'

Dr Shanker Adawal has this to say about Jupiter in our fourth angle: 'Hence Jupiter here gives very good results and provides the native the powers of deciding the fate and fortune of others. He will possess money, wealth and large properties along with honours and favours from the government. In times of crisis, the native will receive divine help. As he grows old, his prosperity and money will increase.'

In practical terms, and in life we have to be practical, Jupiter in the fourth angle stands for: Renovation/decoration/alteration/installation of anything to do with property, statues; Buying/selling/leasing/renting; Gardening/farming/fallowing/mining; Horticulture/flower arrangement or Ikebana; Divination of water; Office/shop/godown/warehouse; Parents, in-laws, elderly people, priests, retired folks, pets and maternal uncle.

By Western astrology, Saturn will remain in your house of health, servants, food, loans, theft, pets, till 20 December 2017. But this year the effect of Saturn will be much less than the two previous years because Saturn will be well placed and in a happy relationship with Jupiter. In simple words, Jupiter is the saviour and the protector. Therefore, have faith and courage. If you believe in astrology, recite the mantra 'Shri Ram Jai Ram Jai Jai Ram' every Saturday in the temple of Hanuman. It is your choice though.

For you very specially, Venus, by Western astrology only, represents everything to do with house, home, friends and wish-fulfilment. Venus will act like a tonic for you between 1 and 25 August; 14 October and 6 November; 5 and 31 July. Make the best use of it.

Mercury represents intelligence, journeys, communication. For you very specially, Mercury also represents foreign affairs and visits to lonely places as well as hospitals and social welfare centres. Mercury will help to push you forward and elevate you to success between 21 June and 25 July; September 30 and October 16; 26 February and 13 March. Be ready to move mentally, physically, spiritually.

Mars, as I am sure you do know, is the energy and warrior planet of the zodiac. Mars will give you added power between 5 June and 19 July; 1 January and 9 March; and 9 and 31 December. It is a good time to achieve your goal and targets. Be bold.

MONTHLY ROUND-UP

January: Marriage, ties, love, collaborations, romance, meeting and reaching out to people and places. **February**: Health, funds, tantra and mantra, change of locale, moving. **March**: Journeys, publicity, ceremonies, collaborations, functions, rites and religion. **April**: Stepping up on efficiency, work, status, prestige, taking care of parents, elders. **May**: Help, socializing, friendship, fraternity, camaraderie. **June**: Expenses, losses, spirituality, helping others, charity, long-distance connections. **July**: Power, perks, promotions, prosperity. **August**: Finances and family. **September**: Contacts and joy. **October**: Property, parents, in-laws. **November**: Joy, creativity, children, hobbies; You make news and win over others. **December**: Work, funds, employment, health and medical check-ups, servants, subordinates.

Money: Cancer is very definitely a money sign. Cancerians know how to earn and also how to save. They believe in having a nest egg for the future. This year, property and job should give you a good deal of money. The months for it could be January, August, October, April and May. Ganesha and Allah say help the poor as much as possible. By helping others you actually help yourself.

Happiness Quota: I give you 87 per cent.

MONTH BY MONTH

January: This is a powerful period. Make the most of it. There is business expansion, and freelancers spread their wings far and wide. There could be international travel, or, at the very least, international associations. You are in expansion mode. Mid-month, the focus shifts to domestic demands. You are filled with verve, vigour and zest. You are also kind and compassionate. As the month ends, there is powerful intensity goading you on. You scorch the tarmac with your innate sensuality. This could also be a creative period when you experiment with new ideas and templates.

February: There is hard work and there is stability. You are determined to prove your point. You are upbeat and positive. Mid-month sees powerful ego drives. You are filled with passion and intensity. There are rewards and awards, applause and accolades. This is a propitious period for work. As the month ends, there could be travel. You are in the mood for adventure. You realize that you need to reach out to the larger, wider world. Family life has its rumbles.

March: You are in the throes of powerful creative energy. Awards and rewards are yours for the asking. This is a strange period with many thrills and chills like a see-saw in the neighbourhood park. Mid-month sees you back on terra firma. You roll up your sleeves and get down to hard work. As the month ends, you sign new deals and expand your business empire. Life is shining on you. You are moving ahead on all cylinders. Nothing can stop you in its tracks. You have sighted your goal and will attain it at all costs.

April: There are emotional moments and many domestic crises. You are at your wit's end. You attempt to sort out your life and work. Mid-month sees domestic issues calling out to you. Children, parents and the spouse need attention. As the month ends, there are new job openings, lucrative freelance offers and new vistas unfolding. You surge ahead. There is peace and harmony in your life. More importantly, there is balance.

May: New opportunities open up at work. Love also comes calling. There are expenses as you invest heavily on business expansion. Mid-month sees you walk down memory lane and spoil an otherwise profitable period with maudlin thoughts. Emotions overwhelm you. As the month ends, you may take to yoga, meditation, alternative therapy and philanthropy to divert your attention from pressing concerns. There are challenges and you evolve as you surmount them.

June: You are in full flow. There could be major business expansion as you explore options. There are powerful ego drives and passions. Mid-month sees travel on the cards.

You could be moving in a group, or solo, but you will be moving in many ways and in different directions. There is also spiritual growth. As the month ends, you open your soul and meet up with people from different climes. You are thirsting for new vistas. You are filled with eloquence and artistry. Those in the media or the arts strike pay dirt. Whatever you start now will reap rich dividends.

July: Your consciousness is raised. You want to be heard, and you will. There is media coverage and you are in the spotlight. There are mood swings and unconscious drives and compulsions. Mid-month sees a semblance of balance in your daily life. You are ambitious. Your emotions are stabilized and the monkey mind is tethered. As the month ends, you forge new alliances and new vistas open up in your life. You lead from the front and earn kudos. Your plate is packed with many bounties. You are magnetic. Those in the fine arts do exceptionally well.

August: You are moving fast and furious. You look ahead and ideate. This is an excellent period for making plans. Your mind is sharp. You sign new deals and surge ahead. Mid-month sees stability and many expenses as you make your presence felt in the world. You take risks and emerge triumphant. You are serenaded by the bounty of life. As the month ends, you are eloquent, flamboyant, articulate, aggressive and affirmative. Success is guaranteed. You meet up with people from different cultures and feel stimulated, invigorated, refreshed and rejuvenated.

September: This can be a powerfully creative period. It all depends on how you optimize it. Family life is exciting; there are pulls and pressures of all kinds. Children and elders could bowl a googly. You are on your toes. Mid-month sees you on overdrive. You meet with people from different cultures and grow with the interactions. As the month ends, there is stability and balance. You know what to do and where you are headed. This is a great time for those in the corporate world. Your ambitions are aroused and you will stop at nothing. There are expenses and indulgences, love and longing, and all the ingredients that make life worth living.

October: This is a propitious phase and whatever you embark on now has a high chance of success. Use this phase well. There are festive occasions too, with an addition to the family, marriages, engagements and anniversaries. Mid-month sees you flamboyantly parade your sensitivities. There are indulgences, mood swings and temper tantrums. As the month ends, you look for spiritual enhancement. You are in an experimental mood. Relationships are intense in this period. Emotions are on fire. This is also a creative phase. Your imagination is torched and you are struck by genius.

November: It is a propitious phase. Make the most if it. There are money and honey, rewards and awards, accolades and applause. Mid-month you are on a business expansion spree and there are rich dividends. There could be foreign travel and you could be elevated to positions of power and responsibility. Love courts you too. You are in the bosom of hope, optimism and joy. There are lucky breaks and windfalls. As the month ends, you are gripped by intensity and achieve miracles. Strong emotional undercurrents accompany the intensity of the period. This is a period charged with philanthropy. If you are a caregiver, or work with NGOs, you reach new heights of compassion. You give selflessly.

December: You are busy reconnecting the old school ties. There are love and bonhomie in the air. You may be looking at taking your love to the altar. There are meaningful associations that garland your life. Mid-month sees stability and balance and you move forward. Work pressures mount. As the month ends, there could be international travel, even pilgrimages. These are indulgent days. If you have artistic inclinations they are showcased. There are many expenses. Love life blooms. You are rejuvenated and transformed. You are knocking at the gates of posterity.

WEEKLY REVIEW (BY PHASES OF THE MOON)

5 January: First Quarter in Aries

I love this quote and will start the astrological predictions with it: 'Even after all this time, the sun never says to the Earth, *You owe me*. Look what happens with a love like that ... It lights the whole sky.' It is variously attributed to both Rumi and Hafiz. This is a great start to the year. This is a powerful period. Make the most of it. If you have started a new project, it will gather steam. There is business expansion, and freelancers spread their wings far and wide. Money wanders into your pocket, and also wanders out. There could be international travel, or, at the very least, international associations. You are in expansion mode. Love follows you like a faithful terrier. Ganesha is happy for you. Now, like I always do, let me tell you a bit about your sign. This helps set the tone for the predictions as you get to know a bit more about yourself. Cancerians can be timid, dull, shy and withdrawn, and the most brilliant. They are fundamentally conservative and home-loving. On the surface they can appear formidable, uncompromising, tenacious, purposeful, energetic, shrewd, intuitive and wise, and deep inside they could be sympathetic, kind, imaginative, romantic, idealistic, filled with insecurities, and sensitive. Their dash and bravado could just be a mask, a façade, a shield to protect them from the vagaries of the outside world. Celebrity Cancerians include Meryl Streep, Jack Dempsey, George Orwell, Mike Tyson, Princess Diana, Hermann Hesse, the Dalai Lama XIV, Sylvester Stallone, Tom Cruise, Pierre Cardin, Ringo Starr, Tom Hanks, Arthur Ashe, Leon Spinks, Harrison Ford, Ernest Hemingway, Gerald Ford, Bill Cosby and Ingmar Bergman, among others. India has had three highly successful cricket captains in Sunil Gavaskar, Saurav Ganguly and current skipper Mahendra Singh Dhoni. As you can see, you are in great company.

12 January: Full Moon in Cancer

The focus shifts to domestic demands. There are a few challenges but you surmount them with the ease of Dhyan Chand getting past the German defence in the Berlin Olympic Games. So mesmerized was Hitler, who watched the game, that he even offered a job to Dhyan Chand! In this phase you may spend time in renovation work or looking into the nitty-gritty of inheritance and other fiscal details. The money angle catches your eye. You have to secure the family monetarily; that is your prime concern. Edison said, 'I have not failed … I have just found 10,000 ways that don't work.' You too work your way into the sunlight through trial and error. You are filled with verve, vigour and zest. You are also kind and compassionate and endear yourself to one and all. Your emotions are rich, eloquent, flamboyant and attractive as they spill over the cosmos in colours that could distract Picasso. Work could take a back seat for the moment. Ganesha smiles.

19 January: Last Quarter in Scorpio

There is powerful intensity goading you on. You scorch the tarmac with your innate sensuality. If you are walking the ramp for the Lakme Fashion Week you are the cynosure of all eyes. 'Don't compromise yourself. You're all you've got,' said Janis Joplin. You certainly won't. You are riding high. There are money and honey. I must add here that astrology never compels. Plus, I am not God and this is a general reading as I don't have your personal horoscope. I have also seen in several decades of making predictions that people can be stuck in ruts and they don't allow the stars to impact them even positively. Use your free will to advantage, I say. Ganesha agrees. You have to help yourself first. Like the fisherfolk, launch your vessel when the tide is in your favour.

28 January: New Moon in Aquarius

This could be a creative period when you experiment with new ideas and templates. You want success, and work hard at your weaknesses. You are looking ahead with hope and optimism. There is a lot to be done and you are figuring out where to begin. There could be a detour too as you take time off to visit art galleries and amusement parks. You may also take the maudlin route but stop dead in your tracks when you realize that it is counterproductive. Steve Jobs in an address to Stanford University said, 'Don't be trapped by dogma: which is living with the results of other people's thinking. Don't let the noise of others' opinions drown out your own inner voice. And most importantly, have the courage to follow your heart and intuition.' This is certainly the period when you break out of the rut and plough your own furrow. You want renown, but on your terms. Ganesha watches.

4 February: First Quarter in Taurus

There is hard work and there is stability too. You are determined to prove your point to the world and will not stop at attempting miracles. You don't hold your punches and realize, like Vijender Singh, the professional pugilist who is making waves, that a quick jab to the nose is all that it takes. You go for the kill and mow down the opposition. 'Sunshine is delicious, rain is refreshing, wind braces us up, snow is exhilarating; there is really no such thing as bad weather, only different kinds of good weather,' said John Ruskin, author, art critic, and social reformer. You are upbeat and positive and send the right messages to the universe. It responds favourably and you hit pay dirt. The fragrance of crisp greenbacks is enticing. There are expenses too, but you are in the lap of honey. Love follows you like mice following the Pied Piper. Enjoy, says Ganesha.

11 February: Full Moon in Leo

Ego drives are high. You are filled with passion and intensity and will not allow your ambitious plans to be waylaid or hijacked. There are rewards and awards, applause and accolades, money and honey. Singles play the field. New love eats into your soul and takes you by the collar into a realm of infinite ethereal possibilities. Call it love or lust, I don't know, even after eight decades of loving. But you are in the throes of amour and nothing can disengage you. This is a propitious period for work too; use your free will to optimize what the stars have in store for you. There are fun times and festivities. Way to go, says Ganesha.

18 February: Last Quarter in Sagittarius

There is a lot of movement in your life in all possible ways. You tweak every technological marvel to get your views across. There could also be physical travel. You are in the mood for adventure and could go bungee jumping without even bothering to check if the straps are secure. You may also go looking for a guru as your spiritual inclinations are buoyed. There are expenses and offbeat and irreverent behaviour as you try to buck trends. Peers and loved ones will find you difficult to fathom. But Ganesha knows what you are wrestling with and that is all that matters.

26 February: New Moon in Pisces

There is a softness which overtakes you. We are all subject to biorhythms which change every single day. You walk down memory lane and shed a few tears. Yes, life could have been better. Yes, certain decisions were taken in haste. But there is no point living in the past. It has to be dusted and forgotten. You have to move on. This is a minor detour and is important to enrich your present as long as you don't indulge it. You realize that you need to reach out to the larger, wider world and are apprehensive about getting out of your cosy shell. Rest there and rot, I say. Ganesha agrees. Family life has its rumbles and children could cause some discontent. But it is all par for the course.

5 March: First Quarter in Gemini

You are moving faster than light. If you are a trapeze artist you would dazzle, even without neon lights. You have the same number of hours per day that Leonardo da Vinci, Thomas Jefferson, Albert Einstein and others had. It is not that you are wasting time; it is simply a matter of checking out all options before the first big move. You are in the throes of powerful creative energy, and, if it is rightly channelled, awards and rewards are yours for the asking. Love runs after singles and those in committed relationships are prone to distractions. You suddenly realize that monogamy has very little going for it. Of course, astrology never compels. This is a strange period with many thrills and chills like a see-saw in the neighbourhood park. Ganesha watches in amusement.

12 March: Full Moon in Virgo

There is balance and you are back on terra firma. You roll up your sleeves and get to the shop floor. There could be an addition to the family and you may even adopt a child from an entirely different culture, like Angelina Jolie and Brad Pitt did. You pore over bank accounts and fiscal instruments with a magnifying glass. Nothing escapes your eagle eye. You are moving ahead, and that is what matters. Elders may need critical care. Ganesha holds your hand.

20 March: Last Quarter in Capricorn

The template of the last week is repeated as you surge ahead. Your focus is on work and nothing else. You have seen how money can change your life and you realize how important it can be in the larger scheme of things. You need money even to be philanthropic. So why make any bones of wanting more. Accept the fact without hypocrisy. You sign new deals and expand your business empire. The employed see promotions and added perks. Life is shining on you. Ganesha smiles.

28 March: New Moon in Aries

You are moving ahead on all cylinders. Nothing can stop you in its tracks. You have sighted your goal and will attain it at all costs. You are greedy and can get unethical. Avarice could get you into trouble with the law. Ganesha also forbids it. I may be of the old school, but honesty is the best policy. There is karma and dharma and you will get your just deserts in life. Learn also to cut your clothes according to your cloth. I am an astrologer and not a preacher but I must insist on ethical ways lest you stray from the path. We are human and fallible. Love breathes down your neck. What you do with it is your call entirely. Family life has nothing to brag about. It trudges along like an old locomotive in need of urgent repairs.

3 April: First Quarter in Cancer

The moon is in your sign. There are emotional moments and many domestic crises. You are at your wit's end. Remember, this is a general reading and nothing is cast in stone. 'When you have eliminated the impossible, whatever remains, however improbable, must be the truth,' noted Arthur Conan Doyle, physician and writer. You attempt to sort out your life and work at untangling the many layers in the maze that it has become. There is passion and powerful bonding. Along with it are jealousy, possessiveness and several extreme emotions. Women, in particular, can go haywire with their hormonal imbalances and extreme reactions. If there has been a break-up, you are unable to handle it. This is a time for peace and calm, yoga and meditation, lest you become a slice of Bollywood's or the idiot box's sordid saga on love and its bizarre consequences. Your life is a page out of Harold Robbins. But all is not lost as Ganesha journeys with you.

11 April: Full Moon in Libra

You are not out of the woods as yet. Inclinations of one week can follow into the next and sometimes for weeks on end too. 'People don't notice whether it is winter or summer when they are happy,' said Anton Chekov. Are you happy? You look at the pros and cons of the situation you are in and attempt to work out solutions. Children, parents and the spouse need attention. Work also calls. How do you prioritize? There are expenses and more lines on your brow. You may visit a shrink or take to a health spa to chill, as they say these days. I have a huge following of young readers and need to update myself with current lingo. You may take to spirituality and get a guru. Life is about challenges. When you are able to handle them you evolve. Ganesha watches without concern. He knows that you have the wherewithal to get on with life.

19 April: Last Quarter in Capricorn

'I can resist everything but temptation,' said Oscar Wilde. You cannot resist getting back on track. Enough is enough, you say to yourself and get into the groove of the legendary Garfield Sobers, who wanted to finish the match in a hurry because he didn't want to miss the afternoon races! You are hitting on the front foot and clearing the boundary with ease. You could be the star of the IPL in the mood you are in. There are new job openings, lucrative freelance offers and new vistas unfolding right before your eyes. You seize them with the enthusiasm of a bee sucking honey and move on with life. Wow, says Ganesha. Love can wait. You have no time for frivolities.

26 April: New Moon in Taurus

The new moon is in Taurus and you are surging ahead. There are peace and harmony in your life. More importantly, there is balance. You are not frittering away your energies. You want to lay a substantive foundation for the future and get down to hard work. You sight money and go for it. You also indulge in helping out the less fortunate. You may even spend time with animal shelters tending to hurt and sick street dogs and cats. You are at peace and your soul hums gently. After the storm comes the lull. You are now ready to take on the world and mesmerize it with your genius. Ganesha is thrilled.

3 May: First Quarter in Leo

As the subcontinent heats up you are in the throes of a bull run. Life is smiling at you and you say cheese. New opportunities open up at work. Love also comes calling. There are expenses as you invest heavily on business expansion. There will be rewards but it will take time. You are busy with bank loans and other fiscal instruments. You pore over the dotted line before deciding on any financial commitment that may hurt you in the long run. Family life rumbles along. It has nothing that adds value to your life in the current circumstances. Ganesha watches.

10 May: Full Moon in Scorpio

You are filled with intensity. This could also be a period when you walk down memory lane and spoil an otherwise profitable period with maudlin thoughts. 'If opportunity doesn't knock, build a door,' said Milton Berle. New openings stare at you but in the mood you are in you don't pick up the signs. There could be issues at home over an inheritance. Elders may need urgent medical support and you are hard-pressed to find peace or 'me' time. Emotions overwhelm you. You take succour in Ganesha and that helps.

19 May: Last Quarter in Aquarius

'It is best and easiest not to discredit others but to prepare oneself to be as good as possible,' said Socrates. The situation of the last week doesn't change much. You could be feeling low if you are prone to depression. You go looking for a guru and explore tantra, mantra and yantra. You feel you need salvation or some sort of spiritual support, or you may just crack up. You take to yoga, meditation, alternative therapy and philanthropy to divert your attention from pressing concerns. There are challenges and you evolve as you surmount them. Ganesha blesses you.

25 May: New Moon in Gemini

Your mind is a zillion time zones. You feel restless and energetic. The monkey mind is on adrenaline. It cannot be tethered. You are on a creative high but it is directionless. You wander around like a puppy that has strayed from its den. This could be an indulgent phase when you let your imagination run wild and do things that you normally wouldn't. Of course, I must add here like I always do, that astrology never compels and this is a general reading. Singles play the field because they don't really know what to do with themselves. It is all a part of the complicated mosaic of life. Ganesha holds your hand.

1 June: First Quarter in Virgo

Mars is in your sign from 5 June to 19 July. You have two weeks when you are filled with energy and raring to go. You are in full flow, like a flamingo in flight or like a cheetah streaking across the Savannah. You come to grips with the reality of your existence and explore solutions. There could also be major business expansion as you explore options. There are powerful ego drives and passions. The best part is that they are harnessed and you work steadily like a cow ploughing the field. Ganesha watches. Mars is like the volcano of vitality inside you and influences endurance, persistence and discipline. Mars was named for the Roman god of war, and is also known as 'the bright and burning one'. Red is the colour of Mars and stimulates the dynamic, potent and fertile drives that power our lives. Mars rules physical energy and action and governs energy, strength, courage, life force and expansion. Well-placed Mars endows powerful energy and an indomitable will to succeed. Mars propels us like an ignited rocket. It is an important energy since it determines how we pursue what we want to achieve in life. In short, Mars represents energy, force, violence, aggression, sports, combat, wars, battles, accidents, operations.

9 June: Full Moon in Sagittarius

There is travel on the cards. You could be moving in a group, or solo, but you will be moving in many ways and in different directions. There is spiritual growth. You find peace and calm and are in a state of balance. 'There are three gates to self-destructive hell: lust, anger and greed,' says the Bhagavadgita. You have seen it all from close quarters and have emerged relatively unscathed. There are scars which remind of the struggle and also warn you to get away from repetitive behaviour. You keep a tab on your mood swings and temper tantrums. This period is propitious for growth. Use it wisely, urges Ganesha.

17 June: Last Quarter in Pisces

The birth period is often a wonderful time for all signs. In this phase Mercury is in Cancer from 21 June to 5 July which can well make it an extremely profitable fortnight. Messages and trips are the special characteristics of Mercury. Mercury, the mighty, all-powerful planet is in your sign now. It favours travels, meetings, conferences, interviews, trips, more brainpower, contacts, communication, correspondence and contracts. Mercury has a special connection with the circuits of the brain. Chess, crossword and other such games belong to Mercury. Also, short-distance runners and spin bowlers are controlled by Mercury. Mercury, in short, is the ambassador and salesman of the zodiac. Mercury is the symbol of news, views, messages, interviews, contacts, communications, travel and transport. Mercury gives an impetus to all of the above in the sun sign where it is located. The moon is also in Pisces and your sensitivities are aroused. You open your soul and meet up with people from different climes. You are thirsting for new vistas and want to get out of the rut. It all happens now. Your dreams come true. Ganesha backs you all the way. You may also feel that you have sighted true love. Is it a mirage? Only time will tell.

24 June: New Moon in Cancer

The new moon is in your sign and your life has a dreamlike quality to it. It bobs on the sea like a sliver of algae and travels where the current takes it. You soak in every type of experience and emerge richer. 'Because you are alive, everything is possible,' said Thich Nhat Hanh. You are filled with eloquence and artistry. Your creative outbursts don't go unnoticed. Those in the media or the arts strike pay dirt. There are rewards and awards, accolades and applause. You may receive grants from the government to pursue your dream project or may even be allotted land to encourage creative arts. Use the waxing moon to advantage. Whatever you start now will reap rich dividends. The gods are with you. Ganesha is with you. Need I say more?

1 July: First Quarter in Libra

'True compassion is more than flinging a coin to a beggar; it is not haphazard and superficial. It comes to see that an edifice that produces beggars needs restructuring,' said Martin Luther King Jr, the civil rights leader. Your consciousness is raised. You are struck dumb by the inequity all around you. You raise your voice and it is heard. You may lead a movement, a rally or a protest march. You want to be heard, and you will. There is media coverage and you are in the spotlight. There may be danger to your life too but you are unconcerned. Of course, astrology never compels, and I am not God. There are mood swings and you vacillate from sheer euphoria to ecstasy. There are many unconscious drives and compulsions. Your shadow side and underbelly express themselves without inhibition. Your soul is torn as it wanders from one room to another. Your peers and loved ones don't know what you will come up with next. Ganesha also doesn't. You are an enigma.

9 July: Full Moon in Capricorn

The full moon is in Capricorn and you are back with a semblance of balance in your daily life. You roll up your sleeves and get cracking. You are ambitious, and a lot remains to be done both at the workstation and in your personal life. Your emotions are stabilized and the monkey mind is tethered. You have the skills and the talent. Nothing can stop you now. Use your free will to advantages, says Ganesha. 'Whatever you can do, or dream you can do, begin it. Boldness has genius, power, and magic in it,' said Goethe. Yes, nothing ventured, nothing gained. As simple as that. You go for it, stake it all, and hit pay dirt.

16 July: Last Quarter in Aries

You are moving ahead fast and furious. Nothing can stop you. You forge new alliances, and new vistas open up in your life. Old confusions, suspicions and misunderstandings just wander off and disappear into thin air. You lead from the front and earn kudos for your leadership skills and the bold stand that you take. You move against the current and there are rich dividends. You work smart. There are passions and ego drives. But they are well directed. Love flows in and out of your life. Ganesha journeys with you.

23 July: New Moon in Leo

The good times continue. There is powerful intensity in everything that you undertake. You are moving ahead with purpose like a rocket that has just been launched. Nothing can distract you from your goal. There are ego drives and expenses. Money flows out of your pocket. Passion rears its lusty head and you are in the throes of amour. It is all happening for you now. Your plate is packed with many bounties. Prioritize and use your free will. Success is yours for the asking. You are like an army general in Siachen. You have sighted the enemy post, and now you dart in with your troops for the annihilation of the enemy. Ganesha watches.

30 July: First Quarter in Scorpio

Venus is in your sign from 1 to 25 August, which is almost the entire month. Enjoy, says Ganesha. The simple rule is that when Venus is in your own sign you will get comforts and luxuries, ornaments and money. This is an important phase. As often discussed, Venus is the planet for love, romance, sex, beauty and good life. This is the planet of attraction, love, wealth, knowledge and prosperity. The compatibility of partners and the type of life the individual will lead are also judged from the placement of Venus in the horoscope. As a planet, Venus is considered to be beneficial, feminine and gentle. Venus symbolizes the force of attraction in the universe. In human beings, this attractive force manifests as love and beauty. When Venus is well placed in the chart, there are love, art, beauty and all the goodies of life that make life worth living. Venus rules Libra and Taurus, though its role in every sign is important. Like other planets, it also has its transits. In Libra, Venus is aesthetic and cultured. In Taurus it is more earthy, materialistic and sensual. Venus rules the venous system, kidneys, urinary tract, throat and larynx, and is responsible for good looks. In short, Venus, in Western astrology, stands for comforts, arts, wealth, relationships, sex, decorations, luxuries and wealth. Additionally, the moon is in Scorpio and you attract love and lust like bees to honey. You are magnetic. Those in the fine arts do exceptionally well. There are fun times and festivities. There could be an addition to the family.

7 August: Full Moon in Aquarius

You are moving fast and furious. You want to be everywhere at all times but that is the sole privilege of Ganesha. You look ahead and ideate. This is an excellent period for making plans. This is not action time as your mind wanders in and out of every crevice. You are just sourcing all possibilities, and when the time is ripe you will go for the kill like Attila the Hun. Your mind is sharp and shorn of emotion. You evaluate the situation on sheer merit. You sign new deals and surge ahead like a speedboat in the choppy waters of the Bay of Bengal. Domestic life is choppy but that is par for the course. Ganesha blesses you.

15 August: Last Quarter in Taurus

There is stability but there are many expenses too as you make your presence felt in the world. You throw the dice like Bond in *Casino Royale*. You take risks and emerge triumphant. You are charging ahead like a shiny new Japanese monorail straight from the factory. There are expenses and indulgences. If you have a weight problem, it gets worse. Ganesha looks at his girth and smiles. This is not the time for any discipline. You live and love large. Tomorrow is another day, and let it come when it does. Till then you are serenaded by the bounty of life.

21 August: New Moon in Leo

The new moon is in Leo and you mount the offensive. You are eloquent, flamboyant, articulate, aggressive and affirmative. You go for the jugular. At the same time, you are a team player. Success is guaranteed. You have strong ego drives but are shrewd enough not to display it when you sight a big deal. You don't back off, but are diplomatic, courteous and charming and get your way across. Ganesha is impressed. Love life is what fantasies are all about. Need I say more?

29 August: First Quarter in Sagittarius

There is a lot of movement and networking. You use every technological tool to get your point across. You meet up with people from different cultures and feel stimulated, invigorated, refreshed and rejuvenated by the exchange of ideas. There is international travel and a quest for the higher reaches of spirituality. You may go looking for a guru and on pilgrimages. You may learn a new yoga or dance. This is a period when your mind expands and you feel like taking in the whole world. Ganesha is awed. There is little time for the family as you surround yourself with distractions. There will soon be time for that too.

6 September: Full Moon in Pisces

The full moon is in Pisces and your underbelly is exposed. You are emotional, even neurotic. Those with underlying psychological problems may have to seek specialized treatment. Please remember that I am not God and this is a general reading as I do not have your personal details. Plus astrology never compels. I add this caveat always, as there are many factors which contribute to a person's actions. There are many slices to life. On the plus side, this is a powerfully creative force and you are capable of literary masterpieces. Family life is exciting; there are pulls and pressures of all kinds. Children and elders could bowl a googly. You are on your toes. Ganesha watches.

13 September: Last Quarter in Gemini

You are on overdrive. You meet with people from different cultures and grow with their interactions. You use every communication tool to advantage. The monkey mind is tethered somewhat and there is direction and purpose in all your endeavours. This is a time for ideating and not for solid work. Even not doing anything is a form of action. From here you spring forth in the weeks to come to emerge as a person to reckon with. Love comes crooning and leaves in a hurry. There is nothing to brag about on the home front. You are left to your own devices and are on a solo trip. You connect with your core and evolve as a person. Ganesha blesses you.

20 September: New Moon in Virgo

There are stability and balance. You know what to do and where you are headed. You finally roll up your sleeves and get down to the shop floor. This is a great time for those in the corporate world. You look at serious business expansion. Money is well spent as you prepare a nest egg. The family is well provided for and you are freed from domestic concerns. Power and glory beckon you. Your ambitions are aroused and you will stop at nothing to achieve your goals. Ganesha backs you.

28 September: First Quarter in Capricorn

You are filled with josh and capable of every jugaad. You are in the throes of irresistible energy. You run through the opposition like a gazelle and triumph over bottlenecks and roadblocks with panache. Along with it is spiritual growth. If you have been working on an increase in consciousness, this is time when you feel that you have been rewarded. You open new vistas and make positive, creative change happen. There are expenses and indulgences, love and longing, and all the ingredients that make life worth living. There is a lot on your plate. This is certainly not a dull phase. Celebrate the colours, says Ganesha.

5 October: Full Moon in Aries

The full moon is in Aries and you are gung-ho. This is a propitious phase and whatever you embark on now has a high chance of success. Use this phase well. There are ego drives and passions at play. Just ensure that they don't hijack your vision of a dream sequence. 'Let everything happen to you, beauty and terror. Just keep going. No feeling is final,' said Rainer Maria Rilke. Yes, this is the phase you are in right now. Go with the flow and like Sinbad you will explore many new climes and profit from the experience. There are festive occasions too, with an addition to the family, marriages, engagements and anniversaries. You are in the party mood and nothing can stop you from wearing your dancing shoes. You are upbeat. Ganesha watches happily.

12 October: Last Quarter in Cancer

The moon is in your sign and the good phase continues, though several emotions are at play. You are vulnerable, and flamboyantly parade your sensitivities. You wear your inadequacies on your sleeve and it is not a pleasant sight. It also weakens you further. There are indulgences, mood swings and temper tantrums. If you can harness this inordinate display of feelings the battle will be won. The idea is to conquer yourself before you attempt to dominate others. 'Thousands of candles can be lighted from a single candle, and the life of the candle will not be shortened. Happiness never decreases by being shared,' said the Buddha. I second that. I have always advocated sharing resources with the less privileged. You do just that and indulge in philanthropy. You take up causes for disadvantaged humans and animals and win kudos. You are the toast of the neighbourhood. The spotlight cannot leave you and you are in thrall. Ganesha smiles. Family life sees powerful bonding. You get to see the many faces of love.

19 October: New Moon in Libra

'A house is no home unless it contains food and fire for the mind as well as the body,' said Margaret Fuller, author, critic and women's rights advocate. You look for spiritual enhancement and court gurus and those with spiritual prowess. You pore over tomes on higher consciousness, and like the Mother of Pondicherry said, you look for the 'highest aspiration to organize your life'. The great revolutionary saint Sri Aurobindo added, 'Man is only a rung in the ladder of evolution and evolution will surpass man.' You are suitably impressed by it all and look to tailor your life into the acme of perfection. It is not easy getting away from the real world or even living in it in the substantive garb of the yogi. There are bills to be paid, a mortgage to be handled, illness in the family, the care of elders and so much more. But you make an attempt and that is creditable enough. Ganesha applauds. In the process, family life too gets a new spin.

27 October: First Quarter in Aquarius

Joseph Addison said, 'What sculpture is to a block of marble, education is to the human soul.' You are in an experimental phase and try out all kinds of things. If you are a chef, there will be new vistas in experimental cuisine. If you are an adventure junkie you may try rappelling or bungee jumping or even a crash course in peak climbing. You attempt it all because you want to grow holistically. You want to be a complete person. Relationships are intense in this period. Emotions are on fire. This is also a creative phase in which poets, writers and film-makers, in particular, come out trumps. Your imagination is torched, you are struck by genius and manufacture masterpieces like a magician pulling our rabbits from a hat. Ganesha is amazed too.

4 November: Full Moon in Taurus

The winter cold is wandering in and the full moon is in Taurus. You bleed the good times for all they are worth. It is a propitious phase. Make the most if it, I say. There are money and honey, rewards and awards, accolades and applause. 'Life shrinks or expands in proportion to one's courage,' said Anais Nin, the writer. There are expenses, love and longing, work challenges that you surmount with the ease of a gladiator spearing a rat, new associations and a lot of fun. The best part is that you are in balance. The monkey mind is at peace and your soul hums a merry tune. This is a great time for placid exchanges bereft of the fury of emotions. Family life is on an even keel and children bring joy. Ganesha is pleased.

10 November: Last Quarter in Leo

You are on the go, propelled by high-octane fuel. You move like the new air force jets that slice the sky in microseconds. You are on a business expansion spree and there are rich dividends. There could be foreign travel and you could be elevated to positions of power and responsibility. Love courts you from all corners and the singles have a wonderful time. Commitment in marriage too is severely threatened in this period. Of course, astrology never compels and as your favourite astrologer I wish you well. These are mere indicators. You are in the bosom of hope, optimism and joy. There are lucky breaks and windfalls. Money comes and goes but your pocket remains full. Most important, you are on the path of high achievement. Ganesha is impressed.

18 November: New Moon in Scorpio

'Inhabit your desires,' says Danielle LaPorte, the life coach. You continue where you left off. You are gripped by intensity and achieve miracles. On the flip side are strong emotional undercurrents which accompany the intensity of the period. Rein them in and all will be well. You have pleasurable times with friends and associates. There are indulgent times and a lot of merrymaking, and why not? The mood is upbeat, life showers goodies on a platter and you hum along like a newly retreaded tyre. Ganesha smiles.

26 November: First Quarter in Pisces

I like to pepper my predictions with quotes as it gives you more value for your buck. It also gives you a break from mundane astrology. 'A human being is a part of the *whole* called by us the Universe. But he experiences himself, his thoughts, and his feelings as something separate from the rest; an optical delusion of his consciousness. Our task must be to free ourselves from this prison by widening our circle of compassion to embrace all living creatures and the whole of nature in its beauty,' said Albert Einstein. You are now widening your circle of compassion. This is a period charged with philanthropy. If you are a caregiver, or work with NGOs, you reach new heights of compassion. You give selflessly like Mother Teresa. This is also a creative phase, and those in the media do well. Your sensitivities are aroused and you lead the way with your heart. Ganesha blesses you.

3 December: Full Moon in Gemini

The year is ending and you are busy making contact with lost friends and loved ones. You are busy reconnecting the old school ties. You may be returning home after a long hiatus, like the prodigal. There are love and bonhomie in the air. 'Time rushes towards us with its hospital tray of infinitely varied narcotics, even while it is preparing us for its inevitably fatal operation,' said Tennessee Williams. You may be looking at taking your love to the altar. There are meaningful associations that garland your life. You look to the future with hope, and junk the past; it will not weigh you down like an albatross any more. Ganesha is happy for you.

10 December: Last Quarter in Virgo

There are stability and balance and you move forward in a definite direction. Work pressures eat up your time but it is well worth the effort. You know that money can embalm your life like nothing else. In the poor developing world, it is the difference between life and death. If you have seen reality at close quarters, you don't need an extra lesson in the value of freshly printed greenbacks. 'Take the first step in faith. You don't have to take the whole staircase, just take the first step,' said Martin Luther King, the American clergyman. You do just that. Ganesha insists on honesty and hard work. They pay well and justly. I second it.

18 December: New Moon in Sagittarius

There is a lot of movement in every possible sense. There could be international travel, even pilgrimages. You could be taking the family on a holiday. These are indulgent days. If you have artistic inclinations, they are showcased. There are many expenses but the money is well spent. Love life blooms like succulent cacti under the resplendent desert sun. If you want more, you are being greedy. Ganesha winks.

26 December: First Quarter in Aries

I love this quote and repeat it often. In a sense, it sums up the human journey. 'Do not pray for an easy life; pray to be a strong person,' said Nadia Comaneci, the legendary Olympic gymnast. The year is ending on a powerful note. You are filled with energy and look forward to 2018 with hope and a new vision for yourself. You are rejuvenated and transformed. You have metamorphosed into a multi-splendoured butterfly. You are knocking at the gates of posterity. Ganesha is thrilled.

LEO

23 July–22 August

Ganesha's Master Key: Love and leadership

'Have an aim. The quality of your aim will determine the quality of your life. Your aim should be high and wide, generous and disinterested; this will make your life precious to yourself and to others.'

– Sri Aurobindo

The important traits are: Egocentric, selfish; Using power to enhance ego, dictatorial, proud; Having an easily bruised and insecure ego; Awakening to one's identity; Becoming self-determining; Integrating the mind into the personality; Self-ruling, having intellectual consciousness; Learning the lessons of selfishness; Aware of the surrounding group; Shifting from self-interest to group requirements; Attaining personality effectiveness and personality control; Being aware of the futility of self-interest; Being aware of the soul as the true self; Having a developed and a definite life plan; Directing one's life with purpose; Concentrating self-consciousness to the divine plan; Manifesting individual will, love and intelligence; Self-mastering; expressing the qualities of the soul on the earth planes; Intelligent disciple; Being sensitive to the soul instead of to the surrounding world; Being conscious of decentralization; Subordinating the integrated personality to the good of the group; Control of group for higher purposes; Conditioning the environment in accordance with the divine plan; Being a centre of a group which is a part of a larger group; Being aware that there is always a larger group and greater centre; Being a centre of a group and relating to other centres of other groups.

Your Beauty-scope: Gold and white are the favoured Leo colours. A sari in full white with a gold border, gold-work pallu, stripes and checks should be ideal. In addition, Leo has a natural personality, brought about by a regal bearing and physique. A Leo has to only walk into a room and the vibrations start acting on one and all. Remember this natural asset, Leo. Others would give the world for it.

Many times, Leos have lovely, rich hair. Use your striking magnificent eyes by keeping a steady gaze. For the night, gold mascara is ideal. The chest is broad and deep, the breasts comparatively small. A little arty padding will help. Yes, the movements are catlike, graceful.

CENTRAL IDEA

Ego, Love, Personality, Selfishness, Generosity

Curiosity, connectivity, communication, compassion, consciousness are the five Cs of our brave new world. You Leos will be fortunate enough to make use of all the five Cs. You Leos will learn to take responsibility for your own actions. While we may continue to believe in fate and God, we will also understand the power and influences of genes, amino acids, carbon gas, and delaying the ageing process. We will understand emotionally, logically and rationally that all of us are in the same boat. We row together or we sink together. We will learn to keep an open mind. Therefore, religion, bigotry, prejudice, egotism will be minimized.

Now I am quoting verbatim from my father's book as it applies wonderfully well to you dear Leos. You Leos should 'wear learning like a watch', correspond 'like the lightning in the sky, instantly and brightly', reach out to people and places 'as if your own arm encircles the world', travel 'lightly and swiftly' and spread 'sweetness and light' like butter and jam on a well-done toast. Wow! We have it certainly laid on thick for you. You ask why and how? Ganesha says, Jupiter in your third slot is the cause of it.

By Western astrology, Jupiter, powerfully placed in Leo in your third angle, ensures that your attitude and approach to life itself will be generous, warm, humane, and thus you will be called an understanding and compassionate person, one of the greatest of compliments in the world. Trips, ties and trading are very probable. You will be improving your mind through a study course, reading books, doing law and learning about religion and philosophy. Advertisements, publicity, correspondence, contacts, communication, community will be the essence of life. Neighbours, relatives, cousins, brothers and sisters see more of you, and what they see they do like and enjoy. Contracts and deeds, documents, will and legacy issues, business affairs will have prominence. That you will be extending yourself in every possible way is the astrological message which is sharp and clear.

Western astrology also says that, Saturn will be very favourable to you. Year-round romance and finance, research and inventions, entertainment and use of technology – all come under the happy influence of Saturn. My father believes in clasping of hands and hugging. I am happy to see this also comes under the orbit of Saturn only for you. That is the real beauty and paradox. Saturn also signifies duty, responsibility and dignity. You Leos are good at all three.

Venus stands for luxury, beautiful objects and fine arts. For you, very specially, Venus will aid you in journeys and communication, loans, funds and joint finance. Therefore, a lot will depend upon Venus. Venus will be in your own sign from 26 August to 19 September; and very favourable from 4 February to 2 April; then again from 28 April to 5 June; and 1 to 24 December. Time to have a ball, as we say.

Mercury signifies news, views and messages. For you Leos, Mercury represents money, oratory, social life, friends, even a wish-fulfilment, group activities and entertainment. You will have the impact of mercury from 6 to 25 July; 2 to 8 September; 14 to 31 March; 21 April to 15 May; 30 September to 16 October; 6 November to the end of the year. Get your travel kit ready.

Mars, as many of you know, is the planet of energy and, therefore, of adventure and courage. For you, Mars also represents house, home, property, foreign travel, journeys, pilgrimages, inspiration, intuition and imagination. Mars works for you from 20 July to 4 September, and you must use all your talents and resources during it. Also, from 21 April to 4 June; 28 January to 9 March; 23 October to 8 December. Mars should help you in contacts and contracts. Therefore, a lot of things will be going for you during these periods. Use it wisely and well.

MONTHLY ROUND-UP

January: Loans, funds, joint finances, domestic matters, job, health. **February**: Love, hate, marriage, divorce, contradictory influences. **March**: Loans and funds, health and pets, religion, spirituality, rites for the living and the dead. **April**: Freedom, intuition, inspiration, publicity, long-distance connections. **May**: Work, parents, status, rivalry, prestige, tremendous pressures. **June**: Friendship, wish-fulfilment, material gains, socializing, group activities, happiness and health. You end on a positive, winning, winsome note. **July**: Expenses, secret deals, negotiations, trips and ties. **August**: Success, projects, ventures, funds, children, creativity, good luck. **September**: Money, family, promises, promotions, perks. **October**: Contacts, communication, contracts, research, import and export. **November**: Home, house, renovation, buying/selling, ill health, retirement. **December**: Fine performances all round; you strike it rich, are lucky and win applause.

Money: The fixed signs Taurus, Scorpio, Aquarius and Leo usually attract money like flies to honey. This year there could be a special emphasis on investment, loans and funds. Great rewards come from it around 2019. Please remember that astrology is not perfect.

Happiness Quota: I give you 88 per cent.

MONTH BY MONTH

January: You are filled with energy and are gung-ho about new projects. There is tremendous expansion in the workspace. You move from strength to strength. There is love and, with it, all the pleasures of life. There are renewed passions and ego drives. Mid-month sees domestic concerns take hold of you. Children could cause a spot of worry, or the health of elders may have you scurrying to the emergency ward. As the month ends, there is powerful intensity in all your dealings. There could be dissension at home. There are inheritance, and several fiscal matters that remain unresolved.

February: There is balance. You make up for the frenzy of the last few weeks with consolidation and solid breakthroughs. You have come into your own and are roaring away. Mid-month sees a massive expansion spree at work. You take risks. There are many purchases, possibly even a new home. There could be international travel and many overseas associations that catapult you into another orbit altogether. The month-end is a period for travel. You want to buck the trend. You want to be free, wild and wanton. There is reckless behaviour as well as strong creative urges.

March: In this phase you are ideating and making useful contacts. You use every technological marvel to get in touch with the world. There are flings, and light affairs of the heart. You live in dreams and fantasy. Mid-month sees you back in practical mode. There is clarity and affirmation in all your dealings. Sundry domestic calls too occupy your time and space. As the month ends, there is balance and equilibrium in your life. You want money and power, and will do all that it takes to get it. Additionally, love entraps you. This is also a good time for creative pursuits and alternative healing.

April: There are maudlin moments that trample you. If you have had previous marriages or intense relationships they come to haunt you. On the plus side, there is bonding with friends and loved ones. You attend alumni meets and renew the old school ties. You are in the throes of regeneration. Mid-month sees you live large and spend like there is no tomorrow. Marriages, engagements, festivities, an addition to the family, even divorces and separations take your time. Your plate is full and overflowing. As the month ends, you are moving spiritedly in the direction of enhanced success and status. There is energy, drive, zeal, zest, enthusiasm and intensity. You are on overdrive. Dame fortune has garlanded you.

May: Apart from the work arena in which you are the gladiator without peer there are many issues on the home front to deal with. Your authoritarian ways will have to be softened. Mid-month sees you filled with powerful intensity. You want to experience life at a very profound level. You take to higher learning. You go on pilgrimages and prospect new vistas for the soul. The energies are powerful. As the month ends, you go in for a complete overhaul. You make profitable contacts and your life gets a new spin. You find yourself, touch your core, and there is evolution.

June: You have become a person of value. There is peer group appreciation and awards and rewards. This pampers your ego drives. You busy yourself with consolidation at work and at home. There could be renovations or even a new home purchase. Mid-month, the pace is fast and furious. Love comes calling too. As the month ends, you are filled with energy, courage and a positive attitude. There are festivities and celebrations. You also excel at business negotiations. This is also a powerfully charged creative phase. You are in experimental mode and there are expenses of all kinds.

July: You strike gold at the drop of a hat. Life is beaming. Make the most of this period. You sight big money and go for it. You are charged and charming. Mid-month sees your creativity touching new peaks of excellence. This is a propitious time. As the month ends, you become a global traveller. New vistas open as you meet new people and savour new experiences. You are learning furiously and evolving to new heights of consciousness. There are passions and ego drives and you often overreach.

August: You doodle with fantasies and embark on new adventures. You take risks, walk down memory lane and sally forth into a wasteland of hallucinations and creations of a restless mind. You are reckless and out of touch with reality. Mid-month sees more stability. You roll up your sleeves and get set to conquer the workplace. There are indulgences and expenses. As the month ends, the good times crowd you. You are on an expansion spree and reach for the moon. The universe pushes you to greater glory. You are flying high both literally and metaphorically. Along with material success you also make substantial progress on the spiritual plane.

September: You live in the mind. You are here, there and everywhere. You showcase your creativity with flamboyance. Love blossoms. Mid-month sees flights of fancy entomb you and you are prone to indulgences. Your life is a maze of contradictions, shadow sides, blind spots and irrationality. As the month ends, you get down to facing the realities of life. This is a good period. Family life too finds a semblance of balance. You take risks and they work.

October: There are strong passions and ego drives. You lead from the front. There could also be business travel. You could be asked to chair important meetings and you are the toast of your peer group. Mid-month sees you in the throes of a metamorphosis. There are many changes in the domestic scene. As the month ends, you may want to revamp your lifestyle. You seek to add new colour to your life. You are in search of a new identity, and check out travel, alternative healing, gurus, god-men, new philosophies, even relationships. There is regeneration, rejuvenation and several new experiences.

November: Your energies are powerful and you bulldoze the opposition. This is also a time for a spiritual regeneration. You step out and make miracles happen. There is also an enhancement of your consciousness. The esoteric sciences beckon you. Mid-month sees you prepare a nest egg and delve deep into investments. You make prudent fiscal plans to ensure that your loved ones are in comfort. As the month ends, you spend time at home attending to domestic issues. You are indulgent. You are in love with love. What a beautiful way to be! This is also a creative phase and you excel in the arts.

December: You are networking with all and sundry. Film folk make waves. Writers strike pay dirt. You are attractive, expressive, creative, dynamic, charged, rejuvenated and reborn. Mid-month sees you in action mode. You have found yourself and know where to go and what to do. As the month ends, there could be international travel and many new associations. You meet with people from different cultures and there is rapid growth. You end the year with fire in your belly. You spend happily and earn well. The family is well taken care of. Your world is humming along on a full stomach.

WEEKLY REVIEW (BY PHASES OF THE MOON)

5 January: First Quarter in Aries

'Age is no barrier. It's a limitation you put on your mind,' said Jackie Joyner-Kersee, the legendary athlete. You began last year with hope, enthusiasm, energy, drive, persistence, determination, hard work and great dollops of luck. Jupiter was helping you out. Travel back in time and think about it. The start to this year too isn't bad by any means. You are filled with energy and are gung-ho about new projects. There is tremendous expansion in the workspace. You move from strength to strength. There is love, and all the pleasures of life follow. There are renewed passions and ego drives. Keep away from altercations and petty squabbles that can waylay you. Avoid conflicts with the law. Count to ten and take deep breaths before a response. Move away from an altercation as fast as you can. This is a good phase. Optimize it with your free will. Let me tell you about Leo now, like I always do. Leo is a fire sign and can be dogmatic, pompous, intolerant, patronizing, domineering, inflexible, vain, magnanimous, creative, romantic and generous. Leos feel and even behave like they are the lions of the human jungle. You don't care as long as you are the top gun. You take risks and win. That's what matters. Ganesha watches.

12 January: Full Moon in Cancer

'I trust that everything happens for a reason, even if we are not wise enough to see it,' said Oprah Winfrey. Domestic concerns take hold of you. Children could cause a spot of worry, or the health of elders may have you scurrying to the emergency ward. There could be trouble in marriage, or loved ones could run into rough weather, and that affects you as we are all a human chain and cannot remain islands. Like a quake, repercussions are felt all around. Lost love may also be troubling you. Mood swings, expenses and indulgences can get the better of you. Ganesha holds your hand.

19 January: Last Quarter in Scorpio

There is powerful intensity in all your dealings. Use your free will carefully and wisely as you are prone to activities that may cause you harm. Your love life may be in tangles as you play the field. There could be dissension at home. There are inheritance and several fiscal matters that remain unresolved. There is a lot on your plate. You are challenged in all possible ways. Ganesha journeys with you across burning embers.

28 January: New Moon in Aquarius

The new moon is in Aquarius and you are all over the place. Your emotions are going haywire and you could get neurotic and become a control freak. You could be a terror at the workplace. The team suffers, and you too, in the process. You are out of balance and create ripples which don't do your image or self-esteem any good. 'If you don't have a good relationship with yourself, you cannot understand the dharma, and your body and mind will not be properly coordinated,' says ChögyamTrungpa, the Buddhist meditation master. He is bang on. You look for salvation and help with the underprivileged. You go looking for a guru and on pilgrimages as you look to assuage a troubled soul. Ganesha watches closely.

4 February: First Quarter in Taurus

You are finally on stable ground. There is balance as you hold on to terra firma. You make up for the frenzy of the last few weeks with consolidation and solid breakthroughs. You have come into your own and are roaring away like the great lions in the Serengeti National Park. There are determination, resolve, purpose and hard work. You achieve miracles. 'You will always be too much of something for someone. Be yourself anyway,' says Danielle LaPorte, the life coach. You are held in awe by the opposition and your peer group. You are affirmative and are a slave driver. You want results. Nothing less than perfection will do. You want the stars and the moon and you make a go for the unattainable. You also court love like it will go out of fashion; it has its consequences too. As I always do, let me name a few famous Leos. They include Garfield Sobers, Pete Sampras, Rod Laver, Aldous Huxley, Alex Haley, George Bernard Shaw, Alfred Hitchcock, Andy Warhol, Sandra Bullock, Usain Bolt, Whitney Houston, Madonna, Arnold Schwarzenegger, Barack Obama, Robert De Niro, and Roman Polanski, among others. As you can see, you are in the esteemed company of high achievers. Ganesha is happy for you.

11 February: Full Moon in Leo

The full moon is in Leo and nothing can stop you now. You are like a meteor across the night sky. Can it be boxed or shot down? You are on a massive expansion spree at work. You take risks; money flows through your fingers. There are many purchases, possibly even a new home. There could be international travel and many overseas associations that catapult you into another orbit altogether. 'If you want to make the right decision for the future, fear is not a very good consultant,' says Markus Dohle, chairman and CEO, Random House. You venture into unknown territory with only the cosmos (not even a compass) to guide you. You are filled with self-belief; love and longing, money and honey, applause and accolades engulf you. Ganesha applauds.

18 February: Last Quarter in Sagittarius

This is a period for travel. Nothing can hold you down. You are like a tent in the Himalayas that refuses to be pegged down. You soar away at the slightest gust of wind. Adolescent children could pose problems as they will refuse to obey or listen to reason. Give them a long leash lest they just break free and regret it later. You want to buck the trend. You wear inappropriate clothes at blue ribbon functions, blow the horn in a silence zone, break the speed limit when it is clearly outlined, smoke in no-smoking areas, and drink where it is prohibited. You break all the rules without a care. You want to be free, wild and wanton. There is reckless behaviour. On the flip side, there are strong spiritual inclinations as you seek out a higher consciousness. Ganesha keeps tabs.

26 February: New Moon in Pisces

There are maudlin moments and creative urges. Art, music, literature, theatre and dance captivate you. You are also engulfed by the past when you sidestep the pressing demands of the day and take recourse in the arms of flashbacks and regrets. This is not your style and you will soon return to normal. But we are all subject to changing tides, and there are biorhythms and different sets of circumstances at play which mould us along the journey of life. Time and tide wait for no man, and the vicissitudes of life spare no one. Water that has flowed under the bridge will never return. I suggest you move forward and let the past remain where it should. Good times will follow as they should. There are love and longing and moments of ecstasy with your partner. Ganesha blesses you.

5 March: First Quarter in Gemini

Your monkey mind is airborne. You want it all in a hurry. To paraphrase Swami Vivekananda, it is better to play football than read the Bhagavadgita or get ritualistic because when you kick the ball the mind is focused. Action is the only way to tame the mind, now a monkey on a stick. In this phase you are ideating and making useful contacts. You use every technological marvel to get in touch with the world. There are flings and light affairs of the heart, but nothing that scorches you. You live in dreams and fantasy, out of touch with the real world. This is also important as it helps detoxify in these trying times. Family life has nothing to cheer about. Ganesha watches.

12 March: Full Moon in Virgo

The full moon is in Virgo and you take stock of your situation. You count the pennies and connect the dots. 'The next best thing to knowing something is to know where to find it,' said Samuel Johnson. You are back in practical mode and look at enhancing your material situation. There is clarity and affirmation in all your dealings. You strike deals with far-reaching consequences. You are open and receptive and make a good leader as well as a team player. You are busy with fiscal instruments like wills and fixed deposits. You are preparing a nest egg. Children may be leaving home for higher studies as sundry domestic calls occupy your time and space. All this is part and parcel of life, says Ganesha.

20 March: Last Quarter in Capricorn

'In today's rush we all think too much, seek too much and want too much and forget about the joy of just being,' said Eckhart Tolle. You are moving ahead fast and furious like the Rajdhani Express. There are balance and equilibrium in your life as you stand squarely on terra firma. You want money and power and will do all that it takes to get it. A note of caution here: Do not resort to underhand means to achieve your goals. There is karma and dharma and you will have to pay in cash or kind in the final analysis. It is best to be ethical. Family life rumbles along and children bring joy as they excel in examinations and interviews. There could be an addition to the family too. You are a good provider and so there are no complaints. Ganesha blesses you.

28 March: New Moon in Aries

'Love recognizes no barriers. It jumps hurdles, leaps fences, penetrates walls to arrive at its destination full of hope,' said Maya Angelou. The new moon is in Aries and, in addition to the work expansion that is happening surely, albeit slowly, you are in the throes of amour. Love has you entrapped in its anaconda coils and nothing else makes sense. The person you desire hijacks reason and rationale from your life. You live a dream sequence. In the end, you will either be liberated from it or be suffocated by its stranglehold. I have lived and loved to know the intricacies of love and lust. It is compulsive, obsessive and spares no one. This is a general reading and I do not have your personal details. Also, astrology never compels and I am not God. It is another matter that most of the time I am bang on, which makes me your favourite astrologer. This is also a good time for creative pursuits and alternative healing. Those in committed relationships torch ethereal zones of ecstasy. Need I say more? Ganesha winks.

3 April: First Quarter in Cancer

You cannot reach out for anything new if your hands are still stuffed with yesterday's junk. There are maudlin moments that trample you. If you have had previous marriages or intense relationships they come to haunt you. You are buried under guilt as children from previous relationships come knocking with accusations. You have nowhere to hide; even the night sky has eyes. 'Put down your shield and stand in the rain of blessings,' says life coach Danielle LaPorte. That is the only way forward. Just count your blessings. Nothing lasts, and this period will also be a memory soon. On the plus side, there is bonding with friends and loved ones. You attend alumni meets and renew the old school tie. Influences from one week can coalesce into another for weeks, and sometimes not at all. Nothing is cast in stone. Please remember that. You are in the throes of regeneration as new vistas open. You realize that your natural arrogance and ego drives have no place in the current scheme of things. You cannot lord over the home. The great lions in the Serengeti National Park also know this. Ganesha holds your hand.

11 April: Full Moon in Libra

The full moon is in Libra and you are spoilt for choice. You live large and spend like there is no tomorrow. You feel that you deserve it. There is a lot happening on the domestic front. Marriages, engagements, festivities, an addition to the family, even divorces and separations. Your plate is full and overflowing. You keep weighing the pros and cons of a situation and miss the point completely. 'They are ill discoverers that think there is no land, when they can see nothing but sea,' said Francis Bacon, the philosopher and statesman. Remain positive and upbeat. Be at your charming best. Life will beckon you with red roses. Ganesha is sure of that.

19 April: Last Quarter in Capricorn

You are moving spiritedly in the direction of enhanced success and status. You are ambitious and want the stars in your pocket. There are energy, drive, zeal, zest, enthusiasm and intensity. The best part is that you have a purpose and your efforts are well coordinated. You are crowned with success. You are like Arjuna's arrow; it is bullseye from the word go. There are rewards and awards, accolades and applause. You are the toast of your peer group. You chair important meetings, and stardom courts you. Ganesha watches.

26 April: New Moon in Taurus

'Charm is a way of getting the answer "yes" without asking a clear question,' said Albert Camus. The new noon is in Taurus and, along with the innate energy in your sign, this combination is formidable. You are on overdrive. Do not overstep. Pride comes before a fall. You feel that you are the cat's whiskers. The cat may have nine lives but don't exhaust so many lifelines in a hurry. Ego drives need to be reined in and altercations avoided. This is a propitious phase. Use your free will to advantage. Fortune favours the brave and you are the chosen one. Dame fortune has garlanded you. Love courts you unabashedly. Ganesha smiles.

3 May: First Quarter in Leo

The moon is in your sign and the good times continue. Just ensure that your ego drives are kept in check. I repeat this as Leos can be full of themselves and difficult to handle at times. Apart from the work arena in which you are the gladiator without peer there are many issues on the home front to deal with. Children can be a source of joy as well as a challenge. Your authoritarian ways will have to be softened a bit to accommodate differing viewpoints. You may also take time out from the concerns of the day and travel or chill in amusement parks and art galleries. You want to indulge a mellow period. You are planning and, I dare say, plotting all along. One eye is forever on the balance sheet. Ganesha wishes you well.

10 May: Full Moon in Scorpio

'Music gives a soul to the universe, wings to the mind, flight to the imagination and life to everything,' said Plato. You are filled with powerful intensity. You want to experience life at a very profound level. You take to higher learning, seek out gurus and want to master the great spiritual texts. You go on pilgrimages and prospect new vistas for the soul. The energies of this period are powerful. Use them well. Of course, astrology never compels. There is free will and there is also a bundle of other circumstances and variables which can impact your life. Love life is mercurial. Ganesha watches dispassionately.

19 May: Last Quarter in Aquarius

'Your body is precious. It is our vehicle for awakening. Treat it with care,' said the Buddha. You take heed and decide to change your lifestyle. If there have been indulgences you cut them out. There is a change in diet, a new exercise programme, a new wardrobe, possibly even a new hairdo. You go in for a complete overhaul like an old Mumbai taxi just before the road test. You take to yoga and meditation and check into to a health spa. Chronic illnesses are addressed and you emerge looking at life and times with new eyes. You also donate generously to old age homes and the underprivileged. Ganesha is happy.

25 May: New Moon in Gemini

'Life is an adventure in forgiveness,' said Norman Cousins. The new moon is in Gemini and you are all over the place, floating around like pollen in a tornado. You want to be everywhere at all times, which is quite impossible. You use the marvels of technology well and spend time with friends and loved ones. You make profitable contacts and your life gets a new spin. Love flirts with you but there is nothing serious. This is a period of growth. You find yourself, you touch your core, and there is evolution of your being. Ganesha watches as you unfold like a caterpillar into a resplendent, multicoloured butterfly. Life is calling you for the dance and you waltz effortlessly.

1 June: First Quarter in Virgo

'Try not to become a man of success, but rather try to become a man of value,' said Albert Einstein. You are firmly on terra firma and moving ahead like forcefully. In other words, nothing can stop you. You have become a man of value for sure. There are peer group appreciation and awards and rewards. You are a person of consequence and this suits your ego drives well; you love to preen like a peacock. You busy yourself with consolidation at work and at home. There could be renovations or even a new home purchase. You move ahead with the grace and pride of an Arabian stallion. Ganesha is delighted.

9 June: Full Moon in Sagittarius

You move fast and furious. You pick up the baton from the previous week and scorch the tarmac like Niki Lauda, the great motor car driver. He came back from a near-fatal accident to win. You exhibit the same courage and steely determination. 'You must be the change you wish to see in the world,' said Mahatma Gandhi. You lead by example and bat on the front foot like Sehwag on song. You are the lion of the Serengeti National Park and make no bones about it. Your roar is heard for miles on end over the vast tracts of thick bush. Ganesha hears it too. Love comes calling and you play the field with disdain.

17 June: Last Quarter in Pisces

Mars is in your sign from 20 July to 4 September. Mars in your own sign gives energy, courage and a very positive attitude. Mars is like the volcano of vitality inside you and influences endurance, persistence and discipline. Mars was named for the Roman god of war, and is also known as 'the bright and burning one'. Red is the colour of Mars and it stimulates the dynamic, potent and fertile drives that power our lives. Mars rules physical energy and action, and governs energy, strength, courage, life force and expansion. Well-placed Mars endows powerful energy and an indomitable will to succeed. Mars propels us like an ignited rocket. It is an important energy since it determines how we pursue what we want to achieve in life. In short, Mars represents energy, force, violence, aggression, sports, combat, wars, battles, accidents and operations. This is a fortnight of intense activity. Your monkey mind is on overdrive. There are festivities and celebrations on the home front. You also excel at business negotiations. This is also a powerfully charged creative phase and media folk do wonderfully well. Artists, writers and singers strike pay dirt. There is a lot happening in your life and your plate is crowded as though it were stuffed with large helpings of Hyderabadi biryani. Enjoy, says Ganesha. There is a lot going for you. Use your free will to optimize the moment.

24 June: New Moon in Cancer

'You become what you worship,' says Danielle LaPorte, the life coach. So what are you worshipping now? The stars say that you are longing for love, even divine love. You want all the goodies of life that money can buy but there is a vacuum despite several material gains. Do you run after money or do you save your soul? It is not an easy choice as one often doesn't accompany the other. You are in experimental mode and try out things that you had never dreamt of in the past. The focus is also on family life. There are many issues calling out to you, like the higher education of children and the health of elders. There are expenses of all kinds. You are spread thin like peanut butter on brown bread. Ganesha is with you and that helps.

1 July: First Quarter in Libra

Mercury is in Leo from 6 July to 25 July. This is a period when you have the Midas touch. You strike gold at the drop of a hat. Media folk do exceptionally well. There are lucrative offers, rewards and awards, money and honey. Life is beaming. Make the most of this period. Messages and trips are the special characteristics of Mercury. It favours travels, meetings, conferences, interviews, trips, more brainpower, contacts, communication, correspondence and contracts.

Mercury has a special connection with the circuits of the brain. Chess, crossword and other such games belong to Mercury. Also, short-distance runners and spin bowlers are controlled by Mercury. Mercury, in short, is the ambassador and salesman of the zodiac. Mercury is the symbol of news, views, messages, interviews, contacts, communications, travel and transport. Mercury gives an impetus to all of the above in the sun sign where it is located. You sight big money like a whaler sighting a beached whale and go for it. You are charged, your mind is tethered and, most of all, you are at your charming best. There is only one winner and it is you. Ganesha blesses you.

9 July: Full Moon in Capricorn

The full moon is in Capricorn and your bull run continues. 'I have been and still am a seeker, but I have ceased to question stars and books; I have begun to listen to the teaching my blood whispers to me,' said Hermann Hesse. You are seized by genius and your creativity touches new peaks of excellence. There is quality time with family as well as a perfect balance with work. This is indeed a great way to be. You may vacation with the family in an exotic locale. This is also your birth period and a propitious time. Like the Bard said, take the tide at the flood and it will lead to fortune. I agree. So does Ganesha.

16 July: Last Quarter in Aries

You are moving ahead like the new jets in the Indian Air Force. They are lost to the eye if you wink. You are jet-setting. You have become a global traveller. New vistas open as you meet new people and savour new experiences. You grow as a person. You are no longer a frog in the well. Your canvas of expression and experience now encompasses the whole wide world. You are learning furiously and evolving to new heights of consciousness. You realize that travel is the only true education and your perspective of life has changed. New love courts the singles, and those in committed relationships have happy times. Ganesha smiles.

23 July: New Moon in Leo

The new moon is in your sign and you strut around like a twice-born Brahmin. This month has been exceptionally good. You are crowned by success and garlanded by life's bounty. There are passions and ego drives and you often overreach as is your wont. The lion often oversteps. Avoid altercations and your world will be as you want it. Children bring joy and there could be an addition to the family. There are fun times and festivities. It doesn't matter if the sun is scorching or the rains are pummelling everything in sight. You are high and dry and moving ahead with confidence. Ganesha applauds.

30 July: First Quarter in Scorpio

'The two important days in your life are the day you are born and the day you find out why,' said Mark Twain. I love this quote. You are seized by a rare intensity now and go to great lengths to uncover secrets. You snoop around like a hound and if you are with the Federal Bureau of Investigation (FBI) or a private detective you ferret out whatever there is to be investigated with alacrity and accuracy. You excel in undercover operations and could be in great demand as a spy or in overseas counter-espionage operations. The Navy Seals and the Special Forces would gladly have you in their ranks. The intensity of this phase slips into your domestic life too and that could be a mixed, if not nixed, arena. There is always a flip side to an otherwise spectacular period. Also, please remember that astrology never compels. I place this caveat loud and clear as this is a general reading and I am not God. Of course I have been accurate over the decades and so I am your favourite astrologer by a distance. Ganesha agrees.

7 August: Full Moon in Aquarius

'Feeling old wounds is the soul's way of looking for what else can be healed,' says life coach Danielle LaPorte. The full moon is in Aquarius and you live in the labyrinthine alleyways of a fertile mind. You doodle with fantasies and embark on new adventures. You take risks, walk down memory lane, return, cast your nets again and sally forth into a wasteland of hallucinations and creations of a restless mind. You could be a blindfolded motorbike rider without a helmet in the pit of hell at the circus! You don't care. You could bungee without security gear! You are reckless and out of touch with reality. Ganesha ensures that you remain unscathed. Thankfully, this phase too won't last.

15 August: Last Quarter in Taurus

'The pessimist sees difficulty in every opportunity. The optimist sees the opportunity in every difficulty,' said the former British prime minister, the late Sir Winston Churchill. You are back on terra firma. You sight land after being marooned and make the most of it. The moon is in Taurus and you are stable. You roll up your sleeves and get set to conquer the world, which means the workplace. There are indulgences and expenses. You study the fine print with a magnifying glass and sign lucrative deals. You are on the fast track to success. You live and love large. Bees frolic to your honey pot as you prepare a nest egg and sail with the wind. Ganesha is impressed.

21 August: New Moon in Leo

The new moon is in your sign along with Venus from 26 August to 19 September. The good times are crowded and you are spoilt for choice. You are on an expansion spree and reaching for the moon. My guess is that you will even get it. If you use your free will well and move ahead with logic and rationale, you will achieve miracles. The universe pushes you to greater glory; and who can fight the hand of destiny? Ganesha seconds that. The simple rule is that when Venus is in your own sign you will get comforts and luxuries, ornaments and money. This is an important phase. As often discussed, Venus is the planet for love, romance, sex, beauty and good life. This is the planet of attraction, love, wealth, knowledge and prosperity. The compatibility of partners and the type of life the individual will lead are also judged from the placement of Venus in the horoscope. As a planet, Venus is considered to be beneficial, feminine and gentle. Venus symbolizes the force of attraction in the universe. In human beings this attractive force manifests as love and beauty. When Venus is well placed in the chart, there are love, art, beauty and all the goodies of life that make life worth living. Venus rules Libra and Taurus, though its role in every sign is important. Like other planets, it also has its transits. In Libra, Venus is aesthetic and cultured. In Taurus, it is more earthy, materialistic and sensual. Venus rules the venous system, kidneys, urinary tract, throat and larynx, and is responsible for good looks. In short, Venus, in Western astrology, stands for comforts, arts, wealth, relationships, sex, decorations, luxuries and wealth. You have to thank the stars for all the bounty that has landed squarely on your lap.

29 August: First Quarter in Sagittarius

Mercury reappears for a short while again from 2 to 8 September. This is another good period. I won't repeat Mercury's virtues here as I have already done it earlier. But, along with the beneficial influence of Sagittarius, you will be flying high both literally and metaphorically. 'The ones that will create the new culture that is needed are those that are not afraid to be insecure,' said Pema Chodron, the monk. Along with material success you also make substantial progress on the spiritual plane. You evolve, grow and glow as a person and possibly give your quest for a higher truth a new leash and lease. There are pilgrimages, search for a guru, tantra, mantra and yantra as you migrate into a more holistic being and reach the higher rungs of consciousness. Ganesha blesses you.

6 September: Full Moon in Pisces

'Even if I knew that tomorrow the world would go to pieces, I'd still plant my apple tree,' said Martin Luther King. You live in the mind. Finally, we are our minds and that is why counsellors are having a roaring time these days, as the mind often gets derailed by the obsessive consumerism on display. Your mind is whirring like the wings of a kingfisher steadying itself for the kill. You are here, there and everywhere. You may feel weak and lethargic and may take time off from the mad rush for some much needed 'me' time. You feel beaten and defeated, lost and forlorn. This is also a passing phase. But we are all victims of our biorhythms and circumstances and there is no escaping that fact. On the plus side, you showcase your creativity with flamboyance. Love blossoms and you spend ecstatic moments with your beloved. Ganesha is happy for you.

13 September: Last Quarter in Gemini

You continue from last week, conjuring up images in the mind. You live an unreal life totally out of touch with reality. Flights of fancy entomb you and you hallucinate at will. If you are prone to indulgences you need to crack the whip now or it may sadly get out of hand. 'Every great philosophy is a species of involuntary and unconscious autobiography,' said Nietzsche. Your life now is a maze of contradictions, shadow sides, blind spots, irrationality, brazen outbursts, loneliness and offbeat associations. Loved ones find you hard to handle, if they understand you at all. No one can fathom you in the mood you are in. Of course, I repeat, astrology never compels. Ganesha holds your hand.

20 September: New Moon in Virgo

There is stability. Terra firma calls and you get down to facing the realities of life. This is a good period and you can move to higher ground if you use this period well. 'Clouds came floating into my life, no longer to carry rain or usher storm, but to add colour to my sunset sky,' said Rabindranath Tagore. Beautiful lines! Your sky too is blessed with colours. You roll up your sleeves and hit the shop floor. A lot needs to be done and there is no time to waste. Life is calling. Are you ready for the dance? Family life too finds a semblance of balance as your mental meanderings slowly come to a halt. Ganesha watches.

28 September: First Quarter in Capricorn

You move ahead with zeal and confidence. You are ambitious and make no bones about it. You take the opposition on squarely like the great Muhammad Ali. You are moving like a butterfly and stinging like a bee. You take risks and they work well for you. There are money and honey and you watch the greenbacks flood your account like the Ganga in spate. This spurs you on. There is little time for love and its trappings. Home life hums along without distraction. Ganesha is with you.

5 October: Full Moon in Aries

The full moon is in Aries and you are on the go. There are strong passions and ego drives but life has taught you to channel them well. You lead from the front and, if you are in a subordinate position, also perform ably as a team player. There could also be business travel, and you profit from it. You could be asked to chair important meetings and you are the toast of your peer group. Love hops, skips and jumps with you but it is entirely your call. Health of elders and children could cause concern, Ganesha watches.

12 October: Last Quarter in Cancer

'Change is inevitable, except from a vending machine,' said Winston Churchill. You are in the throes of a metamorphosis. Like in Zen, you have to empty your cup to allow new energies in. Change is not always pleasant and you resist it with all your breath. But without change there is no growth and this may well be in your interest. There are many changes in the domestic equation too. There could be an addition to the family, weddings, anniversaries, separations, court cases, divorces, death, birth, illness and all that domestic life brings forth. Your plate is overflowing. There are many possibilities. Ganesha is with you through it all.

19 October: New Moon in Libra

You examine all the choices facing you with a magnifying glass. There are many options and you deliberate the right move for a considerable length of time. You do not want to take a false step. If there has been an illness it may recur. It may be time to seek out a second opinion. It may also be time to revamp your lifestyle. The routine has got to you; routine kills. You seek the outdoors and some excitement. You seek greener pastures and a new colour to the life that you are currently leading. All this upsets family life but it is par for the course. Ganesha holds your hand.

27 October: First Quarter in Aquarius

'Be yourself. Everyone else is taken,' said Oprah Winfrey. You are in search of a new identity, and check out travel, alternative healing, gurus, god-men, new philosophies, even relationships. You may feel that the relationship you are currently in has run its course and there is nothing new that it can offer you. You also extend your time and resources to the less fortunate and are applauded for it. There is regeneration, rejuvenation, excesses, eccentricities and more. There are several experiences in store and you emerge from it all with new plumage. You are a new person. In this age of third gender, same sex love and the freedom of expression, anything can happen! Ganesha watches from the sidelines.

4 November: Full Moon in Taurus

The full moon is in Taurus and you are bang-on centred. If you are in an archery contest you would hit the bullseye ten times out of ten. Your energies are powerful and you bulldoze the opposition. This is also a time for a sort of spiritual regeneration. You take challenges head-on and emerge the better for it. Children will be leaving home and you could also be emigrating. Better climes call. The family is in a state of shuffle. You are casting your net wide and before you pounce on big fish there will be many ripples in your pond. Ganesha journeys with you across the seven seas.

10 November: Last Quarter in Leo

The last quarter of the moon is in your sign and your soul is humming merrily. All is well in your world. 'Go beyond your boundaries and enjoy the vast cosmic dance,' says David Simon, the life coach. You do just that. You step out and make miracles happen. It is not only in the material world that you attain success but there is also an enhancement in your consciousness. You spend time in introspection, reading, writing, travelling the lesser known trails, and get to know yourself and the world you live in a little better. The esoteric sciences beckon you. Family life rattles along as you are far away from domestic concerns. You do not want to be bothered with what you think are trivia and mundane affairs. Ganesha watches.

18 November: New Moon in Scorpio

I shall quote Wayne Rooney, the English footballer, here, when asked about his preparation before a match: 'You are trying to put yourself in the moment and trying to prepare yourself to have a memory before a game.' Rooney is talking of visualization, which is being touted all over the place by counsellors and life coaches. The year is ending and you make plans for the future. You prepare a nest egg and delve deep into investments. You make prudent fiscal plans to ensure that your loved ones are in comfort irrespective of the vagaries of your earnings. You visualize a better world for yourself and the family and do all that it takes to make it happen. Ganesha is impressed.

26 November: First Quarter in Pisces

The mood of the last week filters down to this week too. It is a soft phase. You spend time at home. If you are a grandparent, the kids bring great joy. You are indulgent, and cater to their every whim and fancy. There are leisurely walks in the woods and fun times at amusement parks and at malls. You shop for others, as giving is also a form of receiving. You are in love with love. What a beautiful way to be! This is also a creative phase and you may take to the arts and excel in them if you already haven't. Even accountants and bureaucrats discover their artistic skills and showcase them with flamboyance. 'Truth is a pathless land,' said J. Krishnamurti. Wise words. Even without anything tangible on your plate you exult in timeless, infinite happiness. Your soul soars high above mortal greed like the eagle in the Andes. You are like a kite with broken manja soaring away without a care in the world. The best things in life can also come free! Ganesha is happy for you.

3 December: Full Moon in Gemini

Another year is fast coming to an end and you are making contact with the globe. You are networking with all and sundry. Film folk make waves. Writers strike pay dirt. This is a great way to end an exciting year. You are attractive, expressive, creative, dynamic, charged, rejuvenated and reborn. You are sparkling with ideas. Love seeks you out at the slightest pretext. The singles ride on poesy and the committed bond like never before. 'Let your highest aspiration organize your life,' said the Mother. You do just that. Ganesha is thrilled. So am I.

10 December: Last Quarter in Virgo

There is stability and you get down to action mode. You have found yourself and know where to go and what to do. That is more than half the battle won. Leonardo da Vinci said, 'A well-spent day brings happy sleep, so life well used brings happy death.' You are bereft of regrets as you have given your all in the quest for a better life for you and the family. You have reined in your ego drives and swallowed your pride where it mattered. Destiny will favour you as you have used your free will wisely and well. You bask in the afterglow of a life well lived. Additionally, you do not rest on your laurels. Instead, your roll up your sleeves and burn the midnight oil. Ganesha is impressed.

18 December: New Moon in Sagittarius

'Instead of getting depressed or falling into guilt when we see what is wrong in ourselves, we need to say, "Wow! Creator, thank You for letting me see my demons. Now how can I go above them?"' said Karen Berg of the Kabbalah Centre. You are moving in the right direction. The new moon is in Sagittarius and there could be international travel and many new associations. You meet with people from different cultures and there is rapid growth. You also make profitable strides at work and could be opening branches of your business in different countries. Youngsters excel in examinations and interviews. As the winter chill envelops you, you are in a happy and positive frame of mind. What a way to be, says Ganesha. I agree.

26 December: First Quarter in Aries

You end the year with fire in your belly. You are like a fierce Maori warrior who has just passed the rituals into adulthood with flying colours; you could have scalped a lion. You are back at work, scorching the tarmac. Nothing can pin you down. You are like Sushil Kumar in the ring. You spend happily and earn well. The family is well taken care of and health niggles are covered by insurance. Your world is humming along on a full stomach. I shall end the forecast with the profound words of Leo Tolstoy: 'What a strange illusion it is to suppose that beauty is goodness.' Ganesha wishes you well as he joins you in ushering the new year!

VIRGO

23 August–22 September

Ganesha's Master Key: Purification, perfection and discrimination

'Service to humanity is service to God'
— Vivekananda

The important traits are: Overly particular, nagging; Critical of self and others; Nit-picking, emphasizing trifles; Cold and unloving; Overly emphasizing the material; Being obsessed with purification, cleanliness and hygiene without understanding the reasons behind them; Analytical, discriminating; Being a master technician; Being a master craftsman; Being talented at detailed work; Applying the logical mind to the material plane; Becoming aware of the purpose of form; Being precise and accurate; Being aware of the purposes of purification and perfection; Consciously preparing the personality for receiving higher energies; Beginning to be aware of the soul's presence; Continual refining of the physical, astral and mental bodies; Maintaining good physical, emotional and mental health so that the soul may begin to express itself; Consciously assimilating life experiences in preparation for a fuller soul life; Discriminating between what is healthy and unhealthy for the soul's growth; Consciously nurturing the soul by nurturing the form; Blending the mind with the higher energy of wisdom; Using technical and craftsmanship skills to refine the material plane so that it can better accommodate higher energies.

Your Beauty-scope: Discriminating, methodical and exact, Virgo could find beauty aids a bit of a problem, since everything must be just so. First of all, please forget that only certain dresses and saris and make-up can and should be worn. Cleanliness can be an obsession. Let your personality expand. On the physical side, Virgo, you have assets galore – the foremost being you can wear young, smart dresses in vogue for the simple but glorious reason that you never show your age! The features, specially the eyes, are beautiful. Body hair is scanty, the skin pale and clear. And to top it all, the forehead is usually rather high, the eyebrow fine. In other words, the face, said to be a woman's fortune, is natural showpiece. Once in a while flaming, even bizarre, make-up would do splendidly. It will make you look feminine. Though the movements are easy and quick, there's a certain amount of fidgety mannerism. Try to appear carefree. An open neckline could help here. Also gay clothes.

CENTRAL IDEA

Craftsmanship, Analysis, Criticality, Technicality, Wisdom, Logic

Jupiter will be in your second angle. In a nutshell, the second angle refers to the three Fs, namely, finance, food and family.

Very evidently, all these three features will be highlighted. In food I include taste, flavour, aroma, layout and ambience. Ambience means surrounding or atmosphere. There is a fine Yiddish proverb, 'With money in your pocket, you are wise and you are handsome and you sing well too.'

The additional spin-offs of this placing will be: Buying and selling; Trade and commissions; Mutual funds, joint finances, joint holdings; Rental estate duties, taxes – almost the entire gamut of money matters is to be dealt with; Romance, sexual powers, physical rather than totally emotional involvements will also hold and attract you; Retirement, a job change, a move away from your regular profession could also happen now; Securities, mortgages, home finances will have to be dealt with too; probably also a second home.

From 25 December 2015 to 19 December 2017, Saturn has turned hostile towards you. But this does not mean that the whole period will be bad and useless. The main reason for it is that astrology is really a combination of all the different planets and not only one or two planets. In fact, Jupiter will be in a good relationship with Saturn in 2017 and therefore the full impact of Saturn will not be felt. If you want to buy and sell property, cars or other valuable goods there is a fine possibility that you will succeed. Ganesha says, take care of all the elders in your family and that of your spouse. I agree with my father that astrology is not always accurate. Astrologers do go wrong from time to time. Prayers and self-confidence really help all of us. I repeat that astrology is not perfect and accurate.

Mercury is your main planet. Mercury will be in your own sign from 26 July to 1 September. And again from 9 to 29 September. This will help you launch new projects or expand old ones. You will not only look young but also very personable and pleasing. During the period from 26 February to 13 March you will be in the limelight of publicity. People will notice you. From 7 June to 5 July your work will be appreciated and your prestige will soar. The period from 30 September to 16 October is money time, food time, family time. For love, romance, finance and family, you have the days from 11 January to 25 February.

Mars, the planet of courage and sports will help you in travel, communication, contacts and even spiritual consciousness, specially from 5 September to 22 October. From 21 April to 4 June is a good time for you to give your best and achieve much. The third phase is from 23 October to 8 December.

For you, Venus symbolizes finance, food, family, pilgrimage, journey, parents, religion, rituals, foreign countries and affairs. The time to give it a shot is from 20 September to 6 November and from 25 December to the end of the year 2017.

MONTHLY ROUND-UPS

January: Love, romance, the luck of the draw, creativity and children, family and fun and fortune. **February:** Health, employment, pets, servants and colleagues and a few problems connected with these. **March:** Love and hate, marriage and making merry, but paradoxically, in a few cases, separation and legal cases. That is why life is so complex, uncertain, full of contradiction and surprises. **April:** Funds, loans, capital formation, shopping. **May:** Inspiration, journey, name and fame, good luck. **June:** Power, prestige, parents, profession, awards and rewards, money, home, house and office. **July:** You will be off and away to a really flying start, says Ganesha, and as you know, well begun is half done. **August and September:** Expenses but also progress, therefore mixed results. **October:** Excellent for finances, family affairs and earned income. **November:** Reaching out to people through all media of transport and communication. **December:** Important for peace, buying, selling, renovating, decorating; a home away from home.

Money: This year could very well be a thumping money year and your pockets could overflow. I do remember I am always waiting at the sideline. But on a serious note, I have a real request for you. If you really make good money, please help the poor, the unfortunate, the sick and the ailing and the needy. Please understand that your sign itself is that of service to others in every possible way. In helping others, you will be helping yourself and God will really and truly bless you.

Happiness Quota: I give you 83.5 per cent.

MONTH BY MONTH

January: You are powered, filled with hope and raring to go. There are many plans on the anvil and great times with the family and loved ones. But the focus most certainly is on the work front. There are money and honey, rewards and awards. Mid-month sees you caught up in domestic issues. Elders may need medical attention; a residence that you are buying or planning to sell gets delayed; and there are unseen expenses and several emotional snafus. As the month ends, you are powered by a rare intensity and are in soul-searching mode. An old illness may recur, the debris of the past resurfaces and mood swings swamp you.

February: You are encouraged by the swell of greenbacks in your account and roll up your sleeves and work harder. You are ambitious and ready to go the whole hog. Success and love serenade you. Mid-month sees you power away. This is a propitious phase. Make the most of it. There are expenses and rapid business expansion. As the month ends, there could be geographical and spiritual movement. In other words, you grow as a person. There are new vistas and interesting encounters. Your canvas has multiple colours that bleed sense out of your very being. There are also powerful creative urges which throw up works of genius.

March: There is a lot of intellectual movement and you use every technological marvel to get your point across. You are at the forefront in activism and media campaigns. There are strong ego drives. There could be travel and several group activities. Parties, picnics and alumni meetings glue you to the old school tie. Mid-month, you take stock of your life and times. You look at making far-reaching investments. As the month ends, you are centred and focused. The energies are powerful. There are family gatherings and everyday issues of ill health and house repairs.

April: You are on an emotional roller coaster. There are expenses. Your emotions are taxed. You are prone to irrational outbursts. There are negotiations, conferences and discussions. Ego drives are high. Mid-month sees love knocking at your door. As the month ends, you attempt to make a go at life. You are normally practical and efficient and are able to handle the vicissitudes of life with aplomb. There are energy, passion, hard work and determination. You lead from the front and your ego drives are strategically orchestrated.

May: You are moving ahead at a frenetic pace. You live and love large. You make giant strides at work and may also go overboard with your expansionist tendencies. You push ahead like a rebel without a pause. There are many expenses too. Mid-month sees you intense and on tenterhooks. This is a powerful period and if you use your free will to advantage you could strike pay dirt. As the month ends, your mind is whirring all over the place and you are filled with insecurities that have no basis. You meet up with people from all walks of life and spend time in relief centres and halfway homes. Family life is riddled with questions. But children bring joy.

June: You roll up your sleeves and get cracking at work. You also attend to domestic calls and ensure that the family is well taken care of. You are moving ahead with purpose and that is what matters. Mid-month sees you making contact with people from all over the world thanks to all the gizmos at your disposal. You want to be heard and acknowledged. As the month ends, there is poetry in your life as the softer side of you is showcased. There are outbursts of creative genius.

July: You are assailed by multiple choices. There are indulgences and escapist tendencies. Love life is tricky. Mid-month sees you balanced and earthed. There is stability. You are in fourth gear, powering away on the highway of success. You excel at meetings, conferences, debates and arguments. You are fired by fierce determination. You are a visionary and make the right choices. Love comes calling too. As the month ends, you are in the right place at the right time and clinch deals that blow the mind off your competitors. You are well prepared, driven and open to new ideas. You mean business and will not settle for half measures. Along with it there are the love and compassion for the underprivileged.

August: You strike pay dirt. There are new associations and new horizons as you pioneer entirely new vistas and surge ahead of the competition. Mid-month sees you mow down the opposition. You leave the competition behind by a distance. There are expenses as you are in expansion mode. There are indulgences too. As the month ends, you rewrite the rules of the game. This is your moment in the sun. You sign big deals. There is movement on all fronts. You could be travelling overseas. There could be additions to the family and even immigration. There are several possibilities

September: You move ahead with ferocity. This is also a profitable period. You are on a winning streak. Your creative juices get a leg-up and you excel in the arts. Writers, painters and composers strike pay dirt. Mid-month sees new vistas open. There are new associations and a growth in consciousness. You use every gizmo to connect with the world. As the month ends, there are stability and also fun times. You make expensive purchases. There could be a new home on the anvil. You live in abundance. You are in expansionist mode and this is a great period for bankers and those in the higher echelons of the corporate world. There are perks and promotions.

October: You take wondrous strides at work. This is a period of beauty and bounty. There are family reunions and you bask in the aroma of love and bonhomie. Mid-month sees maudlin moments which threaten to derail the creative process. Family life can get suffocating. It is a mixed period. As the month ends, you are in a state of emotional unrest.

Relationships are churning. You go on pilgrimages and take to yoga, meditation and alternative healing. You take to philanthropy and look to the universe for answers. These are passing clouds. Do not get unduly worried.

November: You are back on terra firma. You get down to hard work and make up for lost time. You do a complete revamp. Children bring joy and there are fun times to be had. Your life is beginning to look up. Mid-month sees reckless love and shooting expenses. There are indulgences and escapist tendencies. Passions and ego drives run high. As the month ends, your emotions, drives and energies are at a peak. This is a profitable period for those in detailed work like doctors, professors, scientists, even craftsmen. You busy yourself with the deep and profound issues of life in a bid to unravel the mysteries of time and space. This is a powerful phase. Use it well. This is also a creative period. If you are a professional performer there are renown and applause.

December: You are networking furiously. You want to belong to someone or something; you do not want to be left out or isolated. This can be a period for real growth. You are also in the throes of creative energy. Mid-month sees you stable, balanced and sitting tight on terra firma. You roll up your sleeves and work hard. You are filled with confidence and oozing bravado. You also manage to share time, space and resources with the less fortunate. As the month ends, there is accomplishment, and a foundation laid for new plans that will take you into orbit. You enter the new year with hope, confidence and enthusiasm.

WEEKLY REVIEW (BY PHASES OF THE MOON)

5 January: First Quarter in Aries

'True sacrifice consists in sharing your wealth, strength and qualities, which are derived from society, with everyone,' said Sai Baba. Last year began on a maudlin note. You sped through the maze of emotions to find semblance and sanity in a world full of mischief and intrigue. The start this year is dramatically different. You are powered, filled with hope and raring to go. There are many plans on the anvil and great times with the family and loved ones. But the focus most certainly is on the work front. You surge ahead like a spacecraft to Mars. There are money and honey, rewards and awards. Certainly, a great start to the year. Your foot is on the pedal from the word go, like the 100-metre runners in the Olympic Games. Like I do every year, let me give you a sampling of the celebrities who share your birth sign. You are in the esteemed company of Michael Jackson, Sophia Loren, Stephen King, Mickey Mouse (created on 19 September 1928 by Walt Disney), Mother Teresa, Ingrid Bergman, Agatha Christie and Jesse Owens, among others. I must also add that Virgos are generally careful and trustworthy, but sometimes too critical and cautious. They are sensible, practical and logical. You are ruled by Mercury and have diverse interests. You will make good copy editors because you are good at finding fault; you are overly fastidious and this helps. You have a critical eye and can be a perfectionist. You can also make good doctors and surgeons as you are methodical and meticulous to a fault. In relationships, you could get too nagging. Of course, these are generalizations. Astrology never compels! Ganesha agrees.

12 January: Full Moon in Cancer

While you are moving ahead with gusto there are domestic issues which catch your attention. Elders may need medical attention, a residence that you are buying or planning to sell gets delayed, there are unseen expenses, and several emotional snafus threaten to trip you like a neighbourhood power cut. Children bring joy but they may also be leaving the family fold for greener pastures, and the joy of progress is tempered with a lump in your throat. Family life is exciting thanks to all these developments. Ganesha journeys with you.

19 January: Last Quarter in Scorpio

'Wanting more for your future is not a betrayal of your past,' says Danielle LaPorte. You are powered by a rare intensity as you move like a meteor subject to the law of gravity. You are in soul-searching mode. An old illness may recur, the debris of the past resurfaces, mood swings swamp you, along with a host of other domestic demands. Sibling rivalry gets unpleasant as ghouls from times gone by come flooding out of the woodwork. Ganesha helps you navigate tough times and you emerge from the cesspool with even the matchbox in your back pocket dry. You are unaffected by it all but, indeed, you have learnt many lessons. Time heals and teaches. You are the beneficiary as you surge ahead to new heights of accomplishment.

28 January: New Moon in Aquarius

The new moon is in Aquarius and you chart an offbeat trail. You get off the beaten track, give status quo the heave-ho and set off to the beat of an unknown drummer. Your idiosyncrasies are in full display, as flamboyant and multihued as the soldiers on Republic Day parade. If you are on Siachen you would take the enemy post single-handed. This is the mood you are in. You take risks and seek out adventure. The softer side of you is also showcased as you help out with the underprivileged and make time and resources available for charity. You have no time for the family and such mundane matters. Ganesha watches.

4 February: First Quarter in Taurus

You are counting your pennies and you realize that they amount to a sizeable sum. You praise the lord for this generosity, little realizing that it has been your hard work and determination and, of course, penny-pinching that has got you this far. You are encouraged by the swell of greenbacks and roll up your sleeves and work harder. Money buys a lot in the developing world and it can be the difference between hunger and death. You know how powerful it is without prompts from Madonna. 'Intelligence without ambition is a bird without wings,' said Salvador Dali, the Spanish surrealist painter. You are ambitious and ready to go the whole hog. Nothing comes in your way and success courts you. Love also serenades you along with a host of other worldly indulgences but you cannot be distracted from your path. You continue penny-pinching and build a sizeable bank balance. The family is taken care of and there are no domestic rumbles. Ganesha smiles.

11 February: Full Moon in Leo

You are powering ahead like the new rockets launched in the war games. A new intensity pushes you. You are on rocket fuel and overpower the opposition like Sushil Kumar in the ring. If it is Olympic time, the gold medal is yours for the asking. This is a propitious phase. Make the most of it. There are expenses and rapid business expansion. Money slips out of your fingers despite the penny-pinching. But it is money well spent as you pore over every expense with a magnifying glass and very thick reading glasses. Lawyers and chartered accountants are called in to assist. You leave nothing to chance. The preparation is detailed and deliberate. Ganesha is happy for you as he foresees the lip-smacking rewards to come.

18 February: Last Quarter in Sagittarius

You are moving in every way. There could be geographical and spiritual movement. In other words, you grow as a person, and that is the best way to be. You junk values and methods that have played out their worth. You clean out the closet and de-clutter. To paraphrase Darwin, it is not the species that is the strongest or the fastest that survives, but it is the species that adapts to change. You spring-clean your inner and outer spaces and become sharp and swift like a Red Indian's arrow; you could well be a Sioux brave scalping away on a hunting orgy. Singles play the field, and those who have taken the vows of monogamy swear silently under their breath. The temptations are enormous and something must give, sooner or later. I must add here that astrology never compels and I am not God. These are mere indicators and I don't have your personal chart. Having said that, I must also add that, more often than not, my predictions are right. There are new vistas and interesting encounters. You are on the ascendancy in more ways than one. Ganesha is impressed.

26 February: New Moon in Pisces

'You must love in such a way that the person you love feels free,' says Thich Nhat Hanh. Love obsesses you. The need is compulsive. Nothing else makes sense as your world goes into a tailspin like a jet on Air Force Day. This obsession takes over your entire being. It is as though you are in the coils of the world's largest anaconda and loving every moment of it. Reason, rationale and logic desert you as you sink deeper into the quicksand of amour. I have been there several times and have still been unable to decode lust from love. Youngsters may elope and elder, more mature partners may also lose themselves in the arms of their partners as though their world has been confiscated by opium dust. Your canvas has multiple colours that bleed sense out of your very being. At least let me be discreet by not mentioning gender and age. In these liberated times, any and every romantic liaison is conceivable. Let me not be a conservative and throw a spanner in the works; to each his own. Those who are cynical of such temptations are consumed by creative urges and can throw up works of great genius. Which side are you on? Ganesha flips the coin and watches.

5 March: First Quarter in Gemini

There is a lot of intellectual movement and you use every technological marvel to get your point across. You are at the forefront in activism and media campaigns and are screaming from the rooftops in all your online outlets. You are like a banshee, in the process attracting some support and also a lot of criticism. But you are not doing anything for popularity. You believe in what you stand for and do not care if the brownie points come. There are strong ego drives, you are intellectually competitive and your passions are aroused. There could be travel and several group activities. Parties, picnics and alumni meetings glue you to the old school tie. Family life holds nothing to shout about; in fact, the less said about it the better. Ganesha smiles.

12 March: Full Moon in Virgo

The full moon is in your sign and you take stock of your life and times. If you are an accountant, you come into your own now. You count numbers many times over, burning the midnight oil in the process. You want to be exact. You evaluate your assets and the taxes to be paid, and spend long hours with your calculator. You call in the fiscal experts and they examine your portfolio as though you were a developing nation making huge investments in start-ups. But that is the mood you are in. This is a powerful phase and you could make far-reaching investments with the right guidance. Your gut instincts are also sharply honed. You do well. Ganesha blesses you.

20 March: Last Quarter in Capricorn

You are on terra firma, making the right choices and moving ahead with the ferocity of a hound that has sighted a succulent rodent. Your emotions are in check and there is balance. You move up the ladder rung by rung. Bankers and builders of big industry strike pay dirt. You win every shoot-out, like Clint Eastwood in his heyday. You are centred and focused. The energies are powerful, goading you to name and fame, rewards and awards. The goodies fall on your lap and you are not one to look a gift horse in the mouth. Family life merrily chugs along like a toy train in the Nilgiris. Ganesha is pleased.

28 March: New Moon in Aries

You are like the cheetah in the Serengeti National Park. You have sighted game and there is a family to feed. There is simply no way you can get sidetracked from a meal. While the work front is moving smoothly, the domestic scene also comes into focus. There are family gatherings and everyday issues of ill health and house repairs. Relatives and friends drop by and the house is filled with the buzz of entertaining. This is par for the course; life is gift-wrapped with several ingredients. Enjoy, I say, as no one gets out alive. Ganesha watches nonplussed.

3 April: First Quarter in Cancer

'Love has no other desire but to fulfil itself. Know the pain of too much tenderness. Bleed willingly and joyfully,' said Kahlil Gibran. You are on an emotional roller coaster. There are expenses and you just hate money flowing so effortlessly out of your clenched fist. Your emotions are taxed and they fly off the walls like a boomerang in the Australian outback. You are neurotic and prone to irrational outbursts. There are negotiations, conferences and discussions. Ego drives are high and there could be altercations and court cases, divorces and separations, birth and death. Your plate is as crowded as a large helping of halal food. Use your free will when you respond and do not fly off the handle at the slightest pretext. One type of Virgo breaks all the rules, the other type is just too scared to do anything of the kind. Which type are you? Ganesha smiles.

11 April: Full Moon in Libra

'Opportunity is missed by most people because it is dressed in overalls and looks like work,' said Thomas Edison. It may just happen to you as you weigh the pros and cons of a new opportunity till the cows come home. By that time, the opening is lost and you are way back in the queue. Love comes along, knocking at your door, and you do the same thing: should you or shouldn't you? Frustrated, it also slips away. You are in fantasy land and out of touch with the reality of the times. Opportunity never knocks twice, certainly not in the same place. If you don't use your free will to guide you, the situation may well get out of hand. Of course, astrology never compels and I am not God. There are many variables which work on a person and I am the first one to admit that. Ganesha watches from close quarters.

19 April: Last Quarter in Capricorn

You get out of the dumps and sort yourself out. You realize that a lot needs to be done and have wasted valuable time in allowing the vagaries of an unsettled mind to take over the reins of your life. You brush it all aside like a golden retriever who has emerged from his weekly bath, and attempt to make a go at life. You are normally practical and efficient and are able to handle the vicissitudes of life with aplomb. 'There is no triumph more praiseworthy than surrender,' said Sai Baba. You bow down to the higher powers and the universe acknowledges the situation that you are in. Soon, you are back on the hunting trail like the king cobra seeking out quarry and all is well with your world. Love and passion, money and honey, awards and rewards, name and fame, accolades and applause consort with you. Life is multi-hued and there is magic in the air. Ganesha blesses you.

26 April: New Moon in Taurus

You are playing on the front foot on a barren wicket like Chris Gayle on a good day. Need I say more to accentuate my point? You rock. 'Close both eyes to see with the other eye,' said Rumi. You do just that. Your instincts are finely honed and your third eye opens up like Lord Shiva. There are energy, passion, hard work and determination. You triumph.

Like Sardar Singh, the Indian hockey captain, you sidestep the opposition deftly with the hint of a body feint and lay a match-winning pass to a better-placed teammate. I know the game. You lead from the front and your ego drives are strategically orchestrated. There are money and love and you are spoilt for choice. I am delighted for you. So is Ganesha.

3 May: First Quarter in Leo

'The moment you change your perception is the moment you rewrite the chemistry of your body,' says Dr Bruce Lipton. You are moving ahead at a frenetic pace. You live and love large. You are like a walking advertisement for fizz; you bubble over without cause. You make giant strides at work and may also go overboard with your expansionist tendencies, which may not meet with brownie points. But you are not standing for elections and you are not here to please the laity. You push ahead like a rebel without a pause. Singles play the field and those in wedlock make the best of the situation. There are many expenses too, but you cope. Ganesha blesses you.

10 May: Full Moon in Scorpio

You are intense and on tenterhooks. You have made investments and they may or may not bear fruit. This fear sends you to the couch. You are worried that if the investments don't work in your favour you could be bankrupt. But please remember that anxiety does not empty tomorrow of its sorrow, but only empties today of its strength. 'By plucking her petals, you do not gather the beauty of the flower,' said Nobel laureate Rabindranath Tagore. Life is filled with uncertainties and your fears are well founded. But hold on. There is also the likelihood that you are on the verge of a jackpot. It can work either way. This is a powerful period and if you use your free will to advantage you could strike pay dirt. Ganesha watches.

19 May: Last Quarter in Aquarius

'Just as a cautious businessman avoids tying up all his capital in one concern, so, perhaps, worldly wisdom will advise us not to look for the whole of our satisfaction from a single aspiration,' said Sigmund Freud, neurologist and founder of psychoanalysis. Your mind is whirring like the latest ceiling fan. It is all over the place and you are filled with insecurities that have no basis. You try to put your finger on the situation but cannot find it. The monkey mind has taken over your being and it may be a good idea to get away from it all and watch the action from a distance. You need 'me' time. You need a technological detox. Take a break in the woods or give yoga, meditation and alternative healing a chance to rejuvenate you. These are passing phases and should not be allowed to take control of your soul. Ganesha walks with you.

25 May: New Moon in Gemini

The trends of last week spill over. You are lost in the jungle without a compass with a hungry tigress eyeing you from a distance. You step into no-man's-land and wander without direction. You take to social media and blogging. You begin journaling. It helps; it is therapeutic. You meet up with people from all walks of life and spend time in relief centres and halfway homes. You realize that most people are worse off than you, and you return home feeling pleased with life; the world is not such a bad place after all and it was simply the machinations of your mind that cast such an unholy spell on you. Family life is riddled with questions. But children bring joy. Ganesha carries you through troubled waters.

1 June: First Quarter in Virgo

As the subcontinent sizzles you find stability. The moon is in your sign and you are back in balance. 'I am not a woman, I am a world,' said the queen of Sheba. You go beyond your everyday identity and look at the larger picture. You realize that one lives and dies in the mind. You roll up your sleeves and get cracking at work which has piled up and is gathering dust. You attend to domestic calls and ensure that the family is well taken care of. Relations with women, regardless of your gender, will be unusually powerful. You may meet someone from another culture who deeply impacts you; it need not be a sexual relationship, but it will most certainly be a great learning experience. You are moving ahead with purpose and that is what matters. Ganesha is delighted.

9 June: Full Moon in Sagittarius

'Come, live in my heart and pay no rent,' said Samuel Lover, songwriter, composer, novelist and artist. You are moving ahead like a zebra escaping a predator. You make contact with people from all over the world thanks to all the gizmos at your disposal. You want your ideas to resound across the cosmos. You want to be heard and acknowledged. Your soul also sings of love. You feel lonely and reach out to partners. They come and go in quick succession, like footfalls in a mall. You love the patter of feet and the exchanges that follow, some not so amorous, some business-like, some passion-packed. You are enlivened by it all. Singles have a great time and those in wedlock wonder why they got into it in the first place. Ganesha smiles.

17 June: Last Quarter in Pisces

You are fired by ambition. 'Shatter the legacy that's holding you back,' says Danielle LaPorte. You want to make things happen and are ready to break all the chains. You want renown and will cut corners for a piece of the limelight. You may even get unethical, and I don't second that. Neither does Ganesha. I am old-fashioned and the world has changed, but the basic tenets of life should never be mangled for short-term gain. There is also poetry in your life as the softer side of you is showcased. There are outbursts of creative genius. Those in the media excel. Way to go!

24 June: New Moon in Cancer

The new moon is in Cancer and life could turn into quite a tizzy. There are expenses, love triangles, circles and squares, divorce and separation, court cases and cops. You are at your neurotic best and will not listen to anyone. You may just run away with the plumber who comes home to repair the faucet, as a mark of defiance. As you may have noticed, I refrain from gender identity as the world has opened up and anything can happen! You are entangled in the mesh and maze of life. Emotions get the better of you as reason takes a break. Of course, astrology never compels and I do not have your personal chart. This is merely a general reading, and you could use your free will to advantage. Ganesha agrees.

1 July: First Quarter in Libra

You are assailed by multiple choices. To be or not to be is the question. You are out of focus and your wandering mind is as lost as a minstrel seeking manna in the wilderness. Sai Baba advises you to focus on the five Ds: dedication, devotion, discrimination, discipline and determination. Get centred.

You may also suffer from low self-esteem issues and may feel that you are a loser. This discourages you from making bold claims on life as you feel that you are just not worth it. There are indulgences and escapist tendencies. You are unable to read the writing on the wall, and you walk all over burning coals. Love life is tumultuous. You are indiscreet and could indulge in risky behaviour. Of course, astrology never compels. Luckily, Ganesha is at hand.

9 July: Full Moon in Capricorn

Your boat is set right in the nick of time. You halt the downhill slide and roll up your sleeves before you keel over. You are earthed, finally. There is stability and balance replacing the confusion and uncertainty of the past few weeks. You are in fourth gear, powering away on the highway of success. Your mind is sorted out and your world is at peace, not in pieces. Your ego drives are high and you mean business. You excel at meetings, conferences, debates and arguments. You present papers that win peer group approval and are nominated for awards. There is deafening applause. You are on cloud nine. Notice how quickly the cookie can crumble and then revive! This is how life is. Amazing. One moment one is in the dumps and the next moment one can fly high. Ganesha watches. He knows.

16 July: Last Quarter in Aries

You are powered by high-octane fuel. You are hard-working and disciplined. You are fired by fierce determination and nothing can derail you from your objectives. You want to win at all costs. Your critical faculties are sharp and you work your way through the swamp, ethically. You are a visionary and make the right choices. The team looks up to you. There are perks and promotions coming your way. Your standards are exacting as you look for precision and perfection. Love comes calling too but your priorities are clear. Ganesha is impressed.

23 July: New Moon in Leo

Mercury is in your sign from 26 July to 1 September which is a long time. This is a great period and you make miracles happen. Your world is beautiful. Oprah Winfrey said, 'Luck is when preparation meets opportunity.' You are in the right place at the right time and clinch deals that blow the mind off your competitors. You are well prepared, driven and open to new ideas. You are a visionary and use your ego drives strategically, with opportunism and panache. Messages and trips are the special characteristics of Mercury. It favours travels, meetings, conferences, interviews, trips, more brainpower, contacts, communication, correspondence and contracts. Mercury has a special connection with the circuits of the brain. Chess, crossword and other such games belong to Mercury. Also, short-distance runners and spin bowlers are controlled by Mercury. Mercury, in short, is the ambassador and salesman of the zodiac. Mercury is the symbol of news, views, messages, interviews, contacts, communications, travel and transport. Mercury gives an impetus to all of the above in the sun sign where it is located. This is a fantastic period. Make the most of it. Ganesha applauds.

30 July: First Quarter in Scorpio

You carry on with a relentless and scary intensity. You are like a headmaster with a whip in a government school in the backwoods of India insisting on perfection and the truth.

Nothing escapes your eagle eye. You mean business and will not settle for half measures. 'You must cultivate your heart to raise a harvest of truth, righteousness, peace and love,' said Sai Baba. Along with it, love and compassion for the underprivileged are also there. You give heart and soul to the downtrodden. Of course, you are the toast of the neighbourhood. Ganesha is delighted.

7 August: Full Moon in Aquarius

You work in an offbeat manner and use the path infrequently trodden; you hear the beats of a drummer others cannot fathom. Winners do the same things differently and you have hit that formula on the head. You strike pay dirt. As the Bard suggested, you take the tide at the flood and it leads you to fortune. You have the Midas touch. There are new associations and new horizons as you pioneer entirely new vistas and surge ahead of the competition. Love life is in tangles, but who cares? You have other more meaningful and profitable distractions. Ganesha is impressed.

15 August: Last Quarter in Taurus

You have the earthiness of the moon in Taurus supporting you. You have the stamina of a horse and you mow down the opposition. You sprint the last 100 metres of the marathon and leave the competitors behind by a distance, gasping for breath. You are clearly on a long lease of the bull run. There are expenses as you are in expansion mode. There are indulgences too. Love comes calling, and you may just take a break from work! After all, all work and no play makes Jack a dull boy! Family life is roaring away and the singles have a ball. You return rejuvenated and surge further ahead. Ganesha watches.

21 August: New Moon in Leo

Marilyn Monroe once said, 'It's better to be absolutely ridiculous than absolutely boring.' You are certainly not boring in the phase you are in. You rewrite the rules of the game. If you are in the IPL you are the new find, the new wunderkind on the block. You have the skills of Messi, the cunning of Neymar, the arrogance of Sehwag, the calmness of Dhoni, the staying power of Dravid and the tenacity of Sachin. The gods favour you like they did with Achilles. This is your moment in the sun. You sign big deals, are in expansion mode like Genghis Khan, and hope to rule the waves like Bill Gates. You had it coming, says Ganesha. You are certainly not complaining.

29 August: First Quarter in Sagittarius

'To have great poets, there must be great audiences,' said Walt Whitman. There is movement on all fronts. You could be travelling overseas. There could be additions to the family and even immigration. There are several possibilities that stare you in the face. There are also love and longing. You sizzle like a kebab on the slow burn and take intimacy to ethereal heights. Love and life come calling. They leave their visiting cards behind and you date them with the enthusiasm of Rasputin. There are windfall gains. Ganesha is thrilled.

6 September: Full Moon in Pisces

'I am driven by two main philosophies: Know more today about the world than I knew yesterday, and lessen the suffering of others. You'd be surprised how far that gets you,' said Neil de Grasse Tyson, the American astrophysicist. This is an interesting period. You move ahead with ferocity. Mars is in your sign from 5 September to 22 October.

Additionally, Mercury also makes its presence felt from 9 to 29 September. This is also a profitable period. I have already talked about the beneficial effects of Mercury and so won't repeat it. But, rest assured, you are on a winning streak, like Lester Piggott, the legendary jockey. Now, let me come to the presence of Mars in your own sign. Mars gives energy, courage and a very positive attitude. Mars is like the volcano of vitality inside you and influences endurance, persistence and discipline. Mars was named for the Roman god of war, and is also known as 'the bright and burning one'. Red is the colour of Mars and it stimulates the dynamic, potent and fertile drives that power our lives. Mars rules physical energy and action, and governs energy, strength, courage, life force and expansion. Well-placed Mars endows powerful energy and an indomitable will to succeed. Mars propels us like an ignited rocket. It is an important energy since it determines how we pursue what we want to achieve in life. In short, Mars represents energy, force, violence, aggression, sports, combat, wars, battles, accidents and operations. Along with it is the full moon in Pisces. Your underbelly is up for display and there is nothing to be ashamed of. Your creative juices get a leg-up and you excel in the arts. Writers, painters and composers strike pay dirt. You are also in the throes of amour. Take your pick. I am jealous. Hey, I am joking. Ganesha smiles.

13 September: Last Quarter in Gemini

You are moving ahead in every sense of the word. You are ideating with the speed of a cement churning machine on potholed Mumbai streets a day before the monsoon. New vistas open. There are new associations and a growth in consciousness. You go on pilgrimages and for searching a guru. You look at metaphysics, astrology, natural healing, the occult, tantra, mantra, yantra, god-men, yoga, meditation and esoteric sciences. You use every gizmo to connect with the world. You feel that you have something of great value to share. There is little time for family life as you are lost in the intricate designs of your mind and its cravings. Ganesha blesses you.

20 September: New Moon in Virgo

This is a period of stability and fun times. You make expensive purchases. There could be a new home on the anvil. You spend as easily as you get, and money is in circulation. You live in abundance and that is the key. You send the right messages to the universe and it responds appropriately, showering you with bushels of good tidings. All your plans work out and Ganesha is thrilled. Venus is in your sign from 20 September to 13 October. Your birth period is indeed turning out to be fabulous. After the beneficial impacts of Mercury twice in quick succession you have Venus serenading you for almost a month. Wonderful. Way to go! The simple rule is that when Venus is in your own sign you will get comforts and luxuries, ornaments and money. This is an important phase. As often discussed, Venus is the planet for love, romance, sex, beauty and good life. This is the planet of attraction, love, wealth, knowledge and prosperity. The compatibility of partners and the type of life the individual will lead are also judged from the placement of Venus in the horoscope. As a planet, Venus is considered to be beneficial, feminine and gentle. Venus symbolizes the force of attraction in the universe. In human beings, this attractive force manifests as love and beauty. When Venus is well placed in the chart, there are love, art, beauty and all the goodies of life that make life worth living. Venus rules Libra and Taurus, though its role in every sign is important. Like other planets, it also has its transits. In Libra, Venus is aesthetic and cultured. In Taurus it is more earthy, materialistic and sensual. Venus rules the venous system, kidneys, urinary tract, throat, larynx, and is responsible for good looks. In short, Venus, in Western astrology, stands for comforts, arts, wealth, relationships, sex, decorations, luxuries and wealth.

28 September: First Quarter in Capricorn

You are pushing ahead without remorse. You move on jet fuel. Your mind is tethered and you don't spare the horses. You are in expansionist mode and this is a great period for bankers and those in the higher echelons of the corporate world. There are perks and promotions, rewards and awards, money and honey. You invest in properties and gizmos. You could take the family out on an exotic holiday, maybe a cruise down the south of France. There are festivities, marriages and anniversaries, even additions to the family. It is all happening with you. With the home fires burning well, the belly full and the mind at peace, your world is humming along merrily. Ganesha is happy for you. So am I as your favourite astrologer.

5 October: Full Moon in Aries

'Routine has nothing to do with repetition. To become really good at anything you have to practise and repeat, practise and repeat, until the technique becomes intuitive,' says Paulo Coelho. You do just that and excel. You take wondrous strides at work and scorch the tarmac, leaving the opposition behind by a distance. This is a period of beauty and bounty.

There are many beautiful moments crowning your life. There is domestic bliss and new love for the unattached. Youngsters pass examinations with flying colours. There are family reunions and you bask in the aroma of love and bonhomie. Ganesha is thrilled.

12 October: Last Quarter in Cancer

'Your soul is rooting for you,' says Danielle LaPorte. This is a time when genius can flower as you express yourself from the inner core of your being. There are maudlin moments too, which threaten to derail the creative process. You hark back to the good old days and what could have been if you had made a few course corrections. All this is spilt milk and the sooner you distance yourself from the heartbreaks of the past, the better you are. Family life groans and grunts like a bad belly. It can get suffocating and you may leave home for a while to gather some much-needed 'me' time. On the plus side, media folk have creative rushes and strike pay dirt. It is a mixed week. The dishes on the menu are sweet, salty and bland. Life serves you all the colours of the rainbow. Take your pick. Ganesha watches.

19 October: New Moon in Libra

Your monkey mind is busy slaying demons from the past, present and future. You are in a state of emotional unrest. You cannot put a finger on the leak but it is there inhabiting your soul, your very existence, every breath you take. You look for counsellors, gurus and god-men to alleviate the emotional pain. Relationships are churning in the cauldron, and the curry is messy. You are at your wit's end wondering what to do. These are passing clouds, and we all have our share of life's snafus, assures Ganesha. Hang in there and the sky will soon be clear.

27 October: First Quarter in Aquarius

The trends of the last week continue. You go on pilgrimages and take to yoga, meditation and alternative healing. You may go for a thorough medical check-up to determine if there is some underlying medical issue that needs urgent attention. An old skin ailment may recur. You run short of money and that weighs heavily on your mind; bankruptcy is not an option. Family life is in disarray and those who are courting may decide to call it off. You take to philanthropy and are resigned to fate. You feel that there is nothing more you can do. You look to the universe for answers. Of course, astrology never compels. These are mere trends from a general reading. Ganesha holds your hand.

4 November: Full Moon in Taurus

'The greatest happiness of life is the conviction that we are loved – loved for ourselves, or rather, loved in spite of ourselves,' said Victor Hugo. Your boat is being set right finally. The full moon is in Taurus and you are back on terra firma. There are emotional highs and lows, especially for women, but, by and large, you are back on an even keel. You get down to hard work and make up for lost time. You change your sartorial style and do a complete revamp. A new you is emerging from the complexities of the past. Family life is also peaceful as the clouds have cleared. Remember, unhappiness, like happiness, never lasts for long. Children bring joy and there are fun times to be had. Your life is beginning to look up. Ganesha is happy for you.

10 November: Last Quarter in Leo

'Nobody has ever measured, not even poets, how much the heart can hold,' said Zelda Fitzgerald. While you are back on stable ground, this is also a time for reckless love and shooting expenses. You are in the throes of amour and it refuses to uncoil you. You spend carelessly on your partner and empty your pockets. There are indulgences and escapist tendencies and it may be a good idea to cap it as soon as possible lest it get the better of you. Passions and ego drives run high and you could get into scuffles with the law. On the plus side, there can be rapid business expansion. It all depends on your personal chart. These are general indicators. Ganesha watches.

18 November: New Moon in Scorpio

The new moon is in Scorpio and your emotions, drives and energies are at a peak. You want to know more and more of less and less; you look at super-specialization. This is a profitable period for those in detailed work like doctors, professors, scientists, even craftsmen. You busy yourself with the deep and profound issues of life in a bid to unravel the mysteries of time and space. You go inwards, plumb the recesses of your soul, and comb the truth. There are no compromises, no dilution or adulteration in your thought processes. This is a powerful phase. Use your free will to steer it your way. This can be the period of genius or even a futile, wasted phase, depending on how you plan to work the energies. Ganesha blesses you.

26 November: First Quarter in Pisces

You take a step back from the fire and fury of life and decide to chill. You hang out at the mall, watch films, attend plays, visit art galleries and spend time with friends. You may indulge a lot in comfort shopping and buy things that you don't need and possibly will never, ever use. But you feel good about it and that is what matters for now. This is also a creative period and you could take to dance and music classes. If you are a professional performer there is renown and applause. The softer side of your personality is on show. It is a pleasant break. Love comes calling on gossamer threads. The possibilities are enormous. Take your pick, suggests Ganesha.

3 December: Full Moon in Gemini

As the year ends you are reaching out to friends and lovers from across the globe. You are networking furiously. You want to belong to someone, something; you do not want to be left out or isolated. 'The closing years of life are like the end of a masquerade party, when the masks are dropped,' said Arthur Schopenhauer, the philosopher. These are the closing weeks of the year that has nourished you all along. This can be a period for real growth as new vistas open and new associations blossom. You are in the throes of creative energy and can come up with a master class. The soft winter sun makes you scurry for warmth and your world is pleasantly rumbling along. It is a beautiful life and you have no complaints. You are blessed. Ganesha is delighted.

10 December: Last Quarter in Virgo

Work and you are never really divorced. You are practical and know where your bread is buttered. The moon is in your sign and you are stable, balanced and sitting tight with both feet on mother earth. You are as stable as a road roller on a newly built national highway. While the party folk are calling out to you, this is not the time to waste. You roll up your sleeves and hit the shop floor. There are deals to be struck and headway to be made in the real world. You are filled with confidence and oozing bravado and take calculated risks that work out in your favour. Family life is stable and health is good. Ganesha is happy for you.

18 December: New Moon in Sagittarius

You are in the frenzy of communication and travel. You reach out to all comers and use the latest gizmos to the hilt. There could also be international travel or, at the very least, a holiday with the family. The Dalai Lama said, 'I think technology really increases human ability. It makes a lot of things much easier. But technology cannot produce compassion.' Thankfully, your heart is also filled with compassion as you spend time in philanthropy and share time, space and resources with the less fortunate. You could extend your compassion to the rescue and rehabilitation of birds and animals too. There is happiness in your soul for all the blessings that the universe has showered on you so ungrudgingly. Ganesha blesses you.

26 December: First Quarter in Aries

The last week of the year sees you moving ahead on turbo fuel. You are like the legendary race car drivers who know no fear. There is accomplishment and foundations laid for new plans that will take you into orbit. You are ambitious and sight fame and name. Nothing comes easy and you are ready to go that extra mile to make it all happen for you. There is love and new adventures. Youngsters excel at examinations and interviews and also play the field. They seem to have taken Mark Twain seriously when he said, 'If you can't do anything with your life, at least waste it.' You are in action mode and certainly not wasting valuable time. You enter the new year with hope, confidence and enthusiasm. Ganesha wishes you well.

LIBRA

23 September–22 October

Ganesha's Master Key: Relationship, artistry, lovingness, harmony

'When your creativity comes to a climax, when your whole life becomes creative, you live in God ... love what you do. Be meditative while you are doing it – whatsoever it is!'

– Osho

This is a powerfully creative phase. You express yourself in every possible way. Your mind is clear; you are alert and sharp.

The important traits: Wanting to please everyone; Overly dependent on other people and relationships; Imbalanced in self and life, fickle, indecisive, vacillating; Being torn between two things; Overemphasizing either the partner or the self; Bewildered by personality life versus soul life; Lacking awareness of the higher self; Failing to realize that the partner acts out the consciousness part of the self; Developing a sense of values; Striving to balance personality life and soul life; Seeking moderation in all areas of life; Being aware of the responsibility of choice; Being aware of the existence of the higher self; Being aware of the larger whole; Achieving a balance between personality and soul life; Attaining equilibrium between material desire and intelligent spiritual love; Being able to project inner spiritual purposes into manifestation; Being effective upon the physical plane; Making intelligent choices and taking responsibility for them; Attuning to the higher mind or higher self while functioning in the personality; Being a partner to the higher self; Understanding the law of attraction; Being aware of the perfect justice and order of the universe; Being aware of the organic and structural nature of the whole; Being aware of the holistic nature of the self and the universe; Being aware of one's role as a part of a larger whole.

Your Beauty-scope: Libra is usually a dimpled darling, or has, at the least, a very winning smile. A swan-like neck is natural for an ornament, say, a heavy necklace, preferably of turquoise. Generally, however, the feet are very clumsy. Closed shoes and sandals are the answer to it. No silver anklets either. The Libra movements are graceful, and Libra dancing is a symphony in beauty. Asparagus, almonds, brown rice, peas, oatmeal, beets, raisins, wheat, strawberries, apples, spinach and corn are typical Libra food for both health and beauty. The use of milk and fruits is advocated. A meat diet is not so important in your case. Fish, yes. Flowers like daisy, golden red, ground ivy, orchids, poppy, rose can do wonders in adorning you. But sugars and starch should be shunned like the plague.

CENTRAL IDEA

Ganesha says that by Western astrology the most beautiful signs are Taurus and Libra. The simple reason is that the main planet of both the signs is Venus, the recognized astrological planet for beauty and the arts. But this does not mean that the other ten signs are not beautiful and artistic.

Jupiter, your life's blood astrologically, moves in your own sun sign. Astrology is all about timing; that is the right person, right place, right time: 2017 is the right time. I am writing this forecast on 17 October 2015, during the Navratri religious festival. The other benefits of Jupiter in your sun sign will be the following:

a) House, home, land, warehouse, vehicles, shares, property all come into focus now, with the emphasis on buying/selling/renovation/decoration/alteration/acquisition. You may be laying foundations not only of a new home, but also of a new project, even a new attitude to your immediate kin (family, neighbourhood) and larger environment (society, shifting your base of operations). A change of ambience is almost definite around this time.

b) You may also be motivated towards making household and security improvements. Alongside – and this is important – you'll now place more value on your inner resources, especially the ability to perceive and decide future trends. In that respect, says Ganesha, you may be close to a launch into a different lifestyle and life cycle – in short, a different stratosphere;

c) Marriage, alliance, collaborations, journey with a stopover, advertising and publicity, confirms Ganesha.

d) Journeys, ceremony, job, correspondence and communication and the latest in technology will be extremely useful and profitable for you.

This year Saturn and Jupiter will be in good formation and therefore communication and contacts will result in contracts and cool delight and joy. In other words, Saturn will help you and not hinder your plans. But delays are possible because Saturn is a very slow-moving planet.

Ganesha says most of you know that Venus is your main planet or boss planet. Venus will be in your own sign from 14 October to 6 November. It will open out a window of opportunity in every possible way from 1 to 24 December, 5 to 31 July, and possibly from 28 April to 5 June. Money, marriage, love, alliances are indicated.

Venus, in short, is your greater planet. Friends help each other. Mercury is the planet of communication and trips. Mercury will be in your sun sign from 30 September to 16 October. Foreign travel, ceremonies, inspiration and intuition, artistic genius could all be your own territory. The periods from 6 to 25 July and 7 to 25 February could be memorable. Travel and ties are possible from 14 to 31 March and 21 April to 15 May. I am sure you will agree with me that this is a good list of goodies.

Finally, we talk of Mars, the planet of power. Mars will be in your sign from 23 October to 8 December. Mars will also help you between 21 April and 4 September. Be ready to catch the chances which come your way. Remember, catches win matches.

MONTHLY ROUND-UP

January: Home, house, family, shopping, renovation/decoration, alteration. **February:** Trips, ceremonies, rites, name and fame, future plans. **March:** Work, health, rewards, services, pets, projects, colleagues, promotion. **April:** Love, marriage, law cases, relationships, travels, contracts, communication, enemies. **May:** Joint finance, loans, funds, immigration, moving, shifting, capital formation, passion, sex. **June:** Joy, publicity, travel, ceremonies, functions, parties, irritations, import and export, collaborations, contacts, contracts, happiness because of abundance. **July:** Up and about, hard work, you will be really ready to be on the go be it home/office. **August:** Fun and games, friendship and fraternity, gains and gaiety. **September:** Too many things happening all together; see that you conserve your energy/vitality. **October:** Month of progress, prosperity and getting things done, as said before. **November:** Loans and funds and deals and transactions, buying/selling. **December:** Assignments, communication, transport, ties, trips, relatives.

Money: Promotion and perks and bonus should help you considerably this year. Salesmen, teachers, writers, artists and actors, commission agents, import and export should be in the money.

Happiness Quota: I give you 84 per cent.

MONTH BY MONTH

January: What a start to the year! I cannot but exult. Cast your sails and fly into the wind. New work, new love and all the goodies of life serenade you. Mid-month sees you busy sorting out relationship tangles. There could also be a lot happening on the domestic front. Your hands are full. As the month ends, there is powerful intensity in all your undertakings. You could also be in throes of love. You are emotional, excitable and impulsive. This is also a creative period.

February: There are stability and rapid growth in all areas of life. You have purpose and direction in your gait. You are confident, take calculated risks, and action your ideas. There are rewards and awards, adulation and applause. Mid-month sees work expansion. Your thoughts are clearly focused on money making. You are fired, passionate and ego-driven. As the month ends, there is international travel. Also, there are several monetary arrangements to be made. There is romance, and the unattached are spoilt for choice. The health of the spouse or children could cause concern. Your health too may need to be attended to.

March: If you are in a high-profile job, international travel reaps rich rewards. For everyday folk there are new job opportunities and a rise in status. You reinvent yourself, open your chakras and optimize them. You are working your way to a higher consciousness. Mid-month sees more stability. If you are prone to indulgences you get a handle on it. You carefully monitor your expenses and work your way through balance sheets. Your mind is sharp and alive. As the month ends, you walk down memory lane and cry over spilt milk. You look back at old loves and opportunities lost and are in the throes of despair. There are fancies and illusions, daydreams and inertia.

April: Domestic responsibilities weigh you down. Your health and the health of loved ones are a cause of concern. There are expenses of all kinds. There is a lot on your plate. Mid-month sees the moon in your sign and you are rocking. As the month ends, you roll up your sleeves and hack away. There are determination and fire in your actions. Success crowns you. You live in ecstasy. Your world is shining. Use your free will to steer this profoundly productive period to advantage.

May: There is global travel and an expansion of business interests on the cards. There is new intensity and direction to your life. Mint the moment. Mid-month sees more intensity in your life. There is a lot to be done, and karma and dharma call. As the month ends, your sensitivities are aroused. You network with ferocity using every gizmo at your disposal. You want to be in touch with friends, lovers and acquaintances and feel insecure and vulnerable. On the home front, you could be selling, renovating or moving to a new country altogether. New vistas open.

June: This is a period of relentless hard work. There is marked achievement as you move at full throttle, set targets and meet them. You may be travelling overseas to meet with your children who are studying there. Or if you have business interests, you will be looking at global conquests. Those of you who have taken to yoga and meditation see a visible rise in consciousness. Mid-month sees your mind torment you. There is an unrest that you cannot fathom. As the month ends, there are many indulgences and escapist tendencies. You are hard-pressed for time and resource.

July: There is a lot of sifting and prioritizing as you metamorphose from a caterpillar to a butterfly. You are powering ahead on all cylinders. Mid-month sees you all fire and brimstone. Passions and ego drives are aroused. Love courts you and singles play the field. Your life opens up to infinite possibilities. As the month ends, you mow down the opposition in a blatant display of court craft. There is new zeal, structure and architecture to your life. You are touched by a rare intensity. You scorch the tarmac and the sparks fly. There are maudlin moments too, and creative rewards. An interesting month.

August: You are in the throes of creative triumph. You win peer group approval, accolades and applause. This is a powerful phase and if you tweak it to advantage there will be windfall gains. Mid-month sees indulgences. Family life is stable and children bring joy. As the month ends, you are moving ahead fast and furious. This is a favourable period for discussions and negotiations. Big business folk thrive. You will be offered lucrative deals and there will be a rise in prestige and perks.

September: You give in to indulgences. It is a tough phase. You are living in your heart; rationale and logic gets a shove down the drain. Lovers elope, youngsters go haywire and even senior citizens scout for partners. You take risks and throw caution to the winds. Mid-month sees sustained effort and you forge ahead. This is a powerfully creative phase and accolades pour in. As the month ends, you get down to serious hard work. The bull phase has begun and success serenades you. The goodies roll out unabated. Nothing can stop you from courting the aroma of greenbacks.

October: Make the most of this propitious period. Expand, take risks, make investments, buy, sell – it will all be in your favour. Of course, do your calculations well and the payback will be enormous. Love also comes calling. Mid-month is a time for domestic calls. Marriages, engagements, anniversaries, additions to the family and fun times beckon. As the month ends, there are expenses, purchases, travel, love, lust, new vistas and growth in all areas of your life. This is a fantastic time for creative folk. You excel.

November: There is buying and selling, celebrations and festivities, love and longing, crazy ecstasy and new discoveries of the self through the joyousness that pervades your entire being. Mid-month sees you speed ahead on the fast track without a bump. You continue making waves without a pause. As the month ends, there are love, passion, lust, expenses, romance and good times. You are also curious about esoteric issues like life after death and the occult. There is also philanthropy. This may also be a creative phase and you put your energies into writing, painting, music, dancing and the arts.

December: As the year ends, you network furiously. You are filled with big ideas and dreams and want to share it with the world on loudspeakers. There is travel and new love. Mid-month sees a steadiness in your affairs. As the month ends, you party away. Friends and loved ones drop by from all over the globe and there is bonhomie all around. There are family gatherings and fun times. For those keen on travel there are exotic discoveries. Love and longing make their presence felt. You are pumped up for a great start to 2018.

WEEKLY REVIEW (BY PHASES OF THE MOON)

5 January: First Quarter in Aries

What a start to the year! I cannot but exult. Jupiter is in Libra till 9 October which is an exceptionally long time. There will be many subtexts in between and several other influences but the general trend is more than just favourable. Make the most of it. Cast your sails and fly into the wind. New work, new love and all the goodies of life serenade you. Only you can shoot yourself in the foot. Additionally, the moon is in

Aries. In recent times, at least comparing the last two years, this is the best start that you could have ever hoped for. It is a dream start: it is like Rohit Sharma and Shikhar Dhawan putting together a 100 runs for the first wicket in the finals of a T20 tournament with overs to spare. You cannot ask for anything better. It is like Powell winning the hundred metres by the halfway mark. The gods are kind. Need I say more? Jupiter in your own sign gives you prosperity, spirituality, expansion, joy and confidence. Jupiter is the planet of plenty. Jupiter signifies or shows that it is harvest time. It is time for awards and rewards. I have put it in very simple terms so that you understand it completely and clearly. Jupiter means good luck. Cornucopia is the horn overflowing with flowers, fruit and corn. It shows abundance. Jupiter is also the great teacher, the religious head, and bestows position, pelf and prosperity, the three Ps. As is commonly understood, Jupiter rules higher learning. In the spiritual realm, it lords over religions and philosophy. Jupiter also rules long-distance travel. Luck and good fortune are associated with Jupiter for good reason. Jupiter is considered a kind and benevolent planet. Success, accomplishments and prosperity are within Jupiter's realm. Sports of all kinds and games of chance are also ruled by Jupiter. Jupiter often presages great wealth. Traditionally, Jupiter is known as the 'Greater Fortune'. Ganesha applauds.

12 January: Full Moon in Cancer

The full moon is in Cancer and you are busy sorting out relationship tangles. You could be prospecting new partners. There could also be a lot happening on the domestic front. Children, their partners and, possibly, their children, parents, grandparents, and the entire family tree is in focus. Of course, this is a general reading but these are the indicators. Astrology never compels. Please remember that. You are besieged by domestic issues. Your hands are full. But it all works out in the end. Illness in the family may also make an appearance and you will douse the fires instantaneously. This is all a part and parcel of life. No one escapes the vicissitudes. Ganesha journeys with you.

19 January: Last Quarter in Scorpio

There is powerful intensity in all your undertakings. The focus could well be on relationships. You are either breaking up with someone or forging a new alliance. Librans thrive on relationships and unfortunately hold on to dead ones long after the expiry date, and then it is too late. You could also be in throes of love, or lust as you may prefer to call it. It takes you by storm like a hurricane that leaves nothing in its wake. 'Mistakes are part of the dues that one pays for a full life,' said the legendary actor Sophia Loren. Perfect. Ganesha is at your side as you navigate the maze of life.

28 January: New Moon in Aquarius

You are ideating with the speed of a shuttlecock in a badminton final between China's Lin Dan and Malaysia's Lee; their smashes are like rockets let loose. You weigh the pros and cons of every decision you make and that wastes a lot of time. Also, in the end, you may be left with a poor decision. You are emotional, excitable, impulsive, and attract offbeat types. You experiment with situations, cuisines, people, events and almost everything that crosses your path. This is also a creative period and there could be international travel. You may take to yoga, meditation and natural healing. The possibilities are endless. Ganesha watches.

4 February: First Quarter in Taurus

The moon is now in Taurus and there is stability and rapid growth in all areas of life. Your agenda is clear and you have purpose and direction in your gait. You are confident, take calculated risks, and action your ideas to advantage. You work diligently with the stamina of a horse. There are rewards and awards, adulation and applause and peer group approval. You are on a high. Life smiles at you. Say cheese. Family life is pleasant. Singles have a gala time. Your world is on song. Ganesha is also happy for you.

11 February: Full Moon in Leo

There is a lot of expansion at work. You want big money, you want to live large and well. You want to be surrounded by comforts and luxuries. There is only one life, you reason with yourself, and why not go the whole hog while the sun shines? 'All action results from thought, so it is thoughts that matter,' said Sai Baba. Your thoughts are clearly focused on money making. You send the right energies of abundance and wealth to the universe. You are willing to do whatever it takes to make it all happen for you. There is new intensity in all your dealings. Love drops its calling card but it all depends on you. Use your free will here. There is a lot on your plate. You want to make miracles happen. You are fired, passionate and ego driven. Luckily, the energies are well directed. I must add here that Librans are generally lucky with money. This is a subjective statement, but they get more than they deserve. Money tends to follow them. Ganesha blesses you.

18 February: Last Quarter in Sagittarius

There is international travel. Also, there are several monetary arrangements to be made. If you are into business, there is rapid expansion. Freelancers get blue chip deals, there are money and honey at your beck and call. Way to go! If the family is scattered there could be reunions and if they live with you there could be a holiday together. There is romance, and the unattached are spoilt for choice. Family life is in a state of pleasant upheaval. Ganesha watches.

26 February: New Moon in Pisces

The new moon is in Pisces and there are domestic concerns that take over your being. The health of the spouse or children could cause concern. Your health too may need to be attended to. 'The things people really want are love, connection and purpose,' says Mallika Chopra, the healer. Bang on! If you have reached a point of monetary stability you will be looking for purpose in life. If you haven't, the quest will be centred on mere money making. There are light-hearted flirtations, new experiences and many new acquaintances but you are driven to make things happen and no distraction has the marrow to derail you in your quest for a better you in a better world. Ganesha is impressed.

5 March: First Quarter in Gemini

You are networking with all and sundry, across continents. It is easy now thanks to all the technological marvels at hand. If you are in a high-profile job, international travel reaps rich rewards. For everyday folk fighting mounting inflation, there are new job opportunities and a rise in status. It is a great time for media folk as you are fired by creative urges and come up with masterpieces. 'If you are blinded with your worries, you cannot see the beauty of the sunset,' said J. Krishnamurti. You reinvent yourself, open your chakras and optimize them. You are working your way to a higher consciousness. Ganesha applauds.

12 March: Full Moon in Virgo

There is stability. If you are prone to indulgences you get a handle on it. I must add here that Librans are also prone to addiction. Of course, this is a generalization and a lot depends on your personal chart. Astrology never compels, and I am not God. Please remember this, dear readers. You carefully monitor your expenses and work your way through balance sheets. Your mind is sharp and alive. You weigh the pros and cons before making a decision and, I am afraid, you could be a little too late sometimes. Opportunity never comes knocking twice. It is like boxing. You unleash the knockout punch in the wink of a nanosecond; a dither and you are at the receiving end. Ask Muhammad Ali or the new Indian sensation Vijender Singh. Family life has nothing to boast about; it drags on. Ganesha feels that it is not a bad way to be.

20 March: Last Quarter in Capricorn

'The world is impermanent. Birth is a misery. Old age is a misery. Be careful,' says a Sanskrit poem. You are rushing ahead fast and furious. But there are maudlin moments that threaten to sabotage your peace. You walk down memory lane and cry over spilt milk. You look back at old loves and opportunities lost, and you are in the throes of despair. You revisit old indulgences and your life is like a paper boat navigating a tsunami. You have a heightened perception of the past and refuse to believe that it is all over. If a partner has left you, memories haunt and torment you. There is no point in crying over spilt milk but you will not listen to reason. At the cost of repetition, I would like to add a bit about Libra here; it is always nice to understand your sign, though it is a generalization. Libra is considered to be one of the most desirable signs of the Zodiac. Librans look for peace and harmony, and are conflict settlers. They seek beauty, luxury and drama. Libra is a cardinal air sign and Librans can be indecisive, flirtatious, self-indulgent, dependent and fickle. They are charming hosts and are the diplomats of the zodiac. They gravitate towards showbiz. Amitabh Bachchan and Rekha are classic examples among a host of other Bollywood and Hollywood celebrities. Ganesha blesses you as you wade your way through muddy waters.

28 March: New Moon in Aries

The new moon is in Aries and you are marching ahead like Genghis Khan's army, obliterating all the roadblocks in your path. There are many emotions at play but your energies are thankfully well directed. There are fancies and illusions, daydreams and inertia, many subconscious influences working overtime on you. They hang on to your sides like lichen on a whale. It is a disturbance and an irritant but you sally forward despite it all. Family life is turbulent. Illness in the family also catches you off guard. But this is all a part of the ebb and flow of life. On the flip side, it can also be a powerfully creative phase. You conjure up works of art. Use your free will to optimize the energies. Ganesha holds your hand.

3 April: First Quarter in Cancer

Domestic responsibilities weigh you down. Your health and the health of loved ones are a cause of concern. There could also be celebrations as there may be an addition to the family. What the stars indicate is that the focus is entirely on the family. There are also love and lust. There are expenses of all kinds, including travel. There is a lot on your plate, like overflowing Mughlai curry. There are pressures of different kinds and not all of it is unpleasant. You can have fun times too. Now, like I always do, let me tell you about the great company you keep. The list of celebrity Librans includes Michael Douglas, Catherine Zeta-Jones, Kim Kardashian, Doris Lessing, Serena Williams, Martina Navratilova, John Lennon, Manmohan Singh, Mohandas Gandhi, Oscar Wilde, Groucho Marx, Alfred Nobel, Bruce Springsteen and others. Is there anything to grumble about? You are in esteemed company. Ganesha blesses you.

11 April: Full Moon in Libra

The moon is in your sign and you are rocking. In addition to upward mobility, you charm the Gods with your philanthropy. To paraphrase Guru Nanak, what you give is yours and what you keep is not yours. You revel in the giving and feel good about it. You allocate quality time for less fortunate humans and animals and may even spearhead an NGO espousing veganism or some such cause. You earn peer group applause. 'You give but little when you give of your possessions. It is when you give of yourself that you truly give,' said Kahlil Gibran, echoing the great Sikh guru's sentiments. The universe watches and responds appropriately. Ganesha also watches, very pleased.

19 April: Last Quarter in Capricorn

You are on firm ground and your vacillations cease. 'To the mind that is still, the whole universe surrenders,' said Lao-tzu. You are back in balance and on terra firma. You roll up your sleeves and hack away. There is determination and fire in your actions. Success crowns you. There is little time for the family but they are not a cause for concern.

You move with the ferocity of Mad Max and achieve a lot. Your communication skills are enhanced and ego drives capped. There are money and honey, applause and accolades. Ganesha is thrilled.

26 April: New Moon in Taurus

There is continued growth. You spread your wings wide and enjoy success without a pause. You are like a carnivore in the Serengeti National Park in the spring; there is enough game to last a lifetime. 'We cannot cure the world of sorrows, but we can choose to live in joy,' said Joseph Campbell. You live in ecstasy. Your world is shining. Unless you have serious psychological issues, nothing should faze you now. But we all have underbellies and shadow sides that rock stability out of our lives. You are no exception; it is the destiny of man. Use your free will to steer this profoundly productive period to advantage. Ganesha watches over you.

3 May: First Quarter in Leo

You continue on the upward spiral. There is global travel and there is an expansion of business interests on the cards. There are new intensity and direction to your life. This is a wonderful phase and to paraphrase the Bard, take the tide at its flood and it will lead you to fortune. Mint the moment. You have the Midas touch. Love looms larger than life and there will be many unspoilt moments with the object of your dreams. Love conquers all and you surrender to its charms. It is time well spent, I say. Having lived a long life I know the smouldering impact of love. You can get as senseless as when Joe Frazier sends an upper cut to your brain. Go for it. It is sent by the universe. Of course, you don't need my advice. Librans, ruled by Venus, gravitate towards affections of the heart and body quite naturally. Ganesha knows.

10 May: Full Moon in Scorpio

'Courage is grace under pressure,' said Ernest Hemingway. There is intensity in your life. Some ghouls from the past and present and even the future visit and revisit. You are bowled over by the onslaught. It is like grappling with Sushil Kumar in the wrestling ring. You go down, but you are back on your feet in no time and want to leave it all behind as an unhappy episode. There is a lot to be done, and karma and dharma call. You will soon cruise through life with the ease of Edward Bear Grylls's knife slicing a melting carcass in the Andes. Ganesha knows and is not unduly perturbed.

19 May: Last Quarter in Aquarius

The monkey mind is up to many tricks. It plays with you like a puppet on a string. Your sensitivities are aroused and you could behave in a neurotic fashion. You feel that the sky is falling on your head and imagine all sorts of troubles. You hallucinate and think of ghosts and ghouls. You could also become a hypochondriac and feel that the slightest rise in temperature is a new virus from the Amazon jungles. Friends and loved ones find it hard to understand your moods, which swing around like a baboon in the jungle. If you are in a committed relationship, it could be very tough for your partner, who will be dialling for help with all the urgency he can muster. 'Be like a flower and turn your face to the sun,' said Kahlil Gibran. Apt advice for the mood you are in. Of course, like I always say, this is a general reading and astrology never compels. Ganesha watches over you and that is a consolation.

25 May: New Moon in Gemini

The new moon is in Gemini and you are networking with ferocity using every gizmo at your disposal. You want to be in touch with friends, lovers and acquaintances and feel insecure and vulnerable. The monkey mind is at its old tricks. You have to summon your free will and steer a course away from its distractions. On the home front, you could be selling, renovating or moving to a new country altogether. On the plus side, new vistas open and there is new learning. You are with people from different cultures and there is powerful exchange of ideas and visions. You will learn a lot, says Ganesha. Love walks in and out of your life like wreaths of sunshine passing by a window sill.

1 June: First Quarter in Virgo

This is a period of relentless hard work. The sun is merciless on the subcontinent; you can fry an egg in the shade. And you show no mercy to colleagues, subordinates and to yourself as you whip the team into shape and insist on adherence to deadlines. This is a significant time. There is marked achievement as you move at full throttle, set targets and meet them. Ganesha is impressed. Love tries to sidetrack you, along with domestic calls. But the koel cannot distract the tigress on the hunt in the Serengeti National Park.

9 June: Full Moon in Sagittarius

There is a lot of movement of every kind. You may be travelling overseas to meet with your children who are studying there. Or if you have business interests, you will be looking at global conquests. 'If you follow the inner path using truth and clarity as your compass points, the outer world cannot help but respond to your intention,' says Deepak Chopra. Those of you who have taken to yoga and meditation see a visible rise in consciousness. There are better health, more clarity and an increased sense of well-being.

On the flip side, intimate relationships need a realignment. They may have just shot past their expiry date and you have little patience to deal with a partner shackled by the past. Ganesha blesses you.

17 June: Last Quarter in Pisces

Your mind is in a whirl. It spins like a million tops in an Indian mela. The monkey mind, as Swami Vivekananda called it, is unforgiving. If you believe you can, you can. And if you believe you can't, you can't. It is as simple as that. We live and die in our minds. In this phase, you torment your mind needlessly. There is an unrest that you cannot fathom. You have it all and yet the vacuum is unquenchable. You decide to simplify your life and return to the basics. You take a break from work, maybe a holiday in some exotic locale, or do something different from the everyday routine. You hope to emerge rejuvenated and recast. Life is calling and you have to be ready for the dance. Ganesha holds your hand.

24 June: New Moon in Cancer

The new moon is in Cancer and you are being tested. There are many indulgences and escapist tendencies at play. Domestic calls are numerous and you are running around tending to ailing parents, children and the extended family. Bills have to be paid and bank loans looked into. You are hard-pressed for time and resource. According to Meher Baba, 'God has been everlastingly working in silence, unobserved, unheard, except by those who experience His infinite silence.' You look for benevolence from above. You clutch at straws. Ganesha journeys with you through the quicksand.

1 July: First Quarter in Libra

The moon is in your sign and there is a lot of sifting and prioritizing. There is a new you in the making and you metamorphose from a caterpillar to a butterfly. You astound onlookers; the family is in a daze. You are a changed person, internally and externally. You wear a new sartorial style and a new halo with elan. Now you set out to conquer the world like a junglefowl with new plumage in the rutting season. Ganesha watches.

9 July: Full Moon in Capricorn

You are powering ahead on all cylinders. You are like the new motoring marvels that reach 100 kmph in seconds. You remain on the fast track as you gallop like an Arabian steed across the plains. Money beckons; so does fame. After all, these are the two main ingredients which make the curry of life tasty. They catch you by the scruff of the neck and lead you to the waterhole. You may also resort to unethical means; the temptations are tremendous. I quote Ramakrishna Paramahansa here: 'The magnetic needle always points to the North, and hence it is that the sailing vessel does not lose her direction. So long as the heart of man is directed towards God, he cannot be lost in the ocean of worldliness.' You live hard and large. There are no full stops. Ganesha holds your hand.

16 July: Last Quarter in Aries

The moon is in Aries and you are all fire and brimstone. Passions and ego drives are aroused and there could be altercations, court cases and the law staring at you. Steer clear of it all, I say. Astrology never compels and one's life is packed with many variables and circumstances, including everyday biorhythms. We are constantly in a churn. There are even miraculous remissions which medical science cannot fathom. I am your favourite astrologer but I must add the caveat that I am not God. Love courts you and singles play the field. Your life opens up to infinite possibilities. Ganesha blesses you.

23 July: New Moon in Leo

The new moon is in Leo and you mow down the opposition in a blatant display of court craft. You deftly feint past barbs, accusations and enemies, and leave the opposition floundering in a brilliant display of the principles of Chanakya. There are new zeal, structure and architecture to your life. You make plans and achieve your targets. Of course, all expansion entails risk taking and expenses. You don't hold back. You want to fashion your life with artistic strokes, come what may. You are disciplined, your mind is sharp and you are filled with optimism and positivity. You are in the fast lane and holding your ground. There is love and longing with all the melodrama of a Bollywood potboiler. Ganesha smiles.

30 July: First Quarter in Scorpio

Your movement is now touched by a rare intensity. You scorch the tarmac and the sparks fly. The Buddha said, 'Through zeal, knowledge is gotten; through lack of zeal, knowledge is lost; let a man who knows the double path of gain and loss thus place himself that knowledge may grow.' I love to garnish my predictions with quotes so that you, my dear readers, get full value for your money. I call it 'Predictions Plus'. Love life throws up ugly twists and turns and you are left wondering what happened. Who did what – you or your partner? How did it all go so wrong all of a sudden when it was coasting along like a dream? This is a period of introspection, as the devil may lie within. Librans, despite their natural charm and good looks, often have disquieting love lives. There are maudlin moments too, and creative rewards. An interesting week, admits Ganesha.

7 August: Full Moon in Aquarius

The full moon is in Aquarius and there are moments of genius. You are in the throes of creative triumph. You win peer group approval, accolades and applause. This is a powerful phase and if you tweak it to advantage there will be windfall gains. On the flip side, you will also exhibit eccentric behaviour. The irrational side of your personality will be on eloquent display and you can easily be misunderstood; for that matter, even you will be unable to understand your innermost longings. The full moon is significant and always auspicious. It was said to have enlightened Buddha. G.I. Gurdjieff, an influential spiritual teacher in the early twentieth century, believed that the moon influenced our innermost lives. In astrology, the moon highlights your emotional self and the unconscious part of your personality. There are several lores about the moon but I will not go into all that now. But it is interesting to know that moon madness and werewolves were said to be brought about by the full moon. The *Farmer's Almanac* still suggests certain phases of the moon to plant everything from flowers to trees. On a personal level, the full moon impacts people differently. This has been scientifically and medically documented and is not strictly confined to the domain of esoteric sciences. Ganesha knows it all.

15 August: Last Quarter in Taurus

'I am not upset that you lied to me. I am upset that from now on I can't believe you,' said Friedrich Nietzsche. I love this line. It sums up the entire conundrum of the human temperament. Luckily, the moon is in Taurus and there is stability. You are on terra firma and working hard. There are indulgences of course. But you are able to take the team along as your heart is filled with compassion and you understand human frailties. You also lead from the front and success garlands you. Family life is stable and children bring joy. Love life rocks. Need I say more? Ganesha implores me to stay with the understatement.

21 August: New Moon in Leo

The new moon is in Leo and you are moving ahead fast and furious. This is a favourable period for discussions and negotiations. Big business folk thrive. You will be offered lucrative deals and there will be a rise in prestige and perks. The employed get promoted and freelancers cast their net wide. There are fancy purchases, possibly a second home. You may even purchase a fancy vehicle, much to the delight of family members. Children do exceptionally well at examinations and interviews, and the home fires burn with an extra spark. Ganesha is happy for you.

29 August: First Quarter in Sagittarius

You look to save your soul. It becomes a pressing need. You may go on pilgrimages, turn extra spiritual or seek out gurus and god-men. You look for deliverance. Your world is humming well but there are many questions that mere greenbacks cannot answer. There is money in the kitty and there are name and fame. But the vacuum persists.

You explore tantra, mantra and yantra. You spend time in meditation and yoga resorts in a quest for answers. 'You alone are the explorer of your inner world. Of all the ways to unfold your inner potential, by far the most powerful is to use the flow of evolution. Evolution isn't just a theory, but a force that has been working in every cell of your body since you were born,' says Deepak Chopra. I leave you to ponder over it. Ganesha leads the way and that helps.

6 September: Full Moon in Pisces

The full moon is in Pisces and your sensitivities are aroused. They garland you. You get emotional over every little thing and have little control over your actions as they are not prodded by rationale. You give in to indulgences. You may hang on to relationships that mean nothing to you just because you are afraid to be alone. It is a tough phase. You are living in your heart and rationale and logic goes down the drain. 'Life without liberty is like a body without a soul,' said Kahlil Gibran. You have the liberty in the material sense but you are shackled by the limitations of a mind surrendering to the heart. Lovers elope, youngsters go haywire and even senior citizens scout for partners. It is also a creative phase and media folk are crowned with success. You take risks and throw caution to the winds. Ganesha watches.

13 September: Last Quarter in Gemini

The inclinations of the last week spill into this week too. Of course, astrology only impels and never compels. Use your free will to advantage. You are communicating with all and sundry and using every gizmo on the market. If you are leading a political protest you will be front-paged. There is publicity, and the spotlight hugs you in its gaze. There is sustained effort and you forge ahead. You don't barge the opposition with a sledgehammer. Instead, you skirt past them deftly and reach your goal, leaving them wondering. You are like Lin Dan, the badminton legend, who catches his opponent on the wrong foot at match point. Osho rightly said, 'It is one of the fundamental laws of life that compassion cannot be defeated by hostility. Compassion simply changes the hostile person. Just start looking into people's eyes with grace.' This is a powerfully creative phase and accolades pour in. There could be innumerable affairs of the heart as they slice away on your soul like sculptors working on granite. You don't melt; you just play the field. Ganesha holds your hand.

20 September: New Moon in Virgo

There is an element of steadiness creeping into your affairs. You don't go helter-skelter. You touch firm ground, and the feel of terra firma is most reassuring. You roll up your sleeves and dirty your elbows. You get down to serious hard work. The monkey mind has been tethered. You plan out your life and get into action mode. You are riding high. The bull phase has begun and success serenades you without complaint. You are open to all the goodies that the universe will soon usher in. Zen-like, you are a vessel that has been emptied, and you are ready to partake of the bounties that await you. No one can stop you from realizing your true potential, barring yourself. I repeat this as Librans have a tendency to shoot themselves in the foot. Ganesha smiles.

28 September: First Quarter in Capricorn

Mercury is in your sign from 30 September to 16 October. The goodies will roll out unabated like a Japanese plant churning out a new generation SUV in the thousands. This is turning out to be an awesome year, first with Jupiter hogging centre stage and now Mercury. 'This turning towards what you deeply love saves you,' said Rumi. You automatically gravitate to your intrinsic skills and strike pay dirt. Readers will understand that Mercury is swift of foot, very fast, because he has wings, and therefore does not stay in one sign for a long period. Mercury, the mighty, all-powerful planet favours travels, meetings, conferences, interviews, trips, more brainpower, contacts, communication, correspondence and contracts. Mercury has a special connection with the circuits of the brain. Chess, crossword and other such games belong to Mercury. Also, short-distance runners and spin bowlers are controlled by Mercury. Mercury, in short, is the ambassador and salesman of the zodiac. Mercury is the symbol of news, views, messages, interviews, contacts, communications, travel and transport. Mercury gives an impetus to all of the above in the sun sign where it is located. You are determined and capable of hard work. You love the good life and know what money can buy. Nothing can stop you from courting the aroma of greenbacks. Ganesha is happy for you.

5 October: Full Moon in Aries

The full moon is in Aries and you are powering away like one possessed. Make the most of this propitious period. Expand, take risks, make investments, buy, sell – it will all be in your favour. Of course, do your calculations well, with a team that understands the fiscal market. Invest in help. The paybacks will be enormous. The late Nelson Mandela once said, 'After climbing a great hill, one only finds that there are more hills to climb.' You are in the throes of success. Like Alexander the

Great, you march undefeated. You seize the tide at the flood and smile at fortune; it readily smiles back. You are courted by dazzle and frazzle, and everything wonderful and brilliant as you extend a lengthy lease on the bull run. Love comes to your altar pleading for an appointment. Ganesha winks.

12 October: Last Quarter in Cancer

Venus is in your sign from 14 October to 6 November. You are ruled by Venus and this double whammy is like a lottery ticket. With the moon in Cancer, this is the time for attending to domestic calls. Marriages, engagements, anniversaries, additions to the family and fun times call. Venus is another important planet and is of great significance. This is an important phase. As often discussed, Venus is the planet for love, romance, sex, beauty and good life. This is the planet of attraction, love, wealth, knowledge and prosperity. The compatibility of partners and the type of life the individual will lead are also judged from the placement of Venus in the horoscope. As a planet, Venus is considered to be beneficial, feminine and gentle. Venus symbolizes the force of attraction in the universe. In human beings this attractive force manifests as love and beauty. When Venus is well placed in the chart there are love, art, beauty and all the goodies of life that make life worth living. Venus rules Libra and Taurus, though its role in every sign is important. Like other planets, it also has its transits. In Libra, Venus is aesthetic and cultured. In Taurus it is more earthy, materialistic and sensual. Venus rules the venous system, kidneys, urinary tract, throat, larynx, and is responsible for good looks. In short, Venus in Western astrology stands for comforts, arts, wealth, relationships, sex, decorations, luxuries and wealth. There are domestic issues which you solve with alacrity and then move ahead to work on consolidation and expansion. You are going great guns. There could be marriages, engagements, births, festivities and fun times calling out to you. There could be exotic travel, new love, money and honey, awards and rewards, accolades and applause. Whew. I am at a loss for words. But I am sure that you get the picture. Ganesha applauds.

19 October: New Moon in Libra

Mars is in your sign from 23 October to 8 December. Mars is like the volcano of vitality inside you and influences endurance, persistence and discipline. Mars was named for the Roman god of war, and is also known as 'the bright and burning one'. Red is the colour of Mars and stimulates the dynamic, potent and fertile drives that power our lives. Mars rules physical energy and action and governs energy, strength, courage, life force and expansion. Well-placed Mars endows powerful energy and an indomitable will to succeed. Mars propels us like an ignited rocket. It is an important energy since it determines how we pursue what we want to achieve in life. In short, Mars represents energy, force, violence, aggression, sports, combat, wars, battles, accidents, operations. The new moon is also in your sign and the cards being dealt are in your favour. Unless you do something really bizarre or there is some other aspect in your personal chart which I do not have, your world is a bed of roses. Of course, Mars can put you in a spin and you have to watch out for that. Hold on to passions and ego drives with a strong leash till early December. In this period you display the pace of Usain Bolt, the dancing feet of Nureyev, the vision of Stephen Hawking, the genius of Bill Gates, the passion of Rasputin, the stamina of Yifter the Shifter, the erudition of

Rabindranath Tagore, the dazzle of Marilyn Monroe, the stick work of Dhyan Chand, the doggedness of Tendulkar, the guile of Shane Warne and the flair of Brian Lara. There are expenses, purchases, travel, love, lust, new vistas and growth in all sectors of your life. Ganesha is spellbound.

27 October: First Quarter in Aquarius

You are at your creative best and are inoculated with the stroke of genius. This is a fantastic time for creative folk. You excel. Writers and composers strike pay dirt. Kahlil Gibran wrote *The Prophet*, his most famous book, when he was only twenty-one years old. He couldn't better his first book for the rest of his life! I hope you will do one better with time, but, without a doubt, you will be churning out masterpieces by the kilo. 'I believe a leaf of grass is no less than the journey-work of the stars,' said Walt Whitman, the poet. You take care of the little things and keep it simple. In that alone is greatness. In that is also success. Ganesha is happy for you.

4 November: Full Moon in Taurus

The full moon is in Taurus and you continue on the bull run. Good times are aplenty but the only hitch is that the learning process is strengthened during difficult times; gold has to be put through fire. You have had it rather easy. In a way, it is retribution for a difficult period a couple of years ago. The cosmos has its own checks and balances. But let the past remain where it should and let's enjoy the moment in the sun. There is buying and selling, celebrations and festivities, love and longing, crazy ecstasy and new discoveries of the self through the joyousness that pervades your entire being. Ganesha is as excited as you are.

10 November: Last Quarter in Leo

Last year this time you probably went through tumultuous times. Please remember that I do not have your personal details and this is merely a generalized reading. The fog has cleared and this year you speed ahead on the fast track without a bump. Librans love balance and peace. There are ripples of ego excitement, but nothing that can upset your cart. You continue making waves without a pause. Ganesha watches from the sidelines.

18 November: New Moon in Scorpio

'The only way to live is to accept each minute as an unrepeatable miracle,' said Jack Kornfield. You are living on your terms, with incredible energy and intensity. There are love, passion, lust, expenses, romance and good times. You are filled with gratitude for what has been an excellent year and want to share the goodies with friends and loved ones. You are also curious about esoteric issues like life after death and the occult. You may take time off for serious study. There is also philanthropy. Ganesha leads the way.

26 November: First Quarter in Pisces

You take time off and spend the week in the lap of nature. This is a welcome break. You normally want to be with people but you may also take off solo. You want 'me' time and realize that unless you are alone with your thoughts you will not evolve in consciousness. 'In the depth of winter I finally learned that there was in me an invincible summer,' said Albert Camus. This may also be a creative phase and you put your energies into writing, painting, music, dancing and the arts. You may also take to yoga and meditation or a new form of diet and exercise. Ganesha encourages you.

3 December: Full Moon in Gemini

'That sorrow which is the harbinger of joy is preferable to the joy which is followed by sorrow,' said Saadi, the poet. The full moon is in Gemini and you network furiously. Your mind is all over the place. You are filled with big ideas and dreams and want to share it with the world on loudspeakers. There is travel and new love. You flirt like it will go out of fashion by next week. Singles have a field day and those who are in relationships look for holes in their vows. An interesting period, for sure. Ganesha smiles.

10 December: Last Quarter in Virgo

There is a steadiness in your affairs. You are back on terra firma. There is balance in thought and deed. You get down to work and tie up loose ends. This is not the time for the hard slog but your reassuring presence is necessary at the office. You offer the required steadfastness, and others look up to you for justice and peace. Family life is also calm and there are no ripples in your world. Ganesha is not on tiptoe too.

18 December: New Moon in Sagittarius

The fun times have begun. You party away. Friends and loved ones drop by from all over the globe and there is bonhomie all around. 'A pedestal is as much a prison as any small space,' said Gloria Steinem. There are family gatherings and fun times. For those keen on travel there are exotic discoveries. Love and longing make their presence felt and you leave it to your free will to steer the course. Ganesha blesses you.

26 December: First Quarter in Aries

The last week of the year has you energetic and bubbling with life. You are in the 'can do' mode and will not rest till you achieve your goals. This has been an amazing year – unless otherwise indicated in your personal chart – and you are pumped up for a great start to 2018. Every year has its snafus; for that matter, every day and every moment can throw up surprises. As an astrologer I am aware of all this and make the necessary allowances. I wish all my readers well and I am optimistic and enthusiastic by nature. Optimism can carry you very far because we live in our minds. You wear new plumage and say cheese. Way to go! Ganesha is impressed.

SCORPIO

23 October–22 November

Ganesha's Master Key: Life, death, regeneration

'Unseen energies, mysterious depths of marshes, vindictive and poisonous like vipers, mighty healers and heartless murderers; yes, you are the ultimate in contradictions and therefore the most exciting and mysterious.'

– BEJAN DARUWALLA

The important traits are: Unethically manipulating others for selfish purposes; Scheming, overbearing, subtly domineering; Power-driven, sensation-seeking, self-indulging; Lustful, vengeful, resentful, envious; Desirous, belligerent, sceptical; Inwardly fearful, overly intense, mentally cruel; Intolerant, possessive, exploitative of other people; Exploitative of other's energies and possessions; Using psychic powers for selfish motives; Unconsciously struggling with the soul; Conscious of unseen energies, aware of the need for self-transformation; Aware of the existence of the soul, finding the faith that is born of darkness; Turning personal devotion towards higher causes;

Beginning to use personal power for selfless purposes; Learning mental control over the physical and emotional vehicles, becoming charitable; Surrendering the personal will to the light of God, learning about psychic powers and their proper use; Becoming objective about self; Learning emotional detachment, seeking energy exchanges which are for the highest good of all concerned; Consciously struggling with the soul; Transmuting lower energies to the higher centres; Charismatic, transforming conflicts into beauty; Attuned to the soul, conscious of the will of the higher self; Seeing struggles as opportunities for growth; Seeing would-be adversaries as 'testers' sent by the higher self; Being a transforming agent who is sought by others; Stepping down higher energies to be used for the highest good of all; Having mental control over the physical and emotional natures; Using knowledge of unseen energies to help spread the Light of God; Having an automatic positive effect on others; Lovingly healing those who give their consent; Exchanging energies with others in love and light; Being a transmitter of healing energies for the universal good.

Your Beauty-scope: Beauty with Scorpios mixes or rather merges with that elusive quality called personality. The colour for Scorpio is scarlet. It goes with your total self. Yes, Scorpios walk with a swing, and that's where sex appeal comes in very positively. The eyes are magnificent. Play them up with eye shadow, mascara and even false eyelashes. In addition, the voice is husky, often a Scorpio characteristic. The mouth, firmly set, shows character; so never appear grim! The neck is short, strong. No jewellery there please. The hands exude power and the fingertips are square.

CENTRAL IDEA

Secretive, Cunning, Intense, Obstinate, Spiritual Master

Ganesha asks you to expect the unexpected, the mysterious, the strange, the bizarre, the contradictory, the unusual. Therefore 2017 will be both widely challenging and supremely exciting. Here is what Guru Nanak has to say: 'Those who believe in Him get to the gate of salvation. Those who believe in Him are saved with their kin. Those who believe in Him swim across and help others to swim. Those who believe in Him don't have to beg of others. Such is the name of God the Pure. Those who believe in Him, they alone get to know Him.'

Why have I, very specially, emphasized the importance of God for you this year? I know very well that God is always important. In 2017, God will be very specially important because Jupiter will be in your twelfth angle. It will inspire, encourage and motivate you to seek the help of God. Therefore, I have given priority to the universal help you may receive from God as stated by Guru Nanak or any other great spiritual leader. The message is the same: have faith and hope in God.

There are other aspects of Jupiter in your twelfth angle. These are: You will balance between work, personal aspirations, career on the one hand and home, family, domestic responsibilities on the other; A reshuffle, revamping or reorganization may become necessary in the realm of home and family; There will be many financial demands vis-à-vis your home – hypothecation of assets, joint and material funds, even divorce settlements and alimony. They may come in all shapes and guises. The astrological indications are strong. The twelfth angle is that you will be both, the teacher and the student; will have powerful connections with great charitable causes, hospitals, welfare centres, rehabilitation sources and philanthropists, doing away with past errors and attachments which have served their purpose; Another great secret of Jupiter in the twelfth angle is that you will seek knowledge, wisdom, and also salvation. You may even get an inkling of your last birth and your next birth. I am not saying that it has to happen. I am openly pointing out the possibility of it. A few of you could even end up as a spiritual master. But expenses, ill health, losses, looking after the sick and the unfortunate are also a possibility. You must also take great care of your health and that of your dear ones. Hospitalization, extra expenses, medical care is a possibility. These are the negative points of Jupiter in your twelfth angle.

Ganesha says that in life nothing is free; life demands a price. Pending matters will be resolved, giving you satisfaction. Ganesha also says that there's another way of looking at the influence of the twelfth angle of Jupiter for you. In the words of St Augustine, 'The world is a book; those who do not travel read only a page.' You will travel, physically, mentally and spiritually.

This is the last year of Saturn in your money and family slot, but Jupiter, the planet of prosperity, is in fine formation with Saturn. Therefore, compared to the last two years, this year money will flow freely and the family will grow happily. In other words, less tensions and more goodies of life. Here, let me point out that 2018 may seem very far to you now. But in 2018 Jupiter will be in your sun sign by Western astrology. It will not only be a good year; it will be a great year. We will talk more about it in 2018. This is just an appetizer. To me personally, hope is 70 per cent of life.

Mars is your main planet. Mars will be in your sign from

9 December 2017 to 26 January 2018. Therefore, you will be activated and stimulated in all that you think and do. From 20 July to 4 September you will be working at breakneck or full speed. The period 28 January to 9 March is a fine one for work and service, promotions and perks. Loans, funds and investments are due from 21 April to 4 June. I am sure you will agree with me that we have covered a lot of astrological ground for you.

Venus is the planet of money, art and comfort. For you very specially, Venus could lead to alliances, links, ties, marriages, journeys, collaborations, foreign affairs. When? The periods for it are 4 February to 5 June; 7 to 30 November; 6 June to 4 July; and 25 December 2017 to 17 January 2018. Very surprisingly, pilgrimages and visits to holy places fall in complete tune to marriage and alliances.

Most of us know that Mercury is for messages, contacts and journeys. For you Mercury stands for joint finance, loans, investments, socializing, love, entertainment, children, divorce as well as marriage. The periods from 11 January to 6 February; 1 to 20 April; 21 June to 5 July; 26 July to 1 September; and, finally, 17 October to 5 November are positive indicators for the above events for you.

MONTHLY ROUND-UPS

January: Meditation, the domestic scene, renovation and decoration, excellent rapport with people, travel and communication will be highlighted. **February:** Home, house, family, emigration, buying/selling/renovation. **March:** Top of any situation; children, hobbies and creativity are emphasized. **April:** Job, health, pets, projects, colleagues and your relationships with subordinates and servants.

May: Love/hate, cooperation/competition, collaboration/separation, trips and ties, signing of documents and drafts. **June:** Loans, funds, capital formation, buying/selling; do take care of your health and vitality. **July:** You will begin on a positive, winning streak; and journeys, ceremonies, good relationships, should be the happy events. **August:** Changes on the work and personal frontiers will start and they have to be tackled with tact and skill; August is a continuation of July. **September:** Socializing, friendship, gains and a wish-fulfilment. **October:** Expenses, secret deals, looking after the sick and the needy; also you must safeguard your own health. **November:** A progressive, go-ahead month, as pointed out in the special months feature. **December:** Finances, food, family, contracts and comforts.

Money: I repeat Scorpio, Aquarius, Leo and Taurus are the greatest money signs by Western astrology. For example, Bill Gates is a Scorpio. This does not mean that the other eight signs cannot be mighty money makers. Finally, it really depends upon your individual horoscope. My father has taught me to be very open-minded and completely tolerant. Therefore, each and every sign is important and unique. I have been tremendously impressed by what my father told me five years ago. He said, 'Nature is both abundant and full of infinite variety. We are all children of Nature.'

Happiness Quota: I give you 85.75 per cent. I know very well that happiness means different things to different people.

MONTH BY MONTH

January: The start to your year is fantastic. There are new challenges and ambitions and you move ahead with fire and determination. There is zeal, enthusiasm and josh in all your dealings. Mid-month sees new vistas open up and you grow in consciousness. If there are spiritual stirrings, they get activated. As the month ends, you have an intensity of purpose. Those in business and the corporate world meet with success. Your heartstrings are tugged and you give of yourself freely to those who are in need.

February: You are whizzing away to new directions and destinations. Love comes calling. Mid-month sees you propelled by jet fuel. Those keen on business expansion can use the propitious period well. There could also be foreign travel and international collaborations. Success garlands you. As the month ends, you are on a quest for a deeper meaning to life. Ego drives are on hold; you are sensitive to the needs of others and excel in creative expression. This can be a wonderful time for media folk.

March: There are parties, alumni meetings, festivities, celebrations and fun times to begin with. Mid-month sees you get down to the hard slog. You roll up your sleeves and get to work with determination. You are an achiever. Family life is stable. As the month ends, you are racing ahead without a pause. There are money and honey in sight. You are powering away. There are powerful ego drives and passions at play.

April: You are busy with issues at home. The health of elders and children are a cause of concern. Your own health may need attention. Additionally, there are home improvements and renovations. You wear your emotions on your sleeve and your sensitivities are aroused. Mid-month sees you toying with multiple choices. There are expenses that naturally come with business expansion. As the month ends, you are back to work after a brief interlude. This can be a great time for writers and media folk. Your creative juices are fuelled and you conjure up works of genius. New vistas open. Hard work, determination, inspiration, perspiration and genius take hold of you by the scruff of the neck. This is a propitious time and the energies are in your favour.

May: Family life is in a tailspin as you and the others at home have opposing views. You are hard-pressed to keep the peace. Mid-month sees you filled with empathy, sympathy and philanthropic feelings. You help out with the poor and downtrodden. Maudlin moments also pass by like heavily laden monsoon clouds. As the month ends, you want to be free of shackles and float like a summer cloud. You want to be free of restrictions and expectations. You want to get away from the pressing concerns of the real world. You network furiously and want to be known and heard.

June: You are ambitious and determined, and nothing can baulk you on the road to success. You burn the midnight oil and come up trumps. With every challenge overcome, you evolve stronger and wiser. Mid-month sees a lot of movement. Love and creativity walk arm in arm with you. There are inflated expectations and excessive idealism. There could also be solo travel or a slice of adventure sport. The possibilities are infinite. As the month ends, you get away from the hurly burly of life and amuse yourself with idle chatter or simply taking off by yourself in the woods. You sidestep the rat race and look to rejuvenate yourself.

July: There are many loose ends on the work front that call out to you. Domestic life also has urgent demands. Keep away from altercations and court battles. Mid-month sees ambition goading you on. There are big plans on the anvil and you catch the sweet fragrance of money and power. This is a propitious period and, if you use your free will well, miracles can happen. As the month ends, you continue on the upward trajectory. There is more work expansion. Along with it are expenses. There could also be maudlin tunes that distract you.

August: You are networking with all and sundry and also showcasing your offbeat and rebellious side. Mid-month sees you roll up your sleeves, grease your elbows and get down to the shop floor for hard, uncompromising work. You burn the midnight oil and leave the opposition behind by a distance. This is a productive and growth-oriented period. As the month ends, you are powering away. You are able to get a handle on your passions and ego drives and are amiable and joyous. You are agreeable, sociable and friendly. This helps on the work and personal fronts. There is international travel. There is sartorial change, along with a complete metamorphosis of the soul.

September: Your creative energies are sparked and you manufacture masterpieces. You astound your peer group; the competitors and the naysayers are also left spellbound. Your emotions and sensitivities are aroused and you are dripping with compassion and empathy for the less privileged. Mid-month sees your mind in a whirl. But as the month ends, sanity and stability return to your life. You get down to the hard grind of making a living and reap the rewards. You push on all cylinders, obliterating the opposition. You are filled with zest and josh. More greenbacks and perks have you hungering for more.

October: There are pleasant times at home and children bring joy. It is a period of prosperity and bonhomie. Mid-month sees you plunge into new learning. You seek knowledge. You look at super-specialization. Jupiter in your sign allows you to broaden your horizons. Go for it. As the month ends, you are pushed to the wall by deadlines and conjure up masterpieces thanks to the added pressure. Your plate is full and overflowing with goodies. Take the tide at the flood. You are on a bull run and you obliterate all opposition.

November: You live the life of luxury. There are purchases and international travel. Love looms large. There could be fun times and festivities, even an addition to the family. Mid-month sees the good times continue. Expenses mount too. This is your moment in the sun and you are living it up. There may be domestic concerns. There could be illness in the family, and children will have issues that need to be sorted out. As the month ends, you are at your creative best. This is a great time for writers and painters. There are inspiration and perspiration. You are filled with self-belief.

December: You meet with different kinds of people and give your life an offbeat edge. The creative juices continue to flow as you network your skills to legions of fans. Mid-month sees stability and hard work. There will also be some snafus, snares and trapdoors, but it all depends on your personal chart. Rein in ego drives and passions. Avoid altercations at all costs. As the month ends, you may take the family out on an international holiday or even go solo, traversing exotic trails. You have a purpose and a sense of direction. You live and love large.

WEEKLY REVIEW (BY PHASES OF THE MOON)

5 January: First Quarter in Aries

I love this quote. 'It took less than an hour to make the atoms, a few hundred million years to make the stars and planets, but five billion years to make man!' said George Gamow, physicist and cosmologist. As you can see, we humans are so special. The start to your year is fantastic. There are new challenges and ambitions and you move ahead with fire and determination. There is zeal, enthusiasm and josh in all your dealings. You win brownie points and are showered with money and honey, rewards and awards, accolades and applause. There could also be travel, and many tugs at your heartstrings. If you have chosen a suitor among the many who serenade you, you are ready to give your life to that person; there are no full stops here. Ganesha blesses you.

12 January: Full Moon in Cancer

The full moon is in Cancer and domestic responsibilities absorb you. The health of elders and children take your time. There are expenses which you did not anticipate. This is all a part of the mosaic of life and no one is exempt from it, so don't count yourself as particularly unlucky. On the plus side, new vistas open up and you grow in consciousness. If there are spiritual stirrings, they get activated. Ganesha journeys with you.

19 January: Last Quarter in Scorpio

You are not one to be sidetracked for long. You have grit and gumption to rebound from a low phase, effortlessly and swiftly. You certainly do not inhabit a maudlin note for too long. The moon is in your sign giving you an intensity of purpose. You know the calls of the real world and go about answering them without much ado. The challenges on the home front are met pronto and new work interests catch your eye. Those in business and the corporate world meet with success. Ganesha is with you and that is what matters. Like I always do, to give a better perspective to the generalized predictions, I will add those you share your sun sign with. You are in the exalted company of Leonardo DiCaprio, Julia Roberts, Bill Gates, Martin Luther King, Wayne Rooney, Pablo Picasso, Hillary Clinton, Sylvia Plath, Ezra Pound, Charles Bronson, Marie Curie, Albert Camus, Indira Gandhi, Robert Kennedy, Voltaire, Leon Trotsky and Diego Maradona, among others. Scorpios are achievers. They are also very intuitive and can be sensitive and emotional. Scorpios are represented by the scorpion, the eagle and the lizard. Which type of Scorpio are you? All three are very different. Of course, like I always insist, this is a general reading and is not individual-specific.

28 January: New Moon in Aquarius

'We're here for a reason. I believe a bit of the reason is to throw little torches out to lead people through the dark,' said Whoopi Goldberg. The new moon is in Aquarius and this is a great time for creative folk and those in philanthropy. Your heartstrings are tugged and you give of yourself freely to those who are in need. You may even spend time at home with the elderly or take them for a holiday and meet their every little demand, however eccentric or irrational it may seem. Yes, without a doubt, charity begins at home. Ganesha is impressed and wishes you well.

4 February: First Quarter in Taurus

You are on speed. You are whizzing away to new directions and destinations with the speed of an antelope running for its life in the savannah. As Carl Honoré, author of *In Praise of Slowness*, quipped: 'These days, even instant gratification takes too long.' You are on firm ground and in achievement mode. You are hard-working and determined, and make miracles happen. The achievement-oriented Scorpio is simply unputdownable. Which type of Scorpio are you? Love and lust come calling. But so do money and new frontiers. Use your free will and choose wisely. I know you will. Ganesha is always there, offering tips.

11 February: Full Moon in Leo

'What great thing would you attempt if you knew you could not fail?' asked Robert H. Schuller, retired American pastor and author. This is a question directed at you. The full moon is in Leo and you are full on. Impossible is a word that doesn't exist in your vocabulary. At least, it doesn't in this phase. You are propelled by jet fuel. Those keen on business expansion can use the propitious period well. There could also be foreign travel and international collaborations. Those keen on a roll in the hay also find opportunities in plenty. Your plate is overflowing. Success garlands you. Ganesha applauds.

18 February: Last Quarter in Sagittarius

There is movement of every kind. You could be networking till the cows come home, or even covering long distances geographically. You take risks and believe firmly that nothing ventured, nothing gained. You play the inswinger on the front foot and knock it over the boundary with precision and power like Virat Kohli. You are also on a quest for a deeper meaning to life. Yantra, tantra and mantra excite you. There are pilgrimages and a quest for gurus and god-men as you seek out solutions to the complex issues facing man. You ponder love and longing, the loneliness of man and his eternal quest for salvation. You ask yourself if the human being is condemned and there is no escape from the maze it inhabits in body and soul. If you are single, you wonder if there is anything called a soulmate in this lifetime or the next, this one preferably. If you have broken up recently or recovered from surgery you hope that there are rosier tidings to look forward to. Ganesha journeys with you and that helps.

26 February: New Moon in Pisces

The new moon is in Pisces and you take a step back from the hurly-burly of life and examine your piquant situation in great detail. You want more than name and fame. But how do you embark on that quest? You spend time with friends, and all by yourself too. 'Me' time is invaluable. In the silence are many answers. 'The individual must not merely wait and criticize. He must defend the cause the best he can. The fate of the world will be such as the world deserves,' said Albert Einstein. Ego drives are on hold; you are sensitive to the needs of others and excel in creative expression. This can be a wonderful time for media folk. Ganesha blesses you.

5 March: First Quarter in Gemini

You are in the throes of networking. You firm up travel plans and check out new frontiers. If there is an office meeting overseas you make the most of it and extend your stay and visit nearby countries. The travel bug bites you hard. You love the prospect of new people, new experiences and new vistas, as it allows you to grow as a person. You are richer by the experience. There is more ideating than action in this phase and that is equally important. There are parties, alumni meetings, festivities, celebrations and fun times. Enjoy, says Ganesha.

12 March: Full Moon in Virgo

The full moon is in Virgo and you temper your natural enthusiasm and get down to the hard slog. You roll up your sleeves and get to work with determination. You are an achiever, and very little can hold you back once you set your sights on your target. You obliterate everything that stands in your way. 'Every strike brings me closer to the next home run,' said Babe Ruth. Family life is stable as you have looked into the nuts and bolts; it hums along, well oiled and on a full stomach. There is little time or room for the usual distractions of life. Ganesha watches.

20 March: Last Quarter in Capricorn

You are racing ahead without a pause. There are money and honey in sight. The greenbacks in the bank are a source of delight. As your account gets fatter you get increasingly driven. Money has a strange aura to it and you can recognize it from a distance. Along with it is also greater responsibility and added work. Nothing comes free. There are perks and promotions but the slog also increases. The Dalai Lama says that one should follow the three Rs: respect for self, respect for others, and responsibility for one's actions. You do all three and win kudos. Ganesha is happy for you.

28 March: New Moon in Aries

The new moon is in Aries and you are powering away. You do the marathon in record time, even sprinting lengths of it, leaving the opposition behind by a distance. Love comes calling and you may take a break from it all with a little roll in the hay. Singles play the field and those in committed relationships torch ecstasy to delirious heights. There are powerful ego drives and passions at play. Keep cool and all will be well, says Ganesha. Avoid altercations as far as possible; there are no winners once you lose your balance. Count to ten and take deep breaths and allow the moment to pass. Life has many sides to it and astrology understands it. There are no compulsions.

3 April: First Quarter in Cancer

'Be kind to your loneliness,' says Danielle LaPorte. You are busy with issues at home. The health of elders and children are a cause of concern. Your own health may need attention. Additionally, there are home improvements and renovations. There are expenses which are not in your control. This is all a part of the mosaic and maze of life. There are excesses and indulgences. You also wander down memory lane and cry over spilt milk. You wear your emotions on your sleeve and your sensitivities are aroused. You are indecisive, impatient and confused. This shall also pass. Happiness, like unhappiness, never lasts for long. Family life is stretched. Ganesha knows it all.

11 April: Full Moon in Libra

The full moon is in Libra and you are toying with multiple choices. Even a bad choice will not bring ruin and so you are literally spoilt. 'Live life as if everything is rigged in your favour,' said Rumi. This is what you do now. There are expenses that naturally come with business expansion. It is a challenge and a part of evolution, and you cope. You are earning more. Just ensure that there is no hole in the bucket. As the sun scorches the subcontinent you are also filled with love and passion. You court the love of your dreams and are lost in the throes of ecstasy. Nothing can deter you from this single-minded quest of possessing, body and soul, the object of your desires. I have been there and know how compelling it all can be. It is nature at work; let it. Ganesha wishes you well.

19 April: Last Quarter in Capricorn

After this brief interlude you are back to work. Love still hovers around, enchantingly casting its web, but your focus is most clearly on the work front. This can be a great time for writers and media folk. Your creative juices are fuelled and you conjure up works of genius. 'Words are the only things that last forever; they are more durable than the eternal hills,' said William Hazlitt, the essayist. You take the cue and become a formidable wordsmith. There are accolades and applause and peer group approval. You win awards and rewards. New vistas open and you are hailed as the new talent on the block. Ganesha is thrilled for you.

26 April: New Moon in Taurus

There is stability, hard work, determination, inspiration, perspiration and genius that take hold of you by the scruff of the neck. The new moon is in Taurus. This is a propitious time and the energies are in your favour. You live and love large, and go caress your dreams. There are expenses and risk taking. You expand your circle of influence and find many takers. Your idiosyncrasies and shadow side are tolerated, even passed off as signs of a highly evolved mind. Ganesha smiles.

3 May: First Quarter in Leo

Your motivations are powerful and they egg you on regardless of the challenges facing you. Family life is in a tailspin as you and the others at home have opposing views. Children beg to differ and the spouse has other ideas altogether. You are hard-pressed to keep the peace. 'Education is the most powerful weapon which you could use to change the world,' said Nelson Mandela. You may take time off in serious study or even attend a course in the university, whatever your age. You want to increase your knowledge base and you do whatever it takes. This way, your mind will also be diverted from the domestic maze. Ganesha blesses you.

10 May: Full Moon in Scorpio

'Man can never be a woman's equal in the spirit of selfless service with which nature has endowed her,' said M.K. Gandhi. I love this quote and I fully agree. The full moon is in Scorpio and you are filled with empathy, sympathy and philanthropic feelings. You help the poor and downtrodden and give generously to charities. You are consumed by a rare intensity and want to give 'until it hurts' as Mother Teresa said. Maudlin moments also pass by like heavily laden monsoon clouds. You shrug it off with the ease of a golden retriever after its weekly bath. There is a lot to do and you have just begun. Time and tide wait for no man. You know that as well as Ganesha.

19 May: Last Quarter in Aquarius

Your mind is travelling in outer space. You want to be free of shackles and float like a summer cloud or like a kite without a manja from the tallest turrets of Mount Abu. You want to be free of restrictions and expectations. You want to get away from the pressing concerns of the real world. You want to levitate, even leave your body for a while, and wander around the countryside. As I remind readers all the time, astrology never compels. You have your free will and this is a generalized reading. 'Joy is not to be sought outside – joy is your original state of being. If you do not mess up your mind, you will naturally be joyful,' says Sadguru Jaggi Vasudev. In this phase the Sadguru's words have a remarkable ring to it. Ganesha agrees. You live in your mind, so harness it well.

25 May: New Moon in Gemini

You are furiously networking. You want to be known and heard, and this is the era of being online. You decide to market yourself and hog the limelight for a bit. Unfortunately, or fortunately, it is easy these days, even without an image consultant egging you on. Your monkey mind is at several places all at once. You are busy with the three Cs: contacts, communication and correspondence. You are ideating furiously and meeting with people of diverse interests and sharing views and news. New windows open and a new breeze sweeps the debris from your life. Your glass is emptied and new knowledge pours in. You grow in all possible ways. Ganesha is pleased.

1 June: First Quarter in Virgo

You are on the fast track of hard work and achievement. You roll up your sleeves and grease your elbows. You are ambitious and determined, and nothing can baulk you on the road to success. The writer Emile Zola said, 'One forges one's style on the terrible anvil of daily deadlines.' Work and its pressing demands hover over you like a helicopter spraying pesticide on a paddy field. But you don't give in. You burn the midnight oil and come up trumps. More challenges are thrown at you and yet you don't succumb. With every challenge overcome, you evolve stronger and wiser. You have also learnt to adapt and that is the cue. The species that adapts is the species that survives, said Darwin, as I paraphrase him. Family life has no ripples or piranha biting at its underbelly. Children bring joy and your world is cosy unless you decide to upset it; who knows? Ganesha watches.

9 June: Full Moon in Sagittarius

There is a lot of movement now in every sense of the word. There could also be an earnest quest to seek your soul. 'Sometimes the most enlightened thing to do is fight back,' says Danielle LaPorte, the life coach. If the chips have been down lately, you disown loss of any kind and resolve to get back lost ground. On the plus side, love and creativity walk arm in arm with you. There are inflated expectations and excessive idealism as you live in the fantasies of an unreal world. If there are indulgences and escapist tendencies they could get the better of you. Once again, astrology only impels and never compels and I am not God. You may take the family on a holiday to escape the bludgeoning heat of the subcontinent. There could also be solo travel or a slice of adventure sport. The possibilities are enormous. Take your pick. Ganesha journeys with you.

17 June: Last Quarter in Pisces

Last year this time could have been a trying period. Thankfully, nothing lasts forever. Saturn could have pushed you to the wall, depending, of course, on your personal chart.

But this time you are in a pleasant state. You get away from the hurly burly of life and amuse yourself with idle chatter, hanging out with friends at cafes and art galleries or even by simply taking off by yourself in the woods. You slow down. You sidestep the rat race and look to rejuvenate yourself. You are in experimental mode and try out new cuisines, new lifestyles, maybe even indulge in a sartorial makeover. You are probably impressed by Michelle Obama's lines, 'I see myself shift from weight-bearing stuff to things like yoga that will keep me flexible.' Yes, you could reach out to yoga and meditation too. Ganesha watches.

24 June: New Moon in Cancer

The new moon is in Cancer and there could be unrest at home. Petty issues can blow up. You could also be acting irrationally and refusing to see the other's point of view. You could be as stubborn as the Great Wall of China and, frankly, there are no kudos for that. It is vital to disengage and retreat sometimes like the great generals in battle. You could take a cue from Rene Descartes, the philosopher and mathematician, who said, 'Whenever anyone has offended me, I try to raise my soul so high that the offense cannot reach it.' You look at gurus and god-men, at tantra, mantra and yantra, at every mode of deliverance. You look for answers and, luckily, you get them. These are a part of the vicissitudes of life and we all are subject to it. No one escapes the intricate carvings on the mosaic of life. Ganesha holds your hand and that is a great consolation.

1 July: First Quarter in Libra

'You cannot find peace by avoiding life,' said Virginia Woolf. You look to escape from challenges for a while but it may not be a good idea. It is also against your grain to run and hide. If you have been unethical in your dealings it may be best to come clean and ask for amnesty. I am old fashioned and believe that honesty is the best policy. It pays in the long run. There are dharma and karma and the boomerang effect; it all returns in the end with interest. There are many loose ends on the work front that call out to you. Domestic life also has its urgent demands. You may mean well but there are enemies in the undergrowth who want to claw at your underbelly. Watch out. Keep away from altercations and court battles and all will be well. Ganesha will ensure that.

9 July: Full Moon in Capricorn

You are moving ahead with grit and determination. The full moon is in Capricorn and ambition goads you on. There are big plans on the anvil and you catch the sweet fragrance of money and power. It is a great bait and you go for the jugular. The swell of money in the bank has a sweet effervescence. However much I try, I cannot deny its importance; it would be hypocritical. You should watch for booby traps and ensure that you don't overextend yourself. The pace is frenetic. This is a propitious period and, if you use your free will well, miracles can happen. Family life chugs along like a goods train leaving the yard. In other words, there is nothing to brag about. Children do well at interviews and examinations, and your world purrs with contentment on a full belly and many dreams for the future. Ganesha is happy.

16 July: Last Quarter in Aries

You continue on the upward trajectory. The going isn't tough but you have got going. You send the right messages to the universe and it responds appropriately. There are new job openings and new rewards. Freelancers stretch their earnings through new blue chip accounts. 'When you live your life with an appreciation of coincidences and their meaning, you connect with the underlying field of infinite possibilities. This is when the magic begins. This is Synchro Destiny,' says Deepak Chopra. You are right on cue. There are love and longing and you have to make tough choices. Either way, you ascend the peaks of success. Ganesha is impressed.

23 July: New Moon in Leo

The new moon is in Leo and you continue with the powerful energies of the previous week. Often, one week can coalesce into another and sometimes this can happen for weeks on end. This is a significant phase and there is more work expansion. You not only conjure up grand visions but also act on them. There are myriad energies at play including gigantic ego and passion drives. Hold your horses and let the moment pass lest it trap you into behaviour patterns that you may regret later. Quite naturally, along with expansion come expenses. But you are well equipped to handle it all. There are snafus and snares like weeds in the Garden of Eden. Ganesha takes you across the swamp.

30 July: First Quarter in Scorpio

The moon is in your sign and you could be playing a maudlin tune. Matters at the home front may reach the crossroads. It could be lack of harmony or illness. Either way, you are hard-pressed. You could also be indulgent and escapist and wander down memory lane without a lantern, picking up potholes and debris long consigned to the mists of time.

Remember to let the past remain where it should. Scorpios can often be their own enemies and shoot themselves in the foot for no apparent reason. You could also be a hypochondriac and get on everyone's nerves, including the doctor's, leading to an inflated bill! I am being facetious now but a laugh or two will not hurt. This is an interesting period by all accounts. Ganesha watches.

7 August: Full Moon in Aquarius

The full moon is in Aquarius and your mind is everywhere. You are networking with all and sundry and also showcasing your offbeat and rebellious side, much to the chagrin of friends and loved ones who cannot fathom you. 'There is nothing more important to true growth than realizing that you are not the voice of the mind; you are the one who hears it,' said Michael A. Singer. You take time off and help out with the less fortunate. You are also at your creative best and conjure up masterpieces at the drop of a hat. In love you are an enigma. Your shadow side and underbelly superimpose themselves on all aspects of your life. Ganesha smiles. He knows.

15 August: Last Quarter in Taurus

You are back to solid ground. 'Grow or die. It's simple,' says Danielle LaPorte, the life coach. Yes, there are no two ways about it. It is swim or sink. You rather swim. You want to be a winner. Even a nanosecond loss in the Olympic Games, and one settles for silver. You will have none of that. You roll up your sleeves, grease your elbows and get down to the shop floor for hard, uncompromising work. You burn the midnight oil and leave the opposition behind by a distance. There are money and honey, rewards and awards, accolades and applause. This is a productive and growth-oriented period. Ganesha is happy for you. At home too there is a new buzz as you wear a plumage that wins brownie points from all quarters. Way to go!

21 August: New Moon in Leo

The new moon is in Leo and you are powering away. You are able to get a handle on your passions and ego drives and are amiable and joyous. You are agreeable, sociable and friendly. This helps on the work and personal fronts. People like you. 'Of all the things you wear, your expression is the most important,' said Janet Lane, not without reason. This is also a period of reconciliation and consolidation. You overreach on several fronts but it works; that's what matters in the end. Love comes calling. Use your free will to steer it the way you want to. Whoever listens to advice anyway? Ganesha agrees.

29 August: First Quarter in Sagittarius

'You cannot swim for new horizons until you have courage to lose sight of the shore,' said William Faulkner. There is international travel. You could also turn over a new leaf and leave the old you behind. There is sartorial change, along with a complete metamorphosis of the soul. You are a new being; the caterpillar has become a butterfly. You are on the lookout for a guru and spending time on pilgrimages and ashrams. You may join a religious sect or take vows to spread the word of God in the interpretation and form that you believe in. It is fine as long as you do not become fanatical about it. You may even renounce the material world. There are many possibilities. Ganesha holds your hand.

6 September: Full Moon in Pisces

The full moon is in Pisces, the year is slowly coming to an end and soon the winter chill will envelop you like a warm blanket. I am taking liberties here but I love the nuances of the English language. Your creative energies, quite like mine, are sparked and you manufacture masterpieces with the speed of a Xerox machine. You astound your peer group and, of course, the competitors and the naysayers are left standing and spellbound. You also find the time to serenade your love in the most poetic fashion. Success is yours. You take the road less travelled like a military strategist and come up with unique results. It all works in your favour in the end. 'Do you not know yet? It is your light that lights the world,' said Rumi. Yes, it is your light that shines like a beacon now. Your emotions and sensitivities are aroused and you are dripping with compassion and empathy for the less privileged. You look to ending inequity. Good luck, says Ganesha.

13 September: Last Quarter in Gemini

'There are more tears shed over answered prayers than over unanswered ones,' said Saint Teresa of Avila. Your mind is in a whirl. It is moving faster than all the pinwheels put together on the beach. You look for 'me' time to settle down. You want to relook plans for the future lest the monkey mind carry you away on wings of poesy. There are indulgences and escapist trends but there is also free will that can rein them in. That depends on you. Remember that astrology never compels; these are general indicators as I do not have your personal chart. But, as you know well by now, I am bang on most of the time. Singles play the field and those in committed relationships are tempted to stray as they exaggerate the cracks in their harmony. All this is part and parcel of life and no one escapes it. This too shall pass. Ganesha holds your hand.

20 September: New Moon in Virgo

The new moon is in Virgo and sanity and stability return to your life. You get down to the hard grind of making a living. It is never easy. You adopt the old-fashioned, conservative approach of hard work to liberate you from the shackles of inflation and consumerism. Eckhart Tolle said, 'The present moment holds the key to liberation. But you cannot find the present moment as long as you are your mind.' You have shackled the mind; that is the only way. One method is to plunge into work and you do just that. Hard work never killed anybody and you reap the rewards. Most of the day and night is spent at the office and so there is very little room for domestic discord. You realize that hard work is like hitting two birds with one stone and resolve to make it a habit. Ganesha smiles. He has a sense of humour.

28 September: First Quarter in Capricorn

The grind continues. You pick up the baton from last week like a relay race. You push on all cylinders, obliterating the opposition like Genghis Khan in a bad mood. 'The reasonable man adapts himself to the world; the unreasonable one persists in trying to adapt the world to himself. Therefore, all progress depends on the unreasonable man,' said George Bernard Shaw. You are filled with zest and josh. There is little time for play. More greenbacks and perks have you hungering for more. You didn't need Madonna to remind you that it is a material world. You can see the comforts money can buy so clearly. There is a family to be taken care of, and expenses are rising. You continue with the hard slog and reap the rewards. Ganesha applauds.

5 October: Full Moon in Aries

As you approach your birth period you are benefited by the beneficial aspects of Jupiter. It remains in your sign from 10 October to 7 November. The full moon is also in Aries and the times are propitious. Jupiter stays in your sign for almost a month. Make the most of it. Go and turn everything into gold. There are pleasant times at home and children bring joy. It is a period of prosperity and bonhomie. Now let me tell you a bit about Jupiter as its influence takes you to greater heights. As the guardian of the abstract mind, Jupiter rules higher learning. It bestows on us a yen for exploring ideas, both intellectually and spiritually. Jupiter also rules long-distance travel. Luck and good fortune are associated with Jupiter. It is a kind and benevolent planet and helps us to grow and flourish. Leisure time is also one of Jupiter's pastimes. Jupiter also presages great wealth, material and otherwise. It takes Jupiter about twelve years to circle the zodiac. It is masculine energy and rules both Sagittarius and Pisces. Jupiter's glyph, or symbol, shows the crescent of receptivity rising above the cross of matter. This symbolizes Jupiter's role of raising our awareness beyond the physical world. Jupiter encourages us to reach, expand and improve. You will do all this and more in this period, assures Ganesha.

12 October: Last Quarter in Cancer

You plunge into new learning. You seek knowledge. Even senior citizens may enrol for classes. You want to know more about less and less. You look at super-specialization. You want to be the master of your trade. Even homemakers may take to distance learning to enhance their knowledge and boast a few extra degrees. I write this on Women's Day and I know that education is the key. Educate the woman and you educate the family. I am all for it. Jupiter allows you to broaden your horizons. Go for it. The good times roll and you also laugh all the way to the bank. I don't have to tell you to be generous and that what goes around comes around. You know it all. It is dharma and karma. Ganesha agrees.

19 October: New Moon in Libra

When it rains, it pours. Doesn't matter who said it, and I am not talking of the Mumbai monsoon. I am talking about your specific chart. Mercury is in Scorpio from 17 October to 5 November. Messages and trips are the special characteristics of Mercury. Mercury, the mighty, all-powerful planet is in your sign now. It favours travels, meetings, conferences, interviews, trips, more brainpower, contacts, communication, correspondence and contracts. Mercury has a special connection with the circuits of the brain. Chess, crossword and other such games belong to Mercury. Also, short-distance runners and spin bowlers are controlled by Mercury. Mercury, in short, is the ambassador and salesman of the zodiac. Mercury is the symbol of news, views, messages, interviews, contacts, communications, travel and transport. Mercury gives an impetus to all of the above in the sun sign where it is located. This is also your birth period, and the energies are multiplied. Scorpios are indomitable. Most of our beauty queens and several industry stalwarts are Scorpios. They are fiercely ambitious, and once they set their sights on something, they do not give up. 'I don't need time. What I need is a deadline,' said Duke Ellington, jazz pianist, composer and conductor. You are at your creative best. You are pushed to the wall by deadlines and conjure up masterpieces thanks to the added pressure. Your plate is full and overflowing with goodies, quite like an unlimited south Indian thali. Money and its various fiscal instruments catch your gaze. Investments, inheritance and windfalls seek you out. You are not complaining or playing hard to get. You just love it all. Even the fragrance of freshly minted currency gives you a high, and with good reason too. Along with all this is also a rise in consciousness and you are grateful to the universe for the largesse. You make wise investments and prepare a nest egg. Ganesha exults.

27 October: First Quarter in Aquarius

'Forgiveness says you are given another chance to make a new beginning,' said Archbishop Desmond Tutu. You are in a great frame of mind. It is all working out for you and you want to forgive all the naysayers who never gave you a chance in the first place. There have been enemies, and those who discouraged you. It riled you no end but you have come out trumps now. You get larger than them and bow to a higher power. This further strengthens your resolve and you are charged and powered to work more. Inevitably, you court success. In my entire life I have never seen hard work backfire. I have been writing books for years now. The success I wear so eloquently and unabashedly is all thanks to good old hard work. Go for it, I say; create your destiny. Take the tide at the flood. You are on a bull run and you obliterate all opposition and make mincemeat of roadblocks with the frenzy of a butcher in the crowded bylanes of Hyderabad during festival days. There are money and honey, rewards and awards, applause and accolades. Ganesha is speechless, despite knowing it all.

4 November: Full Moon in Taurus

The year is ending and you are on a high in your birth period. Venus is in Scorpio from 7 to 30 November. The simple rule is that when Venus is in your own sign you will get comforts and luxuries, ornaments and money. This is an important phase. As often discussed, Venus is the planet for love, romance, sex, beauty and good life. This is the planet of attraction, love, wealth, knowledge and prosperity. The compatibility of partners and the type of life the individual will lead are also judged from the placement of Venus in the horoscope. As a planet, Venus is considered to be beneficial, feminine and gentle. Venus symbolizes the force of attraction in the universe. In human beings, this attractive force manifests as love and beauty. When Venus is well placed in the chart, there are love, art, beauty and all the goodies of life that make life worth living. Venus rules Libra and Taurus, though its role in every sign is important. Like other planets, it also has its transits. In Libra, Venus is aesthetic and cultured. In Taurus, it is more earthy, materialistic and sensual. Venus rules the venous system, kidneys, urinary tract, throat, larynx, and is responsible for good looks. In short, Venus, in Western astrology, stands for comforts, arts, wealth, relationships, sex, decorations, luxuries and wealth. You have all the comforts of life. The full moon is in Taurus and you live the life of luxury. There are purchases and international travel. Love looms large and you succumb. You may take the object of your desire to the altar; it is serious business now. There could be fun times and festivities, even an addition to the family. Life is dancing with you as an equal partner. Ganesha is impressed.

10 November: Last Quarter in Leo

You are powering away like the new monorail. The good times continue. Expenses mount but you have the money and it doesn't pinch. Despite the comforts you continue with the hard work. You know that it is all thanks to unstinted efforts that you have arrived where you have and there is no letting up. Success breeds success. You have been fashioned well by life to realize that even one slip can demolish a lifetime's achievement. You have taken aeons to climb the mountain and one trip on a loose foothold, like snakes and ladders, and you are back at rock bottom. You take calculated risks. You live large, but a nest egg has been prepared. It is written in the *Dhammapada*, 'A ship which is not well prepared, in the ocean, goes to destruction together with its goods and merchants.' This is your moment in the sun and you are living it up. But it is a wise head that watches every step; one eye is also on the wallet. Ganesha smiles.

18 November: New Moon in Scorpio

The new moon is in your sign and you are on a bull run. Of course, there are domestic concerns to attend to. There could be illness in the family, and children will have issues that need to be sorted out, especially if they are teenagers; you don't want them eloping with unsavoury characters or taking to banned substances. 'If you wish to make an apple pie truly from scratch, first you must invent the universe,' said Carl Sagan, astronomer and writer. In many ways, you are back to square one. You have to care for the simple things of life before they blow up in your face. There are also emotional moments as your sensitivities are aroused. There could be indulgences and escapist tendencies as you wander aimlessly down memory lane picking meaningless debris. Nothing serious, but there is no need to be waylaid from your path. Scorpios can also press the self-destruct button easily. Ganesha cautions you against that.

26 November: First Quarter in Pisces

You are at your creative best. This is a great time for writers and painters. They strike pay dirt. There is inspiration and perspiration and the masterpieces you conjure up showcase genius. You are filled with self-belief, and that is the key. Ramakrishna Paramahamsa said, 'He who has faith has everything, and he who lacks faith lacks everything. It is the faith in the name of the Lord that works wonders, faith is life and doubt is death.' Self-belief and a healthy self-image push you to opening new vistas. You network furiously and are busy with cultural gatherings. There are money and honey, accolades and applause. You are the toast of your peer group. You may win international recognition. Love follows you like an obedient puppy. Way to go, says Ganesha.

3 December: Full Moon in Gemini

The full moon is in Gemini and you are all over the place. You meet with different kinds of people and give your life an offbeat edge. There is new learning. You may meet with someone from an entirely different culture who gives your life an added spin. It may be someone of the same gender and there need not be sexual connotations in the association. This person may influence you like a guru. You are the wiser and enriched by it. The creative juices continue to flow as you network your skills to legions of fans. Ganesha is happy for you. Family life chugs along like an anaconda on a full belly.

10 December: Last Quarter in Virgo

The last part of the year is taken over by Mars. It is in your sign from 9 December till the end of the year. There is stability and hard work. There will also be some snafus, snares and trapdoors, but it all depends on your personal chart. Astrology never compels. Rein in ego drives and passions and count to ten and take deep breaths before you respond or retaliate and all will be well. Discretion is always the better part of valour. Avoid altercations at all costs; you certainly don't need the cops hovering around you. Ambition is fine. But eschew avarice. Mars is like the volcano of vitality inside you and influences endurance, persistence and discipline. Mars was named for the Roman god of war, and is also known as 'the bright and burning one'. Red is the colour of Mars and stimulates the dynamic, potent and fertile drives that power our lives. Mars rules physical energy and action and governs energy, strength, courage, life force and expansion. Well-placed Mars endows powerful energy and an indomitable will to succeed. Mars propels us like an ignited rocket. It is an important energy since it determines how we pursue what we want to achieve in life. In short, Mars represents energy, force, violence, aggression, sports, combat, wars, battles, accidents, operations. Ganesha watches.

18 December: New Moon in Sagittarius

You are on speed. You are moving ahead, fast and furious. You may take the family out on an international holiday or even go solo, traversing exotic trails. There is a lot of movement now in every sense of the word. The world is smaller and you want to smell and taste all that is on offer. You want to smell the coffee in every land. 'When the mind is controlled, all sorrows cease,' said Sai Baba. Your mind is still expressing itself flamboyantly but it is well directed. The monkey on a stick has got a new lease on life. You have purpose and a sense of direction. You take risks but that is a part of the territory you are in now. There are fun times. You live and love large. In a week, the year will end and you are not going to rein in a galloping horse now. You tell yourself that you live just once and life affords no dress rehearsals. You do not want regrets. You go for it and leave the rest to Ganesha.

26 December: First Quarter in Aries

As the year ends you are fired up by the moon in Aries. There are expenses, but they always accompany expansion. You move into fifth gear and set your heart on charting a new course for 2018. You hit the new year with the velocity of gale-force wind. You are like a hurricane that obliterates everything in its path. You have the ambition of Alexander, the ruthlessness of Genghis Khan and the calmness, wisdom and breadth of vision of the Buddha. Your world is brimming with excitement. There are family gatherings and festivities. There could be an addition to the family. There are weddings and anniversaries. 'The entire cosmos is bound by time. It is permeated by time. It is a product of time and is destroyed by time. Time is one of the forms of God,' said Sai Baba. You have no quarrel with that as you use your time well. Time and tide caress you gently. Ganesha holds your hand.

SAGITTARIUS

23 November–22 December

Ganesha's Master Key: Fearless and frank

Sagittarian British prime minister Winston Churchill played a very major part in helping the Allies win the World War II. According to him, opportunity and positive attitude led to success and victory. A fine example to all Sagittarians.

The important traits are: Overly idealistic; Unrealistically carefree; Blunt and sarcastic; Flippant, having a 'know-it-all' attitude; Forcing one's beliefs on others; Adventurous, epicurean; Making jokes at the expense of others; Self-righteous, excessively casual; Expounding wisdom without love; Neglectful of important details; Aspiring to a more spiritual understanding of earth life; Seeking various experiences for a better understanding of truth; Expanding one's vistas to become more open-minded; Becoming one-pointed in the search for higher understanding; Becoming more open-minded; Becoming internationally conscious; Aspiring to new heights of growth and expansion; Cultivating the higher mind; Depending on wisdom through spiritual experiences; Becoming more deeply aware of the sorrows on the earth and the reasons for it; Having an optimistic attitude and living it; Being aware of the practical details which make up the larger picture; Inspiring hope, faith and courage in others; Being the torch which helps enlighten the understanding of others; Practising one's spiritual philosophies on a daily basis; Counselling others with humility and love wisdom; Sharing one's philosophies in a loving, open-minded way with those who are receptive to them; Perceiving the limited nature of the human understanding of truth; Being in tune with spiritual guidance when counselling and teaching; Consoling others who are in pain and sorrow; Helping to encourage optimism among humanity; Helping to spiritualize the mind of humanity; Perceiving life from a world perspective.

Your Beauty-scope: Strange as it may sound, it might be irksome for you to be a prim and proper miss/madam. You were never meant to be one. Wear sporty or at least colourful clothes. Movements are forceful, and I see no need to play them down. The hips are truly wide and here exercise and diet should help a bit. The head is well-shaped, the eyes merry and twinkling and out for a bit of fun. You ought to attract people by your mischievous ways. Mod jewellery is ideal for you. Also large prints. Chunky ornaments also go beautifully. Remember that.

CENTRAL IDEA

Bombastic, Blunt, Adventurous, Wise, Confident

Yes, you will be the right person in the right place, at the right time! You can expect the goodies of life. Thanks to

Jupiter in your eleventh angle, the beauty is Jupiter is your main or chief planet.

You will be full of enthusiasm, zeal, confidence, there will be a fresh new approach to life, to your activities, to your goals. Ganesha has a lot of goodies in store for you as gifts. Some of these will be: passion, romance, rendezvous, the birth of a child, even a secret affair, that's the way it goes; hectic socialization, interactions, good collaborations and contacts; tremendous opportunities for gain and making serious or at least very good money; luck in games of chance and enterprise.

My father always says life is not perfect. Even the greatest men and women are tested and forged in the fire of life. By Western astrology, Saturn will be in your sign till 21 December 2017. Saturn teaches you duty, responsibilities and, often, but not always, gives an added burden in terms of health, wealth and happiness. But this year Saturn will be in a fine relationship with Jupiter. Jupiter is your master planet. Jupiter means all-round prosperity, as we say in our Indian English. Therefore, your troubles and difficulties and delays will be much less. My father always tells me that in the long run Saturn makes you stronger and better. The simple reason is that Saturn represents both karma and dharma.

Mercury, planet of journeys and communication, represents marriage, unions, ties, trips, work, prestige, honours and riches for you very specially. Therefore, for you, Mercury becomes extra important. Jupiter, your main planet, is most important. After Jupiter Mercury becomes the most important planet for you. Mercury will be in your sign from 6 November this year to 10 January 2018. Mercury will also be acting in your favour from 14 to 31 March, 21 April to 15 May, 7 to 20 June, 6 to 25 July and certainly from 30 September to 16 October.

For you very specially, Mars stands for romance, hobbies, children, entertainment, creativity and foreign affairs as well as hospitals and social welfare centres. Mars helps you from 28 January to 9 March, 20 July to 4 September, and 23 October to 8 December. A change of house or office is possible. So also renovation and decoration.

For you Sagittarians, Venus boosts your perks, promotion, service, socializing, entertainment, friendships and wish-fulfilment. Venus acts as your great friend from 1 to 24 December, 14 October to 6 November, 4 February to 2 April and possibly 25 December 2017 to 10 February 2018. You will be loved as well as respected. What more can you want?

MONTHLY ROUND-UP

January: Finances, family ties, adornment, home, buying/selling, vehicles. **February:** Contacts, communication, contracts, crash courses, mental brilliance, new projects, courage and determination. **March:** Home, family, treasure, parents and in-laws, work prospects even for the retired, paradoxically, elderly persons will retire shortly. **April:** Journeys, ceremonies, publicity, children, hobbies creativity, therefore a lively and lucky month. **May:** Jobs, pets, projects, subordinates, health needs care. **June:** Love/hate, partnerships/separations, but all told you do gain and look forward to the future with great confidence, you deserve it. **July:** Legacy, finances, passion but low vitality. **August:** Distant places, research, parents and in-laws, education, children, good fortune through meeting the right people. **September:** Position, prestige, power, parents, home and property, rites and rituals for the living and the dead. **October:** Friendship, socializing, gains and glamour, realization of aspirations. **November:** Travel, restlessness despite good fortune, expenses and health need care. **December:** Good going in terms of health, wealth and happiness; and you should thank Ganesha for it.

Money: Sagittarians are usually lucky in property matters. I am saying usually because my experience is limited. This year January and February, June and August and October could bring you into money. March, September and October will be important for home, house, shop, office, land, farming and so on. Please note that this is only a general forecast. I am not God.

Happiness Quota: I give you 84.5 per cent.

MONTH BY MONTH

January: This is a wonderful start to the year. You are in full throttle. Nothing fazes you, and you go about the business of living, charged and ready for action. Love also smiles at you. Mid-month sees you busy with domestic issues. The health of a parent could be a cause of concern. Children may not see eye to eye. There are many expenses. This can also be an explosive phase, so keep your emotions in check. As the month ends, there is new intensity in all your dealings. Your relationships are charged. Your philanthropic zeal is also strengthened.

February: You are filled with firmness, stability, determination and drive. You roll up your sleeves and get down to the hard slog. You are ambitious and want big things to happen. You are willing to spend for quality. You take risks. Mid-month sees you blazing away. There could be international travel and a reaching out to new experiences. Your life is rich with anecdotes. As the month ends, there is calmness. If you have been suffering from an illness there is remission and if you have just had surgery or a medical procedure you recover well. You are also goaded by powerful intuition and insights. There are creative outbursts and strokes of genius.

March: There is a range of emotions. You are filled with love and longing and yet at the same time you want to be free of all earthly attachment. This is an unusual period as you plumb new furrows and merge with new learning. Mid-month sees you return to terra firma. There is balance in your life. You get down to sorting out your fiscal affairs and plan business expansion. As the month ends, you move ahead, fast and furious. You have direction and determination and are capable of extreme hard work. You sight money and honey.

April: You reach for the stars. There is no limit to your ambitions. Ego drives and passions are exaggerated. You live in awareness and mindfulness and make miracles happen. You are the new genius on the block. Mid-month sees several domestic concerns grab you by the collar. Elders at home may need medical attention. As the month ends, many choices stare at you. Love also sneaks into your life when you least expect it. You make plans for the future and create organizational systems. You lead from the front. This is a propitious phase.

May: You are propelled by energy. You move mountains. There are expenses coupled with expansion, and love that singes your soul. There are ego drives which get the better of you. Mid-month sees new intensity in all your dealings. You are ideating in top gear. You think large, and execute even larger. As the month ends, your mind is on tenterhooks.

There are indulgences and escapist tendencies. You use every marvel of technology to get your point across. There are travel, new horizons, love and longing.

June: You focus on work and fiscal affairs. The home fires need to burn and there are many domestic demands. Mid-month sees a bountiful phase. There are also spiritual pursuits, pilgrimages and new learning. As the month ends, your latent sensitivities are sparked. You are in the throes of creativity. This is a great time for writers and photographers. You are high on life.

July: This is a period packed with several possibilities. Your plate is overflowing with domestic and work pressures. Your heartstrings are also pulled in several directions. There is direction and ambition. You work hard and impress peers, subordinates and employers. You are also suitably rewarded. Mid-month sees stable family life. Make the most of this bull run. As the month ends, there are expenses and travel. The pace is frenetic. You are also wrestling with intricate existential dilemmas.

August: This is a creative phase. Writers and painters strike pay dirt. You also showcase your sensitive side. You may take time off from the pressures of life and indulge in valuable 'me' time. You want to reassess and refocus before you take on the world. Mid-month sees you get down to the business of making a living. There are also domestic demands which take your time. As the month ends, you network with the world and cross borders without a care. There are challenges and you evolve. Love serenades you. Those in realty, the corporate world and big business strike pay dirt. This could be a period of new beginnings.

September: Your sensitivities are aroused. You want to spend time with loved ones and family. You want to be surrounded by beauty. Mid-month is the time for ideating. You move ahead in evolutionary terms. As the month ends, there is a semblance of stability. There will be issues with money and your business dealings are in sharp focus. Fiscal issues dominate your time along with domestic calls.

October: This is a propitious period to forge ahead with your plans and aspirations. You get down to the business of making a living. Mid-month sees your emotions at a peak. This can also be a powerful creative force that throws up masterpieces. As the month ends, inheritances and windfalls make their presence felt. This can also be a great time for writers and artists. You come up with brilliant ideas and execute them with discipline, dedication and determination. This is certainly an interesting period with exciting possibilities.

November: Whatever you embark on leads to success. The employed get perks and promotions, and freelancers bag blue chip accounts. You spread your tentacles far and wide with considerable success and acclaim. The spotlight falls squarely on money and its accumulation. Mid-month sees you live and love large. Lady Luck courts you with all her charm. You have the Midas touch. Accolades and applause, money and honey, follow you like an obedient puppy. As the month ends, you have added intensity and purpose. There is new love and powerful bonding. This is a magical run.

December: In the last month of the year, Venus joins Mercury and large helpings of largesse are bestowed on you. This is a great time for media folk. Writers and playwrights strike pay dirt. There is international travel and new vistas open. Mid-month sees you take time off to recuperate, rejuvenate and catch your breath for future excursions. The year is ending in brilliant fashion. Use your free will well and you will start 2018 on a surer footing. As the month ends, while you continue on the accelerated path of progress, your soul stirs with spiritual calls. There is love, bonding and fun times with family and friends. There are several moments in the sun.

WEEKLY REVIEW (BY PHASES OF THE MOON)

5 January: First Quarter in Aries

I shall start with a quote from Sai Baba which is very profound and is applicable to all of us. He said, 'In money, scholarship, knowledge and intelligence there is no evil. Evil arises only from the activities you carry out using them.' This is a wonderful start to the year. You are in full throttle. Nothing fazes you and you go about the business of living, charged and ready for action. Mercury is in your sign from 6 to 10 January. It comes into your sign again towards the year-end. This is a short stay, but you can optimize it. Well begun is half-done. You are also propelled by the energy of Aries. There are rewards and awards, money and honey. Love also smiles at you. All I can say is – go for it; don't spare the horses and you will be richly rewarded. Messages and trips are the special characteristics of Mercury. It favours travels, meetings, conferences, interviews, trips, more brainpower, contacts, communication, correspondence and contracts. Mercury has a special connection with the circuits of the brain. Chess, crossword and other such games belong to Mercury. Also, short-distance runners and spin bowlers are controlled by Mercury. Mercury, in short, is the ambassador and salesman of the zodiac. Mercury is the symbol of news, views, messages, interviews, contacts, communications, travel and transport. Mercury gives an impetus to all of the above in the sun sign where it is located. Ganesha is happy for you.

12 January: Full Moon in Cancer

'Look as long as you can at the friend you love, no matter whether that friend is moving away from you or coming back towards you,' said Rumi. You are moving ahead but are also busy with domestic issues. The health of a parent could be a cause of concern. Children may not see eye to eye and it will be tough to rein them in. You will have to give a long leash and hold it from a distance. There are many expenses. You have the means but your time is stretched. If you have recovered from an illness, your health too could be delicate. This can also be an explosive phase, so keep your emotions in check. Do not allow your fabled frankness to get the better of you. It is necessary to be diplomatic at times. Love life is also frayed at the edges. Ganesha holds your hand.

19 January: Last Quarter in Scorpio

There is new intensity in all your dealings. Your relationships are charged like reinforced dynamite. I quote Kahlil Gibran from *The Prophet*: 'Your joy is your sorrow unmasked. And the selfsame well from which your laughter rises was oftentimes filled with your tears. And how else can it be? The deeper that sorrow carves into your being, the more joy you can contain.' You may suffer from a persecution complex. You think everyone is out to get you. You look for salvation in gurus and god-men and open every tome on spirituality for answers. There are escapist tendencies and indulgences. You may go on a pilgrimage or join a sect for deliverance. Money slips through your fingers. But Ganesha is not worried. This is a passing phase.

28 January: New Moon in Aquarius

The new moon is in Aquarius and your philanthropic zeal is strengthened. Your offbeat nature is also on show and you unabashedly display your underbelly to all and sundry. Your shadow side wins no admirers but you don't care. You are the elusive centaur. Despite the crocodiles waiting for you in ambush, you are the wildebeest that manages to slip through. You take risks and traverse uncharted territory. In love, you court suitors who share your offbeat ideals. They may just come and go, because such alliances never work in the long run. Ganesha watches. Now let me tell you with whom you share your sun sign. They include Andre Gide, Monica Seles, Britney Spears, Madame Tussauds, Charles de Gaulle, Joseph Stalin, Nostradamus, Woody Allen, Walt Disney, Gianni Versace, Alexander Solzhenitsyn, Kim Basinger and several other celebrities. Let me also add a generalization as I do not have your personal details. Sagittarius is a fire sign and those belonging to it can be tactless, outspoken, frank, quarrelsome, versatile and enthusiastic. They love their space and need freedom, even in friendships and more intimate relationships. Anyone who is associated with Sagittarians knows this to be true!

4 February: First Quarter in Taurus

You enter the second month of the new year with firmness, stability, determination and drive. The moon is in Taurus and you are firmly on land. 'I do not feel obliged to believe that the same God who has endowed us with sense, reason, and intellect has intended us to forgo their use,' said Galileo

Galilei, the great physicist and astronomer. You roll up your sleeves and get down to the hard slog. You are ambitious and want big things to happen. You are willing to spend for quality. You take risks. Love comes calling, family life is stable and children bring joy. It is a happy period with many powerful energies working in your favour. Ganesha smiles.

11 February: Full Moon in Leo

'The enlightened man is the greatest stranger in the world; he does not seem to belong to anybody. No organization confines him; no community, no society, no nation. An awakened person is the master of his own destiny. She/He holds the light of her/his own hard-won truth,' said Osho. The full moon is in Leo and you are blazing away. You are moving very fast. There could be international travel and a reaching out to new experiences as new vistas open in your life. Your life is rich with anecdote and happenings. There could be new paramours and some indiscreet flings in the hay. Your idiosyncrasies are also on full display. It is an eventful period. Ganesha watches.

18 February: Last Quarter in Sagittarius

'The very purpose of life is to seek happiness,' said the Dalai Lama. The moon is in your sign and there is calmness. If you have been suffering from an illness there is remission and if you have just had surgery or a medical procedure you recover well. You are also busy with fiscal instruments and budgets. Money comes in and goes out without ceremony. You play the field and check out muddy waters. You are in an experimental frame of mind and do not think twice about stepping out of line. This is an eventful week. Ganesha holds your hand.

26 February: New Moon in Pisces

Your inner core is charged. Your sensitivities are aroused and you feel stimulated, alive and awake. 'Life finds its purpose and fulfilment in the expansion of happiness,' said Maharishi Mahesh Yogi. You are goaded by powerful intuition and insights. You take to yoga and meditation and join groups for energy healing. If you are already into natural therapies and alternative healing modalities you take it to another level. There are creative outbursts and strokes of genius. New vistas open miraculously. There are new realisations and new dreams that beckon you. Your soul is stirred. Those in stable relationships take ecstasy to ethereal heights. Ganesha watches with interest.

5 March: First Quarter in Gemini

'Love transcends policy and history,' says Danielle LaPorte. Your mind is everywhere. There is no focus. You want to do everything all at once, and that is simply not possible. You are like an elk in the savannah being stalked by a pack of lions. You are frozen; your eyes, ears and nostrils pick up every scent and you don't know which way to run. There is a range of emotions and possibilities playing on you. You are filled with love and longing and yet at the same time you want to be free of all earthly attachment. The contradictions drive you crazy. You want to be consumed in the flames of amour, to blaze like a kebab on a grill, to watch the sunrise entwined in the hormones of your infatuation, and yet you want your freedom. You do not want the accompaniments of love and lust which naturally accrue. Ask me. I haven't lived so many years in vain. Love comes with a lot of baggage. One doesn't come without the other. This is an unusual week as you plumb new furrows and merge with new learning. Ganesha blesses you.

12 March: Full Moon in Virgo

You return to terra firma. There is balance and common sense that takes hold of your life. You want to make up for lost time. If insanity had gripped you earlier, you look back and wonder how and why. I must add here that these are generalizations as I do not have your personal details. Astrology also never compels. These are signposts. Use your free will to advantage. You get down to sorting out your fiscal affairs and plan business expansion. Ganesha helps you along the way.

20 March: Last Quarter in Capricorn

You are moving ahead, fast and furious. You have direction and determination and are capable of extreme hard work. You sight money and honey. That is enough bait. 'You can search throughout the entire universe for someone who is more deserving of your love and affection than you are yourself, and that person is not to be found anywhere. You, yourself, as much as anybody in the entire universe, deserve your love and affection,' said Siddhartha Gautama. You are the centre of your universe. Send the right signals and the universe will affirm them. This is a great time for business tycoons and real estate magnates. The sweet whiff of newly minted currency sends you into raptures. Ganesha always urges you to avoid avarice. I ask you to the stick to the ethical. Pay heed.

28 March: New Moon in Aries

You are powering away like the new air-conditioned coaches on Mumbai's suburban line. You reach for the stars. There is no limit or inhibition to your ambitions. You may also take to activism and let ego drives and passions bleed all over the place like a cheap shirt bought at a roadside bargain. There could be altercations and brushes with the law, but you don't care. 'One who condones evil is just as guilty as the one who perpetrates it,' said Rev. Martin Luther King Jr, the great civil rights leader. Just remember that *now* is the moment that never ends. You live in awareness and mindfulness and make miracles happen. You are the new genius on the block. Of course, astrology never compels but the energies of the period are powerful. Tweak it the way you want to according to your circumstances and station in life. Free will can never be underestimated. Ganesha blesses you.

3 April: First Quarter in Cancer

'Any fool can criticize, condemn, and complain but it takes character and self-control to be understanding and forgiving,' said Dale Carnegie. There are several domestic concerns that grab you by the collar and shake you out of your earlier trajectory. Elders at home may need medical attention and a troublesome teenager may need to be held close with a tight leash. You are pushed to the wall. You want quick answers but your fertile and febrile mind is everywhere, flitting around like a bumblebee, eager to land, but unable to. You court fancies and illusions. There could also be domestic disharmony as you and your partner refuse to see issues with the same eye. There could be separations as emotions are out on display from every chandelier. Dirty linen is laundered publicly. Matters can get messy. Ganesha watches with some concern.

11 April: Full Moon in Libra

'Truth is a pathless land,' said J. Krishnamurti. Sometimes the energies of one week coalesce into another and linger on for weeks on end. There are many factors which influence you, my dear readers. The full moon is in Libra and many choices stare at you like an intersection in a strange locality. You wonder which fork to take. Love also sneaks into your life when you least expect it, like a commando on the assault on a cross-border covert operation. You are ambushed and waylaid. Before you realize it you are in the throes of amour. It takes you by surprise and there is no escaping its tentacles. It has the grip of a fasting crocodile which has finally caught an unsuspecting wildebeest during its annual migratory forays. On the flip side are heavy purchases and a possible business expansion. You are caught in the swamp, in the gnarled vicissitudes of life. You look for truth. Where and what is it? Ganesha knows the answers but he is not letting on.

19 April: Last Quarter in Capricorn

You are somewhat steadied now. You once again succumb to the charms of greenbacks. Nothing has a greater allure. You decide to roll up your sleeves and step on the gas. You make plans for the future and create organizational systems. You lead from the front and shake up the office hierarchy, rewarding those who are on the ball and ejecting deadwood without remorse. You want success at all costs. Money has been taken from the bank to fund your expansion plans and you will not settle for any blot on the balance sheet. You run a comb through every plan, rope in the experts and cover all grey areas. You are meticulous and disciplined. Like a roving hawk you notice even the tiniest disarray in the brush. If you use the energy well, success is yours. If there is love, it plays second fiddle to the call of work. Ganesha smiles.

26 April: New Moon in Taurus

'The best way to pay for a lovely moment is to enjoy it,' said Richard Bach. The new moon is in Taurus and along with work expansion are fun times galore. This is a propitious phase and you could use it to advantage. There are birthdays and anniversaries, additions to the family and meetings with friends and loved ones. You are expansive, exuberant, excited and enthusiastic about life. There are alumni meetings, and you revive the old school tie. You may take to new courses and classes and plough new paths. There is growth on all fronts. You are like Chris Gayle on a good day; you simply blow the opposition to smithereens. Ganesha is thrilled.

3 May: First Quarter in Leo

'Beware lest you lose the substance by grasping at the shadow,' said Aesop. I love this quote. It is so profound and packed with meaning. I make it a point to garnish my predictions with quotes to benefit you, my dear readers. I want to share my knowledge of English with you. I admit, we are both enriched by this sharing. You are propelled by energy in this phase. You move mountains. You are the great lion in the Serengeti National Park. No one can match you. Your will superimposes itself on everything the eye can see. There are expenses coupled with expansion, and love that singes your soul from the inside. You survive it all handsomely. There are ego drives which get the better of you and you are spoiling for a fight. Ganesha holds your hand and wrests you away from the battlefield. There are money and honey, rewards and awards, applause and accolades.

There is upward mobility. Use the energies with maturity and all will be well.

10 May: Full Moon in Scorpio

Leo Tolstoy, the well-known novelist and philosopher, said, 'Truth, like gold, is to be obtained not by its growth, but by washing away from it all that is not gold.' The full moon is in Scorpio and there is new intensity in all your dealings. Even if you walk down memory lane there is a new swagger to your melancholia. You are ideating in sixth gear and also optimizing your plans. You think large, and execute even larger. New vistas open and droplets of new knowledge fall on to your brow. There are challenges, but you rise to meet them. The tough get going when the going gets tough. Yes, for sure. Ganesha applauds. Love peeks in through the curtains. It all depends on how distracted you want to be.

19 May: Last Quarter in Aquarius

Carl Jung, the great psychoanalyst said, 'The world today hangs by a thin thread, and the thread is the psyche of man.' Your mind is on tenterhooks. You are here, there and everywhere, adorning the monkey mind with new ornamentation. Of course, it gets the better of you and you are compelled to do its bidding. You may spend time with offbeat people who catch your fancy. They are not the types you would normally meet socially. But you want to experiment. There are indulgences and escapist tendencies galore. Your underbelly is fully exposed, but you don't care. You believe that if the world sees it, it is their problem and not yours. You also offer to host mismatched and inappropriate relationships. It will do you no good, but that is the mood you are in. Ganesha watches.

25 May: New Moon in Gemini

The new moon is in Gemini and you are interacting with all and sundry. You use every marvel of technology to get your point across. There is travel, and new horizons catch your fancy. There are love and longing, lust and deep bonding. This is not the time for hard, sustained work. Your mind and instincts are on holiday. You will come back refreshed and rejuvenated and ready to fight another day. Until then, it is playtime. Ganesha blesses you.

1 June: First Quarter in Virgo

There is more stability now. You are back in balance and on terra firma. You decide to focus on work and fiscal affairs. The home fires need to burn and you certainly do not want the home to burn. There are many domestic demands which include the health of parents and children's studies. You may be moving too, and with it are instability and upheaval. It could be a posting or even emigration. Einstein said, 'Life is like riding a bicycle. To keep your balance you must keep moving.' Well, you are certainly keeping your balance, despite it all. All movement is good. It removes the deadwood. Eventually, you grow and evolve. Ganesha wishes you well.

9 June: Full Moon in Sagittarius

The full moon is in your sign and this can be a very beautiful and bountiful phase. There are also spiritual pursuits and you could go looking for a guru or delve deep into tantra, mantra and yantra. There are pilgrimages and new learning. You evolve into a better human being. I will now quote an appropriate line from a Buddhist hymn: 'Let me a pure white lotus be, unfolding in Samsara's stream.' In this phase this seems to be your quest. You get the right fellowship from kindred souls. A person from another culture impacts you in a profound way. He or she may not come in the garb of a guru but the association will take you to new realms of realization. You ascend the ladder of evolution. Way to go, says Ganesha. I am also thrilled for you.

17 June: Last Quarter in Pisces

The moon is in Pisces and your latent sensitivities are sparked. You are in the throes of rich creativity. This is a great time for writers and photographers. Media folk mint the moment. You win peer group applause and also make good money. Osho said, 'When your creativity comes to a climax, when your whole life becomes creative, you live in God … Love what you do. Be meditative while you are doing it – whatsoever it is!' Yes, that is the key to success. You do just that and genius garlands you. Love also leaves its calling card repeatedly. You are tempted. Use your free will well. There are many possibilities that swing the pendulum either way. This is an interesting period. Ganesha loves times like these that are pregnant with choices. There are get-togethers, picnics, outings and indulgences replete with happy family times.

24 June: New Moon in Cancer

The new moon is in Cancer and there could be a continuation from the previous week. Sometimes the energies of one week slip into another and this can happen for weeks on end. There are many factors which influence the situation, and astrology never compels. You are on a creative high and strike pay dirt. Even those who do not indulge in any creative activity for a livelihood bring newness and a fresh look at life into their everyday dealings. Rollo May, a mid-twentieth century psychologist who wrote *The Courage to Create*, said about creativity: 'The experience is one of heightened consciousness: ecstasy.' You live in several moments of heightened consciousness strung together in a heady garland. The feeling is mind-blowing, akin to being on speed or recreational mood-enhancing substances. But you are high on life, and Ganesha knows that it is the best way to be. I am envious!

1 July: First Quarter in Libra

Several parts of the subcontinent are steaming. You can fry an egg in the shade. The moon is in Libra and this can be a very interesting period, packed with several possibilities. Your plate is overflowing with domestic and work pressures. There are medical emergencies, calls from children and the spouse, business expansion and your own personal emotional and physical needs. There is no dearth of solutions; in fact, there are several. The problem is which solution to identify with. 'Truth resides in every human heart, and one has to search for it there, and to be guided by truth as one sees it. But no one has a right to coerce others to act according to his own view of truth,' said Mohandas Gandhi. I agree, and so does Ganesha, that truth prevails finally and it should not be compromised. You are also in the thick of multiple affairs of the heart. Your heartstrings are pulled in several different directions. Life is a maze of conflicting emotions right now. This too shall pass, but until then you tear at your hair.

9 July: Full Moon in Capricorn

The full moon is in Capricorn and there is direction and ambition that goads you on. You work hard and impress peers, subordinates and employers. Of course, you are suitably rewarded. Family life too is stable and that is a relief. Singles get away from the party circuit and adopt the straight and narrow work ethic. Michael Jordan, the great basketball player, always said that he was only as good as his last game and his best would be the next game! You agree with that work ethic and steamroll the opposition into submission like Khali, the great WWF (World Wrestling Federation) wrestler. You touch new frontiers of excellence and aspiration. This is an upward curve. You are on a bull run. Well done. Ganesha wishes you well.

16 July: Last Quarter in Aries

The going is good. The bull run continues. There are expenses and travel but it is not a waste. Your heart sings new tunes of love and serenades all comers without quarrel. You are testing the field. New vistas open and you emerge wiser and stronger. Life is more than mere astrology. I am your favourite astrologer and have been casting charts for many years, yet I am humble enough to admit that it is a combination of factors that impacts one's life. Circumstances change and there is free will. Luck is also an 'X' factor. You attract it or it attracts you; it goes either way without logic or rationale. That is the magic of life; the unpredictability that we are faced with every moment of our lives. Ganesha watches as you go about the business of living.

23 July: New Moon in Leo

'What if the things you are resisting are the very things to your homecoming.' This is a quote from the *Way of Mastery* which is as profound as it is relevant to your situation now. The new moon is in Leo and you are charged like a new cycle dynamo in the Indian heartland. Love torches you. Work pressures pile up. You are filled with passion and ego drives. Use them well. The energies are propitious. The pace is frenetic. You are first off the block like Usain Bolt. Success garlands you. Need I say more? But, along with it all, are many questions that still torment the inner recesses of your soul. Outwardly, you are propelling ahead, fast and furious. But deep within you are wrestling with intricate existential dilemmas. There are indulgences and escapist fantasies that grip you tight like a new, chafing dog collar. There is an array of possibilities. Ganesha knows that.

30 July: First Quarter in Scorpio

You are moving ahead with intensity. The purpose and direction may be divided because there is a lot on your mind, and focus may be hard to come by. You also look for a complete overhaul of your personality, from sartorial change to a change in behaviour and everyday habits. There is a search for guru and a study of yantra, tantra and mantra. Health may go through tricky times. Your communication strategies may also falter with your insistence on your way or the highway. Your rigidity, stubbornness and outspokenness dither others. You think they are at fault but this is a good time for some deep and honest soul searching. If you are patient and willing to listen, the answers will show up. Ganesha watches.

7 August: Full Moon in Aquarius

The Buddha said: 'Through zeal, knowledge is gotten, through lack of zeal, knowledge is lost; let a man who knows the double path of gain and loss thus place himself that knowledge may grow.' The full moon is in Aquarius and you are filled with zany ideas. This can be a powerful creative phase. Writers and painters strike pay dirt. You also showcase your sensitive side and spend time with the less privileged. Interestingly, you also spend time in pampering yourself. Women visit beauty parlours and gyms as though they are going out of fashion, and men do their thing. You want to look and feel good inside and out. You may take time off from the pressures of life and indulge in valuable 'me' time. You want to reassess and refocus before you take on the world. Ganesha blesses you.

15 August: Last Quarter in Taurus

You are on stable ground. Terra firma calls, along with the lure of big money. You may not be particularly inclined to hoard currency but the benefits of a rich bank balance do not escape you. There is hard work as you roll up your sleeves and get down to the business of making a living. There are domestic demands which include a parent's illness or even comforting a delinquent or challenged child or sibling. You are pushed to the wall and have to gather all your resources to meet the challenges head on. Ganesha helps you along the way and that is a huge relief.

21 August: New Moon in Leo

The new moon is in Leo and this could well be travel time. You explore new frontiers in time and space. 'Once a friend, always a friend. Why should borders stop that?' said Erin Hunter. This is an era of refugees and terrorism. But it doesn't deter you. You network with the world and cross borders without a care. There are challenges and you evolve. Love serenades you and you take your pick. On the flip side, those in realty, the corporate world and big business strike pay dirt. There are big deals staring you in the face and you do not wince. You are like Sachin facing Shoaib's bouncer in the World Cup and dispatching the ball over the ropes with ease. Ganesha is thrilled.

29 August: First Quarter in Sagittarius

'Understand the present moment and you have understood the whole phenomenon of eternity,' said Osho. The moon is in your sign and this is a profound period. You go deep within the torched recesses of your soul and plumb new heights of self-realization. You take to new learning and are the wiser for it. This could be a period of new beginnings. There is international travel, even immigration, for those so inclined. Children leave home or, possibly, the prodigal returns to the hearth. There are births, deaths, anniversaries, marriages and divorces. It is all happening. Life is calling you to the dance. Go for it, says Ganesha. You don't need prodding.

6 September: Full Moon in Pisces

'Love and sacrifice are the two greatest qualities in life,' said Sai Baba. The full moon is in Pisces and your sensitivities are aroused. You want to spend time with loved ones and family. You want to be surrounded by beauty. If you are moving home, there are butterflies in your stomach. All movement is evolution, but along with it is anxiety. You are not sure if you are doing the right thing. Should you wait some more? Should you move at all? This drives you crazy. You decide to get away from the scene of the action and spend time in the comforting balm of nature. You visit art galleries, take in a movie or hang out at amusement parks and nature trails. You indulge in comfort shopping, in anything that can provide a release. You may also lose yourself in the arms of new love. There is travel too, and you soar like a giant balloon across the beautiful English meadows. Ganesha watches.

13 September: Last Quarter in Gemini

'It is through simple, direct and ordinary things in a person's mind and behaviour that he or she arrives at the realization of the awakened state of mind,' says Chögyam Trungpa, the Tibetan master. Your mind is playing tricks on you. At the very least, it is all over the yard like a Kanjeevaram sari left out to dry in the hot Indian sun. This is a time for ideating and not for action. You check out options at work and relationships and eject what does not suit you. You could also join a sect or be influenced by the tenets of a new spiritual movement. You could enrol in an NGO to green the city, or work with the well-being of stray dogs and cats. There are many possibilities as you torch your core with searching questions. You are moving ahead in evolutionary terms. Ganesha blesses you.

20 September: New Moon in Virgo

The new moon is in Virgo and there is a semblance of stability. There are a few glitches and snafus as Saturn entered Sagittarius on 19 September 2015, and will remain till 20 December 2017, by Western astrology. This is a long stay by any yardstick. Saturn is the taskmaster and you learn a lot about yourself and the world you live in. I must add here that astrology never compels and this is a general reading. I do not have your personal chart. But there is more stability now and you are not hovering in the ozone layer like a kite that has lost its manja. You assess your life and take the necessary steps to right the boat. You use quality 'me' time to chart your course. Ganesha blesses you.

28 September: First Quarter in Capricorn

You seem to have emerged from the maze and haze of life and are moving ahead with conviction. Life has taught you not to take things for granted. You watch your pride and overconfidence and rein them in. Your free, frank and fearless spirit may have also caused many embarrassments. You have learnt to hold your tongue and speak out only where it matters. There will be issues with money, and your business dealings are in sharp focus. Fiscal issues dominate your week along with domestic calls. Doctor's appointments may have to be made. Elders and children give a hard time. You look for succour from a higher power. You give yourself to Ganesha and all is well.

5 October: Full Moon in Aries

The full moon is in Aries and this is a propitious period to forge ahead with your plans and aspirations. You realize that nothing is permanent, more so the very body that you cherish, pamper and nourish so much. This is disconcerting but as close to the truth as it can be. A Zen proverb says: 'If you realize that all things change, there is nothing you will try to hold on to.' Despite the introspection, you get down to the business of making a living. As long as you inhabit this physical body there is no escaping its demands. You roll up your sleeves and get to the shop floor and dirty your knees. Work is a balm. It inures you from negativity and helps pay the bills. Nothing to complain about. Ganesha holds your hand.

12 October: Last Quarter in Cancer

I love to garnish my predictions with quotes. It gives you, my dear faithful and loyal readers, more bang for the buck. Swami Vivekananda said, 'Learning and wisdom are superfluities, the surface glitter merely, but it is the heart that is the seat of all power.' The moon is in Cancer and your emotions are at a peak. The heart may be the seat of all power but it is also the centre of despair. It all depends on how you use the energies of the moment. Harness your free will judiciously. You could walk down memory lane and shed tears. You could also escape in fantasies and indulgences. On the flip side, this can be a powerful creative force that can throw up masterpieces. There are also moments of happiness with family and loved ones. Ganesha journeys with you as you go about finding yourself.

19 October: New Moon in Libra

The new moon is in Libra and you decide on taking the family for a holiday. If you are single, there could be solo journeys too. Those who are grounded by multiple business concerns sign important deals. Inheritances and windfalls make their presence felt. There are expenses too, and money runs out of your pocket as easily as it enters. Romantic interludes pepper your life with excitement. You just want to have fun and are easily misunderstood. Women could get into tricky situations without meaning to. Ganesha says that discretion is the better part of valour. I agree. Avoid troublesome spots and late night revelries.

27 October: First Quarter in Aquarius

'I became insane, with long periods of horrible sanity,' said Edgar Allan Poe. Your mind is allowing you to experiment, and you will certainly not be exposed to long periods of sanity. You showcase your underbelly quite flamboyantly and attract the wrong kind of attention. Of course, you don't care. Take the necessary precautions and all will be well.

This can be a great time for writers and artists. You come up with brilliant ideas and execute them with discipline, dedication and determination. If you are an oddball, you thrive this week. If you aren't, you wear plumage that you would never have in the normal course of everyday events. This is certainly an interesting period with innumerable exciting possibilities. Ganesha watches with interest.

4 November: Full Moon in Taurus

The full moon is in Taurus and this is a good period. Whatever you embark on now leads to success. The employed get perks and promotions, and freelancers bag blue chip accounts. You spread your tentacles far and wide with considerable success and acclaim. The spotlight falls squarely on money and its accumulation. If too many greenbacks have slipped out of your fingers it is time now to get into accumulation mode. You love the whiff of money like everyone else, but generally speaking (I don't have your personal details), you don't have the accumulative tendencies of Taureans and Scorpios, who are considered empire builders. You realize that and get down to preparing a nest egg. You call in the experts and run through every fiscal instrument with a magnifying glass. There are expensive purchases too, but they are more in the nature of investments. They will stand you in good stead in times to come. Ganesha is impressed.

10 November: Last Quarter in Leo

Mercury is in your sign from 8 November to the year-end. To top it, the moon is in Leo. You live and love large, and Lady Luck courts you with all her charm. You have the Midas touch. Accolades and applause, money and honey, follow you like an obedient puppy. You have sent the right messages to the universe and it responds with interest. You are on a bull run and your world is sitting pretty. 'When we plan and rehearse the plan, there are actual physical changes at the quantum level that will bring about the fulfilment of your goal,' says Deepak Chopra. He explains that, on a cellular level, and through your connection to something higher than yourself, your imagination will bring you everything your heart desires, if you just believe. Tweak your free will, along with the bounty the stars have in store for you, and you make miracles happen. I have talked about Mercury in detail in January when it visited you for the first time and so will not repeat its beneficial aspects. Ganesha blesses you.

18 November: New Moon in Scorpio

You continue forging ahead, brushing aside the opposition with some degree of disdain. It may be easy to lose yourself when the going is particularly good. You are probably sure of your footing, but let me caution you that pride comes before a fall. Take the necessary precautions lest a great period be shackled by some immature or hasty act. The words of Lord Krishna in the Bhagavadgita are especially significant here: 'You are all essentially divine, you are eternal and ancient. Do not conduct yourself as a human being nor be bestial in your attitude and behaviour'. This is a special period. Make the most of it. The new moon is in Scorpio, giving you added intensity and purpose. There is new love and powerful bonding. Friends and loved ones find you amiable and affectionate. You win brownie points and score heavily on the endearment index. Ganesha is with you.

26 November: First Quarter in Pisces

You are in a softer and more creative frame of mind. You are not pushing ahead like a giant locomotive from the coach factory. You are also not bludgeoning the ball like Shahid

Afridi. Instead, you are all deft touches like Lin Dan, the legendary Chinese badminton player. Your body feints and court craft leave the opposition stunned. You are at your creative best. As an astrologer I know this feeling. I shall quote Johannes Brahms on creativity: 'Straightaway the ideas flow in upon me, directly from God.' This is the mood you are in. I don't have to add here that there are awards and rewards, accolades and applause, money and honey. Your skills are appreciated across quarters; even your critics bow to your genius. Success breeds success. This is a magical run, to say the least. Ganesha applauds.

3 December: Full Moon in Gemini

'Let us read, and let us dance; these two amusements will never do any harm to the world,' said Voltaire. Venus joins Mercury and large helpings of largesse are bestowed on you. The beneficial effects of Venus will continue till the year-end. This is also your birth period and the full moon is in Gemini. This is a great time for media folk. Writers and playwrights strike pay dirt. You are communicating with the world and winning laurels for blogs, books, plays, musical scores, scripts and everything to do with words and feelings. There is international travel, and new vistas open without caution. Venus is another important planet and is of great significance. As often discussed, Venus is the planet for love, romance, sex, beauty and the good life. This is the planet of attraction, love, wealth, knowledge and prosperity. The compatibility of partners and the type of life the individual will lead are also judged from the placement of Venus in the horoscope. As a planet, Venus is considered to be beneficial, feminine and gentle. Venus symbolizes the force of attraction in the universe. In human beings, this attractive force manifests as love and beauty. When Venus is well placed in the chart, there are love, art, beauty and all the goodies of life that make life worth living. Venus rules Libra and Taurus, though its role in every sign is important. Like other planets, it also has its transits. In Libra, Venus is aesthetic and cultured. In Taurus it is more earthy, materialistic and sensual. Venus rules the venous system, kidneys, urinary tract, throat, larynx, and is responsible for good looks. In short, Venus, in Western astrology, stands for comforts, arts, wealth, relationships, sex, decorations, luxuries and wealth. Ganesha exults.

10 December: Last Quarter in Virgo

I quote Soren Kierkegaard, the Danish philosopher: 'Life can only be understood backwards; but it must be lived forwards.' There is more balance in your life now. It is not that you have slowed down; it is just a pit stop to recuperate, rejuvenate and catch your breath for future excursions. There has been a lot happening in your life of late and you need to withdraw and look at events dispassionately from a distance. You have been moving at great speed. You take time off, examine the compass of your life and give more direction and thrust to your endeavours. The year is ending in brilliant fashion. Use your free will well and you will start 2018 on a surer footing. Every action has a reaction, and what you embark on now will bear fruit soon. Ganesha watches over you.

18 December: New Moon in Sagittarius

The new moon is in your sign and the trends are propitious. 'The touchstone for virtue in a person is their keenness to give up, to sacrifice and develop detachment,' said Sai Baba.

While you continue on the accelerated path of progress, your soul stirs with spiritual calls. You are making money and there is fame. You have all that hard cash can buy and yet a vacuum remains. You plunge into the sacred texts and befriend enlightened masters. There are also love, lust and ethereal bonding. There are fun times with family and friends too. Your plate is crowded with good tidings. You have no complaints. Ganesha smiles.

26 December: First Quarter in Aries

'Wherever you go, go with all your heart,' said Confucius. That is how you plan to spend the last days of the year. You are propelled by the power of Aries and will carry the energy of this period into the new year. There are travel, family outings, close bonding with loved ones, and several moments in the sun. You love to be with people. You are the soul of the party and wear out your new dance shoes in a jiffy. You are filled with gratitude for all that has landed on your plate, for both the good and the bad. If one has nourished your body, the other has blessed your soul. You have been on the fast track of evolution. With every challenge, you have risen like the phoenix. Way to go, says Ganesha as he cradles you into 2018.

CAPRICORN

23 December–22 January

Ganesha's Master Key: Organizer and ambitious

My father has always pointed out that Capricorn is the ruling sign or main sign of India. Capricorn is strongly associated with religion, tradition, organization, spiritual values, a plethora of skills, a cornucopia of thrills, a whole lot of spills, quite a few kills – and, in the distance, inviting hills. My father has a great sense of humour but he is also very serious about India and technology. Also, we Indians must be very tolerant, keep an open mind and learn to live peacefully by listening to the other person's point of view. Our great Indian culture must now accept new and open views and values, go in for greater charitable causes and respect the right of everyone to live according to his or her personal choice. In the next five years our country will be a superpower. New trends must be welcomed warmly and openly. This is the guidance of Lord Ganesha. I am only his humble mouthpiece.

The important traits are: Oriented towards outer world goals only; Rigid, crystallized, close-minded; Heartless, cold, ruthless; Fearful, pessimistic, overly authoritative; Seeking advancement at the expense of others; Achievement-driven; Seeking success through unethical means; Power-hungry and status-conscious; Overly cautious, stingy, emotionally blocked; Persistent, patient; Focused, persevering; Planning ahead, organized; Self-controlled, responsible to others; Honourable, ethical, upright; Using power with love; Dependable, prudent; Having a sense of responsibility for one's life and self; Self-disciplined; Mastery of self and material environment for the purpose of achieving greater good for humanity; Acting as a responsible citizen for God's kingdom; Oriented towards spiritual goals; Helping to implement the divine will on earth; Helping to achieve spiritual perfection on the physical plane; Acting not on the authority of the personality, but on the higher self.

Your Beauty-scope: Beautiful bone structure, as a rule, is found in Capricorns; play up this delicate angle. Generally, the knuckles are seen very clearly, so use a darker shade of foundation. Anti-wrinkle cream is a must for your neckline. Some of you could develop corded necks. So be on your guard. The upper part of the head, very specially, is superb. See that it is exhibited to the full in real life and in a photograph! Normally, you have large feet. Pedicure is a must. For you more than most, diet could be just the difference between beauty and the commonplace. The diet I recommend constitutes figs, greens, cow's milk, oranges, lemons, bone meal (important as the bones could be brittle), egg yolk, cabbage, fish, wholewheat. The herbs and flowers which most astrologers agree are ideal for you will be ivy, pansies, wolf-bane, hemlock.

CENTRAL IDEA

Practical, Efficient, Suspicious, Hard-working, Selfish

I admit that this book follows Western astrology. But only for you Capricorns, I have decided to use Vedic astrology with Western astrology. Matters highlighted include profession, function; source of livelihood, government service, honour from the king; business, status; wealth; political power; fame; progress; nature of work, professional inclination, the treating physician, hidden treasure; prescribed course, teaching capability, self-control, dominance, sacrificing nature; proficiency, father's wealth; well-being; foreign travel; financial status, place of residence, performance of sacred and religious deeds.

You will be in a direct relationship with important people and business giants. Yes, awards and rewards are possible. At the same time, be ready for responsibilities and heavy financial, emotional, physical and even spiritual duties. Remember, this is your fate. Accept it gracefully. By doing so, responsibilities will not be a burden but just a normal part of life and living. Even contacts in business and affairs of the heart are more than possible. I know that you Capricorns are immensely ambitious and therefore overdo everything. It will certainly tell on your health. Like it or lump it, you must learn to relax through exercise, meditation, baths, sleep, sports, yoga and so on. Let me put it all in a different way. You have many things going for you. Why spoil it by overdoing anything? Why indeed? Expenses will multiply. But let me assure you that your credit rating will be high and handsome. Therefore, stop worrying about it.

The last two years, Saturn has been playing tricks with you and causing ill health, mood swings, expenses and depression. This year Saturn will trouble you much less because Saturn will be in a good placing with Jupiter, the planet of honey and money. In other words, Jupiter will balance out Saturn. Foreign affairs, import and export, charitable causes, hospitals, welfare centres, rehabilitation clinics will play an important part in your life. The old, the weak and the very young will have to be taken care of. But I know very well that you know how to manage your affairs and keep your cool in critical conditions. Ganesha, Allah, Zoroaster and Christ are all with you. I know you are hard-headed and practical. But I also know that you are fully aware of your duties.

Mars represents house, home, office, entertainment and socializing for you. Mars will work like a Trojan or a giant powerhouse for you between 21 April and 4 June, 5 September and 22 October, and 1 and 27 January. Go all out for victory then.

Venus, the planet of money and honey, will help you in romance and finance (a good combination), and children, entertainment, prestige and power, between 6 June and 4 July, 25 December 2017 and 17 January 2018, 5 and 31 July, 7 and 30 November. You will have the necessary finance for a glorious romance.

For you Capricorns, Mercury controls service, jobs, servants, colleagues, religion, education, parents. It is a formidable list for sure. Mercury helps you from 1 January to 6 February as it will be in your own sign, 1 April to 6 June, 26 July to 1 September and again from 9 to 29 September, and finally from 17 October to 5 November. The trick is to move fast and communicate effectively. A job hop or promotion or perks or all three are possible.

CAPRICORN

Pluto is in Capricorn till 30 March 2025: I generally don't dwell on the outer planets as they influence countries more than people. But a few lines on Pluto may be interesting. Pluto rules power and the misuse of power. Pluto rules the motives that are hidden within the person wielding power. These deep motives, even if they are unseen, will sometimes explode. Pluto in Capricorn opens your intuitive skills. Pluto pushes you into a direction that you have wanted. However, the journey will have many twists and turns. With Pluto transiting through Capricorn, you may find the spotlight on you.

MONTHLY ROUND-UPS

January: Success, happiness, fun and games, family, victory. **February:** Finances, family, the luck of the draw, buying, selling, investing. **March:** Fanning out to people, places, contracts and contacts, communication channels abuzz. **April:** Home, house, parents, in-laws; renovation/decoration of home/house, parents/in-laws; renovation/decoration of office/shop/home. **May:** Despite changes you do enjoy journeys, and are creative; children give joy. **June:** Work, health, loans, pets and projects. **July:** Off and away to a magnificent start, despite pressures and pulls, says Ganesha. **August:** Windfalls, joint finance, legacy, passion. **September:** Right contacts, success, travel, publicity. **October:** Tremendous drive, like Sourav Ganguly, the Cancerian, ambition honed perfectly. **November:** Good news, pressures, delays, but all turns out well in the end, and you do socialize; **December:** Expenses, losses and psychic powers, glimpses of Ganesha/God/Allah/the Supreme Power, pilgrimages, rites and duties.

Money: My father has invented a digital formula for you. It is Ambitious + efficient + management expert + practical = great money.

Happiness Quota: I give you 84 per cent.

MONTH BY MONTH

January: You have a great start to the year thanks to the beneficial effects of Mercury. There are money and honey. You ride high. Accolades, love, money and all the goodies of life are heaped on you. Mid-month sees you busy with domestic demands. There is also love that singes your soul. There are also fun times with family and friends. As the month ends, your creative side is highlighted. This is also a period when your sensitivities are aroused and your offbeat side gets a leg-up.

February: You are on steady ground. You are also pushed to achieve. Ambition, determination and perseverance make a heady combination. Life purrs along happily. Mid-month sees you charged. Powerful passions and ego drives at play. You explore new ideas, new places, new cuisine and new people. This is a wonderful time for travel. As the month ends, there is a creative surge within you. Your mind is fertile, your critical faculties are sharp and you throw up works of genius.

March: There are indulgences and escapist tendencies. You check out cults, gurus and new spiritual learning. There are powerful and stimulating influences cuddling you. Mid-month sees more stability. You roll up your sleeves and slog away. The moon is in your sign and you achieve success. There is balance and you know what you are doing and where you are headed. You are capable of sustained hard work. As the month ends, you are on a bull run. This is a great time for creative folk. You are also joyous, filled with mirth and a new zest for life. You earn kudos.

April: You want to be surrounded by beauty. There are golden moments spent at home with the family. Children bring joy. You take bonding to ethereal heights. The energies are powerful mid-month and miracles are possible. There are big plans for business expansion. Love also possesses you. As the month ends, you outsmart the opposition and sidestep and obliterate all that stands between you and success. You are in achievement mode.

May: Ego drives are torched. Watch out for altercations. This is also a great time for a complete overhaul of your life. You may want to take to yoga, meditation, alternative healing. Mid-month sees you busy with domestic chores. You are on a good run. Mid-month, your defences are down and you are vulnerable. Loved ones will find it hard to handle you. As the month ends, you embark on new ventures. You are filled with creative and inventive ideas.

June: Your life is on an even keel. You make rapid progress at work. You are happy with yourself. That is the key to life. There could also be travel, unexpected expenses, an addition to the family and much more. Mid-month sees love enter your life. It transports you to another realm of joyousness. As the month ends, you spend a lot of time at home with repairs and renovations. The health of elders may also need attention.

July: The moon is in Libra and you are living your life in your mind now. You are filled with ideas that hop around like a rutting grasshopper. Innumerable choices are presented to you. But you manage to power ahead. There is stability and direction. Mid-month sees fire in your belly. You take risks, spend money and seek out love. Your critical faculties are sharp and success garlands you. As the month ends, you are powered and recharged and think nothing of attempting what you have never done before. You take on new challenges and emerge triumphant. You are a winner all through.

August: The full moon is in Aquarius and you are filled with visions of the future. You may be looking at social change. Your offbeat and dishevelled side expresses itself eloquently. Mid-month sees more balance in your life. Your single-minded dedication to work has its rewards. Love life warms up. As the month ends, you are thirsting for action. You are intellectually alive. New vistas beckon.

September: Your moods are churning; you blow hot, cold and lukewarm. You are overly sensitive. There are expenses, indulgences and escapism. Your mind roams without inhibition. Mid-month sees relative stability. You settle down and plan your life and work in great detail. As the month ends, you mean business and roll up your sleeves and get to work. You gain applause from your peer group. Family life rolls along without quarrel.

October: This can be a propitious time for travel. Also, your fantasy life unfolds in all its splendour. But the mundane demands of domesticity call out. Mid-month sees you meet up with friends and socialize. Love and bonhomie embrace you.

As the month ends, you are filled with zany ideas. You are offbeat, creative and outlandish. You break free from shackles and the status quo and listen to the beat of a distant drummer.

November: The full moon is in Taurus and there are balance and stability in your life. There are also many expenses too. This is also an amorous period. Mid-month sees powerful intensity in your undertakings. This is a great period if you are on a solo run. You are filled with energy, excitement and euphoria. As the month ends, there are odd jobs at home which demand your time, including caring for elders. You also take time off and pore through spiritual texts and meet with gurus and god-men. This is also a creative phase and you showcase your artistic skills.

December: As the year ends, you allow your monkey mind full freedom. You want to spill your plans to the world and use every technological marvel to broadcast them. Mid-month sees hard work take over. The last weeks end in style. Your life is more than just a bed of roses. Your timing is exquisite. You are the right person at the right place. Success cannot elude you. You also ensure that you live in gratitude. You are filled with love, generosity and kindness. What a great end to the year!

WEEKLY REVIEW (BY PHASES OF THE MOON)

5 January: First Quarter in Aries

'If you are depressed, you are living in the past. If you are anxious, you are living in the future. If you are at peace, you are living in the present,' said Lao-tzu. You start the year with Mercury in your sign from 1 to 5 January. For sure, you are living in the present because it is a great start to the year. Mercury is here for a very short period, but, along with the moon in Aries, it gives you a head start over your rivals. Mercury, the mighty, all-powerful planet, favours travels, meetings, conferences, interviews, trips, more brainpower, contacts, communication, correspondence and contracts. Mercury has a special connection with the circuits of the brain. Chess, crossword and other such games belong to Mercury. Also, short-distance runners and spin bowlers are controlled by Mercury. Mercury, in short, is the ambassador and salesman of the zodiac. Mercury is the symbol of news, views, messages, interviews, contacts, communications, travel and transport. Mercury gives an impetus to all of the above in the sun sign where it is located. There are money and honey, my favourite phrase, as you enter the arena of life with the confidence of an unbeaten gladiator. You ride high. To paraphrase the Bard, take the tide at the flood and it will lead to fortune. This is also your birth period. The energies favour you. Accolades, love, money and all the goodies of life are heaped on you. Ganesha urges you to choose wisely lest it all go to your head because it most certainly is a heady time.

12 January: Full Moon in Cancer

'Dance right out of your cage,' says Danielle LaPorte. You do just that. Mercury re-enters your sign on 11 January and stays till 6 February. This is a slightly longer stay, ensuring that you lay a solid start to the year. You are like Chris Gayle giving a walloping foundation to his team in a T20 final. Since I have already waxed eloquent on the beneficial aspects of Mercury I will not repeat it. The full moon is also in Cancer and you are busy with domestic demands. You take a step back from work and ensure that the family is well taken care of. Children bring joy and there is domestic

CAPRICORN

peace. Charity begins at home and you ensure that the larder is well stocked. Like with everything else in life, the family too marches on its stomach. Those in monogamous relationships give new meaning to their love. Singles feel that they have finally found their significant other. The portents are powerful. Ganesha is happy for you.

19 January: Last Quarter in Scorpio

There is powerful intensity goading you on. You want to get to the bottom of things, quite like Sherlock Holmes. The moon is in Scorpio and you take on life with an added zest. Love singes your soul. If its stirrings began earlier, it now reaches critical mass. 'A musician must make music, an artist must paint, a poet must write, if he is to be ultimately at peace with himself. What one can be, one must be,' said Abraham Maslow, the great psychologist. You chase your dreams and live large; you want room on the rainbow. You are direct, honest, aggressive and assertive in your dealings. You think big, and out of the box. Success garlands you. There are also fun times with family and friends. Ganesha is thrilled.

28 January: New Moon in Aquarius

'The soul's first adventure is the fight between two ideas: the wish to return to earth in a human form, and the desire to feel the freedom of having no form,' said Paramahansa Yogananda. The moon is in Aquarius and your creative side is highlighted. This is also a period when your sensitivities are aroused and you showcase a lot of yourself that is otherwise kept hidden. 'The touchstone for virtue in a person is their keenness to give up, to sacrifice and develop detachment,' said Sai Baba. You may also spend time with the less fortunate. You think and act out of the box and give your life and times a new spin altogether. Your offbeat side gets a leg-up. Media folk have a field day. Now, to explain the context in more detail, let me tell you a bit about your sign: Capricorns revel in challenges. They are ambitious, sometimes ruthless, pragmatic and persevering. If anyone can turn a shortcoming into a blessing, they can. Capricorns are generally successful. Like mountain goats, they climb slippery slopes and ensure that no pursuer can reach them. Ruled by Saturn, they look for reputation, money and power, and, more often than not, get it. Famous Capricorns include Nicolas Cage, Denzel Washington, Tiger Woods, Anthony Hopkins, Mel Gibson, Elvis Presley, Richard Nixon, Rod Stewart, Martin Luther King Jr, Muhammad Ali, Kevin Costner, Mao Zedong, Louis Pasteur, Rudyard Kipling and Swami Vivekananda, among others. As you can see, you are in great company. Ganesha is impressed.

4 February: First Quarter in Taurus

'When you make a choice you change the future,' says Deepak Chopra. You are on steady ground, thanks to the beneficial influence of the moon in Taurus. You are also pushed to achieve and you will not be deterred by hard work. Ambition, determination and perseverance make a heady combination. Without a doubt, there is success in your undertakings. You may also be spending a lot, but it is not wasted. You make wise investments with an eye on the future. You busy yourself with fiscal instruments and fun times with the family. Life purrs along happily. Ganesha is happy for you.

11 February: Full Moon in Leo

The full moon is in Leo and you are charged. You want to make it all happen instantaneously. There are powerful passions and ego drives at play. You are hosting new emotions. This is a significant phase and it could backfire if you give vent to misplaced ego drives. Avoid altercations and brushes with the law. Good fences make good neighbours. There could be a family holiday. Children bring joy though they may also be leaving home for better prospects. You are happy for that. Ganesha watches over you.

18 February: Last Quarter in Sagittarius

There is a lot of movement now as you are keen to experience life in all its glory. You want new breeze wafting into your life. You want to be around new cultures and new types of people. You believe that this will invigorate your mind and kick-start it or goad it into opening new vistas. You explore new ideas, new places, new cuisine and new people. You wander around unfamiliar places and are invigorated by new scents. Your sense of adventure is strong and you would love to take risks. This is a wonderful time for travel. You are filled with energy and the key is in channelling it the right way. You play the field as partners drop by, mesmerized by your charm and ebullience. Life calls out to you and you meet it frontally. Ganesha is delighted.

26 February: New Moon in Pisces

'Your dignity depends on your will,' says Danielle LaPorte. The new moon is in Pisces and there is a creative surge within you. Your mind is fertile, your critical faculties are sharp and you throw up works of genius as though it were second nature to you. You network with vengeance and get renown for your blogs, articles, books or musical scores. You win more than just peer group applause. There could be a global ovation. Of course, astrology never compels and I do not have your personal chart. This is a general reading though

I have been proved right most of the time over the decades. Use the energies of the period well. Ganesha is thrilled.

5 March: First Quarter in Gemini

There could be a contradiction of sorts. You want to be alone and yet you want company. This creates a lot of confusion and your signals are misinterpreted; the fault is entirely yours. You take time off the usual grind and hit the road. You meet up with strangers and form an unlikely band of travellers. You are in the mood to try out new things. There are indulgences and escapist tendencies which you may need to keep tabs on. Along with tantra, mantra and yantra you check out cults, gurus and new spiritual learning. You could take to a new form of yoga or martial art. There are powerful and stimulating influences cuddling you. Ganesha is not worried.

12 March: Full Moon in Virgo

Ralph Waldo Emerson said, 'He has not learned the lessons of life who does not every day surmount a fear.' The full moon is in Virgo and you are back on terra firma. You know where to draw the line in your escapades. You teeter on the edge of the precipice and then pull back before you plunge into the ravine. You have a built-in security system that has worked well so far. You have been there and done that. Now you roll up your sleeves and slog away. The faint whiff of freshly printed currency notes grabs you by the collar. The aroma is seductive. You want more of it. If working hard gets you there you don't mind burning the midnight oil. Money has a strange allure and there is never enough of it. Don't you know that? Ganesha holds your hand.

20 March: Last Quarter in Capricorn

'Love the work. Destiny will do what it wants with you regardless,' says Elizabeth Gilbert. The moon is in your sign and you achieve success. There is balance and you know what you are doing and where you are headed. You are capable of sustained hard work and that is the most ancient secret of success which proves itself over and over again, even in this day and age of modern conveniences. No pain, no gain, even if you are not a gym rat. This law applies to all of life. You don't need prodding as you get down to hard work and secure a nest egg. More important, Ganesha is with you. You do your best and he will do the rest.

28 March: New Moon in Aries

The new moon is in Aries and you are on a bull run. There could be great success for writers, musicians and painters in this period. I must add here that artists and art lovers alike have believed that unless you are filled with angst like Bob Dylan, Alanis Morissette, or Ernest Hemingway, you might not be able to tap or delve deep into your creativity. Even Socrates and Plato historically took 'melancholic habitus', or what can be called a sulking holiday to charge themselves creatively. Well, you don't need to do that. You are joyous, filled with mirth and a new zest for life, and you are also at your creative best. Like Osho suggested, you channel your joy and your love of life into creativity. You don't need mind-altering substances to tap the fountain of new ideas within you. You earn kudos and your inner confidence spills over into everything that you do. There are rewards and awards, money and honey, applause and accolades. You break all stereotypes and emerge as the dark horse. Ganesha is impressed.

3 April: First Quarter in Cancer

The moon is in Cancer and you are enveloped by love and longing. You want to be surrounded by beauty. Your sensitivities are aroused and you want to be cuddled by life. There are golden moments spent at home with the family. Children bring joy and the partner is delighted to see more of you for a change. You take bonding to ethereal heights. You may take the brood for a much-deserved and long-awaited holiday and have fun times. There are 'me' time and family time as a sense of peace and happiness takes over your body and soul. Ganesha is happy for you.

11 April: Full Moon in Libra

The full moon is in Libra and you may have many unusual experiences. But, let me add like I always do, that astrology never compels, and this is a general reading as I don't have your personal chart. In this period you may feel a type of clairvoyance or serendipity and may be at a loss to explain it. Let me quote Dr Beitman here: 'Simulpathity [sic] tells us we can connect with the experience of others at a distance without knowing how we do it.' He adds that the human GPS tells us, 'We can find our way to people, things and ideas without knowing how.' I am also learning all the time, along with you, though I know fully well that the world is filled with secrets that science has been unable to explain. Astrology and the esoteric sciences plug many gaps. This may explain somewhat the strange occurrences that may be happening in your life. The energies are powerful now and if you live mindfully and in awareness, miracles are possible. Use your free will well and keep an open mind. Ganesha watches.

19 April: Last Quarter in Capricorn

'Love knows no riches or poverty. It is beyond both,' said the poet Kabir. The moon is in your sign and you are passing through a very practical period. You are slogging away and also making big plans for rapid business expansion. You are clear about your intent and do not spare the horses! There is money to be made and you do not need further inducement. But, when you least expect it, you are smitten by amour. You are in its deathly coil. Nothing makes sense any more until you possess the object of your desire – body, mind and soul. Love or lust, I am not sure which, possesses you and takes over your being. For the moment at least, you are felled by its touch as though you were in the ring with Joe Frazier at his peak. Ganesha knows it all and observes with interest.

26 April: New Moon in Taurus

'I don't need time. What I need is a deadline,' said Duke Ellington, the jazz pianist and composer. The new moon is in Taurus and you are in excellent shape, like a wild horse in the prairie. Nothing can keep pace with you as you gallop away. You outsmart the opposition and sidestep and obliterate all that stands between you and victory. You live and love large. There are many purchases and expenses. Money flows out of your fingers. But you are in achievement mode. Deadlines corner you. There is no escape; not even a vent in the distance. But they also challenge you to deliver, and deliver you do. I know the feeling as I write my books and columns, year after year. One is pushed, and from the pressure exerted, genius emerges. You have the talent, and now life is allowing your innate skills to flower. Destiny cannot be beaten. Ganesha applauds.

3 May: First Quarter in Leo

'If we are creating ourselves all the time, then it is never too late to begin creating the bodies we want instead of the ones we mistakenly assume we are stuck with,' says Deepak Chopra. The moon is in Leo and ego drives are torched and touched. Watch out for altercations; they can be easily avoided. Step away from disputes. You don't need the law barging into your home. This is also a great time for a complete overhaul and change in tack. You may want to take to yoga, meditation, alternative healing, maybe even a sartorial makeover. You are fed up with the old you and look to reinvent yourself. You want to junk routine and wear new plumage. You flirt with love as it lands up on your doorstep as though the stork absent-mindedly dropped it. Ganesha watches.

10 May: Full Moon in Scorpio

'Pray as though nothing else will work, and work as if no prayer will help,' is a German proverb that has stood the test of time. The full moon is in Scorpio and you are busy with domestic and work chores. You also spend time in the arms of amour; it certainly is a good way to be. You may also take time off to reflect on your life and times. You want to make sense of your feelings and impressions. There is a lot happening in your world and you want to distance yourself from it and watch it all. There is progress at work and, as a result, a deep sense of satisfaction. You are on a good run. Don't muck it up, says Ganesha, with indulgences and escapist tendencies which also seek to warm you up.

19 May: Last Quarter in Aquarius

'What dreadful hot weather we have! It keeps me in a continual state of inelegance,' said Jane Austen. Your mind plays tricks on you. The subcontinent is scorching and you can boil an egg in the shade. It is not that you are having sunstroke; the moon is in Aquarius and it is dredging deep within the crevices of your soul and raking up events that have probably been buried for lifetimes. You walk maudlin streets and are filled with self-pity. This is not your style, but it can happen to the best of us. Your defences are down and you are vulnerable. You need cuddling and tender loving care. You may be prone to histrionics and tantrums. Loved ones will find it hard to handle you. This shall also pass, but, until then, you are considered a pain where it hurts the most! Of course, astrology never compels. Use your free will to advantage. Ganesha watches.

25 May: New Moon in Gemini

The new moon is in Gemini and this is a grand time for embarking on new ventures. You are filled with creative and inventive ideas. They burst out of you like creepers on a window sill. It will also be prudent to avoid being brash, reckless and overconfident. Do not react to what people say or do. You could be dealing with sensitive egos, and a stray remark could snowball into gigantic proportions. If you indeed need to critique, do it in a sensitive and supportive manner. In life, diplomacy often wins. Politics, or what you see and read on the idiot box and in newspapers about our leaders, is merely a reflection of everyday life. It is just that the stakes are higher. Family life may also be on the boil. Ganesha holds your hand.

1 June: First Quarter in Virgo

Henry David Thoreau said, 'I find it wholesome to be alone for the greater part of the time.' The moon is in Virgo and there is stability and balance in your dealings. Your life is on an even keel now. The best antidote for any problem in life is to plunge into hard work. You do just that and your mind is as clear as filtered water. You work alone and well. You make rapid progress. You are happy with yourself. That is the key to life. You seem to have stumbled upon it by accident. This may goad you to seek more 'me' time in the future. Ganesha blesses you.

9 June: Full Moon in Sagittarius

The full moon is in Sagittarius and many influences are working on you. This is a propitious period but it all depends on how you tweak it. Use your free will to advantage. 'All that we are is the result of what we have thought,' said the Buddha. Ensure that the monkey mind is tethered, and all will be well. There could be travel, unexpected expenses, new love, searching for a guru, marriages, anniversaries, an addition to the family, and much more. Your plate is full. It spills like the rajma-chawal served in the dhabas of India along the long, winding, national highways. Ganesha journeys with you.

17 June: Last Quarter in Pisces

'Ecstasy is your birthright,' says Danielle LaPorte, the life coach. The last quarter of the moon is in Pisces and your heart blossoms in inexplicable joy. You seem to have glided on to the fountain of happiness. It may be sheer accident: you haven't gone seeking it out with a lantern – but you are the better for it. Life is now a bed of roses. You exult and delight in it. There is love that transports you to another realm of joyousness. Even without it, you live in ecstasy. For no apparent reason, you seem to inhale only the fragrance of the flowers wafting along the corridors of your life. Where are the thorns? You have no idea; it hasn't even crossed your mind. Right now, you bask in the sheer timelessness of the moment. It will change like it has to. But the thought doesn't cross your mind. Ganesha is impressed.

24 June: New Moon in Cancer

'There is an eloquence in true enthusiasm that is not to be doubted,' said Washington Irving, the writer. The new moon is in Cancer, and this could see you spend a lot of time at home. If repairs and renovations are to be carried out, you supervise it all to the tiniest detail. There are other domestic calls too. The partner needs help and children may be leaving home. The health of elders may also need attention. You are also busy with financial deals, wills, inheritances, stocks and realty. You pore over every fiscal instrument with a magnifying glass. No detail skips your expert eye. You realize that you could be in for a windfall. That only encourages you to add up the numbers one more time. Just remember to give freely to the less fortunate. What you give always returns manifold. Ganesha agrees.

1 July: First Quarter in Libra

'Your worst enemy cannot harm you as much as your unguarded thoughts,' said the Buddha. As you may have noticed, I have spoken a lot about the monkey mind. I have always asked you to tether it; and for good reason too. Please remember that we live in our minds. Our world is between our ears. So when you lower the volume of the chatter, or banish it altogether, a new you emerges. A manic depressive can be buoyant and positive within moments. It is all about channelling one's thoughts in the right direction. I emphasize this because the moon is in Libra and you are living your life in your mind now. You are filled with ideas that hop around like a rutting grasshopper. Innumerable choices are presented to you and you don't know which fork in the road to take. Money comes and goes and you could give in to indulgences and escapism. In the process, you may miss out on something important. With your mind all over the place, the 'moment' eludes your grasp. Ganesha holds your hand.

9 July: Full Moon in Capricorn

The full moon is in your sign and you are powering ahead. Thankfully, there are stability and direction in your life as you move forward with the determination of a new Mumbai monorail. Those in the subcontinent may also find themselves in the wet embrace of the monsoon. At one level – if you are not flooded out of your home like a wet rag – the monsoon can be poetic. I am reminded of Rabindranath Tagore's beautiful lines on the monsoon: 'Come pleasant beauty, bring your pleasant companionship and quench the thirst and heat.' In the midst of it all, you are in the throes of the hard slog. You know where you are headed and there are no full stops. There is success. Money and honey garland you. Family life has no hiccups or hurrahs, which probably explains matrimony in general. Ganesha smiles.

16 July: Last Quarter in Aries

'Everything that is happening at this moment is the result of the choices you have made in the past,' says Deepak Chopra. The moon is in Aries and there is fire in your belly. You take risks, spend money and seek out love in the weirdest corners. Your critical faculties are sharp and success garlands you. You mow down the opposition like a speeding car on Mumbai roads. There could also be business travel as you look to expand your interests. Children may also be leaving home. Ganesha watches the nest emptying.

23 July: New Moon in Leo

The new moon is in Leo and you live and love large. You are in an expansive mood and spend time with friends and loved ones. Alumni meetings and get-togethers hog your time. You are powered and recharged and think nothing of attempting what you have never done before. You take on new challenges and emerge triumphant. In the mood you are in you could even walk over Niagara Falls on a tripwire, balancing a heavy load. Nothing fazes you. Love walks in and smiles. You accept the invite. Ganesha also smiles.

30 July: First Quarter in Scorpio

'Meditation is simply seeing reality and acknowledging it with bare honesty,' said Bo Lozoff. The moon is in Scorpio, adding a new intensity to your life. There are several influences at play and you can be pushed to the wall. But you stick to your guns and refuse to buckle down. You are grounded and sure of yourself. Nothing can shake your equanimity. As the week unfolds, people and events butt you, but you manage to look away as though nothing happened, and it riles them even more. You are filled with enthusiasm and energy and your emotions are at an even keel. You are a winner all through, ultimately leaving the opposition as potent as scantily clad cheerleaders. Ganesha is impressed by your deft manoeuvres.

7 August: Full Moon in Aquarius

'Every man is the creature of the age in which he lives and few are able to raise themselves above the ideas of the time,' said Voltaire. The full moon is in Aquarius and you are filled with visions of the future. You may be looking at social change, even revolution. You are possibly disenchanted with the political climate and believe that you have the answers. There are discordant energies at play and they could trip or entrap you. There are mood swings and neuroses. Your offbeat and dishevelled side expresses itself eloquently. Love life goes for a toss as your partners simply refuse to recognize you any more. Marriage is no longer a bed of roses. Of course, astrology never compels and I wish you well. Please remember that this is a general reading as I do not have your personal chart. Ganesha walks with you.

15 August: Last Quarter in Taurus

Luckily, there is more balance in your life now. Instinctively, you return to the old panacea: hard work. You have been derailed from the tasks at hand and there is a lot of catching up to do. You roll up your sleeves and dirty your elbows. Your single-minded dedication to work has its rewards. Love life warms up. Singles play the field and those in committed relationships bond beautifully. There is also time spent with the family as domestic calls hog your time and resources. In all, it's a productive week. Ganesha is happy for you.

21 August: New Moon in Leo

'You may never know what results come of your action, but if you do nothing there will be no result,' said Mohandas Gandhi. The new moon is in Leo and you are thirsting for action. You are intellectually alive, and keen on growing as a person. You want to impact the neighbourhood in a positive way and so may take to tree planting, culling strays or spearheading a garbage collection drive. You are open to new experiences and quite naturally new vistas beckon. There could be travel and a dramatic broadening of horizons. You are pushing hard and the rewards are visible. Ganesha is pleased.

29 August: First Quarter in Sagittarius

'What a strange thing! To be alive beneath cherry blossoms,' said Kobayashi Issa. I like this quote for its originality and freshness. The moon is in Sagittarius and you take a hard look at spirituality. You delve into yantra, tantra and mantra and spend time in pilgrim centres. You may engage in rituals and take significant vows. You could also take love to the altar. The possibilities are endless. You realize that the world you see in its physical form around you doesn't connect to the world that inhabits your soul. It is disconcerting, but there is little you can do about it. Ganesha knows. At best, you can seek out an inner peace. You know that too!

6 September: Full Moon in Pisces

'Every increased possession loads us with new weariness,' said John Ruskin, the social reformer. The full moon is in Pisces and your moods are churning; you blow hot, cold and lukewarm. You are sensitive and take jest and mirth to be Biblical truism. You shed tears at the slightest perceived affront. You simply cannot handle the truth and bare facts. Friends and loved ones will have to couch straight talk in diplomacy. For some reason, your defences are down and your insecurities peak. There are expenses, indulgences and escapism. Ganesha takes you across troubled waters.

13 September: Last Quarter in Gemini

Your mind is everywhere. It roams around without inhibition like a kite that has lost its manja. You soar above the clouds into the cosmos. You want to do big things, but to realize your true potential there is no substitute to good, old-fashioned hard work. Nothing else works. Ask me. This is what I have realized after writing countless books and columns over the years. The Buddha said, 'Ambition is like love, impatient both of delays and rivals.' You are impatient but it does no good to your cause. You hire image consultants, pay them a huge sum, and ensure that you are featured in the papers. Unfortunately, this is the way things are done these days; one needs spin doctors. Youngsters play the field and those in committed relationships have one eye peering out from the lookout tower. Family life is in for a toss. These are passing phases, and harmony will return as it always does. After the choppy waters is the calm. Hang in there, advises Ganesha.

20 September: New Moon in Virgo

The new moon is in Virgo and there is relative stability. The storm clouds have passed. You settle down, and plan your life and work in great detail. A new acquaintance may turn out to be an integral part of your success. Never judge a book by its cover. Appearances can be deceptive; things are not always what they seem. 'God has been everlastingly working in Silence, unobserved, unheard, except by those who experience His Infinite Silence,' said Meher Baba. You get a glimpse of a higher force guiding you and you may join a spiritual movement or busy yourself in evangelical work. Or just simple hard work gives you deliverance. If you have been tossed around like lichen in the Bay of Bengal, there is stability now. The best part is that your mind is at peace. The battle has been won. Now you set out to conquer the world. Ganesha watches over you.

28 September: First Quarter in Capricorn

The moon is in Capricorn and you are rock solid. 'Whatever happens to you, you can either see it as a curse and suffer it, or you can see it as a blessing and make use of it,' says Sadguru, the New Age mystic. If you have been soaked and rinsed in a tumble-dry washing machine, it is the past. You have emerged with flying colours and are now basking in the fragrance of existence. You mean business and roll up your sleeves and get to work. Money and honey follow you like a faithful puppy. You excel and gain applause from your peer group. Family life rolls along without quarrel. Children bring joy. Ganesha rejoices.

5 October: Full Moon in Aries

'A healthy attitude is contagious, but don't wait to catch it from others. Be a carrier,' said Tom Stoppard. There could be a lot of movement in your life now. This can be a propitious time for travel. But this is also not a great time to take risks or to invest large sums of money in any venture. It may be a good idea to take a short holiday. Immigration and any other such big move should be deferred. If you are signing legal documents, scan the fine print with a magnifying glass. This may also not be a good time to invest in real estate. Ride things out for a while and keep your options open. A premature commitment may boomerang. You are most definitely on the upswing but it is always wise to hold on to the railings during a daredevil ride in Disneyland. Ganesha holds your hand.

12 October: Last Quarter in Cancer

The moon is in Cancer and your fantasy life unfolds in all its splendour. You daydream and catch butterflies. But you are pulled back to terra firma and a string of obligations by domestic calls. The spouse needs help, the children have demands and the health of elders needs attention. If you live in a joint family you are hard-pressed to find 'me' time. There is no escape from the mundane demands of domesticity, and, if you pride yourself as someone who performs all responsibilities diligently, you have no space at all for yourself. You are in touch with your feelings and emotions and want to articulate them with some flamboyance. You want to give free rein to your inner dreams and desires, but this is certainly not the time. I shall end with a quote from George Bernard Shaw: 'The single biggest problem in communication is the illusion that it has taken place.' That seems to be the theme of the moment. Ganesha wishes you well.

19 October: New Moon in Libra

The new moon is in Libra and you are spoilt for choice. You travel and meet up with friends. You are in a jovial mood and socialize. Love life is intense as you coat intimacy with a new fury. Love and bonhomie embrace you. You indulge in leisure activities and feel happy for yourself and your world. It purrs merrily. Ganesha is happy too.

27 October: First Quarter in Aquarius

The moon is in Aquarius and you are filled with the zaniest of ideas on the planet. You are an inventive genius in the mood you are in. You are offbeat, creative and outlandish. You are like Steve Jobs when he chanced upon the idea of Apple.

You break free from shackles and the status quo and listen to the beat of a distant drummer. Like secret dog whistles, only you hear the call. You are in the mood to do something different and there are several eureka moments. Of course, all this may not render family life great stability, but that is not your priority at all. You are now brandishing your scimitar against windmills. Ganesha watches in disbelief.

4 November: Full Moon in Taurus

As the Greek philosopher Heraclitus said, 'There is nothing permanent except change.' The full moon is in Taurus and there are balance and stability in your life. There are also many expenses as money finds a hole in your pocket. You make detailed plans for the future and identify possible pitfalls. You are troubleshooting before there is trouble. Like they say, it is better to be safe than sorry. It is just that you want to be in charge of the situation and not caught unawares. You want to be ahead of the pack, so you plan with meticulous precision. This is also an amorous period. You and love are conjoined twins. Those in committed relationships take bonding to great heights. Life is calling out to you and you are all dressed up for the dance. Ganesha supports you.

10 November: Last Quarter in Leo

The moon is in Leo and passions and ego drives run rampant. You are a control freak in this phase and want it all your way, come what may. This can lead to altercations and possible trysts with the law-enforcing agencies. I would advise you to take a step back and retreat from the heat of battle. 'Two people have been living in you all of your life. One is the ego, garrulous, demanding, hysterical, and calculating; the other is the hidden spiritual being, whose still voice of wisdom you have only rarely heard or attended to,' said Chogyal Rinpoche in *The Tibetan Book of Living and Dying*. There is powerful intensity in your undertakings, which is both good and bad, depending on the context. You are on fast forward and may go overboard when it is not necessary. This is a great period if you are on a solo run. As a team player you are caught wanting. There could be travel and many affairs of the heart. An exciting time indeed! Ganesha chuckles.

18 November: New Moon in Scorpio

The new moon is in Scorpio and this is a period of energy, excitement and euphoria. 'The best time to plant a tree was twenty years ago. The second best time is now,' says a Chinese proverb. Quite rightly, you want to mint the moment. The past is over and the future is fantasy. So you go for it. There is business expansion and there may even be overseas forays. Freelancers cast their net wide and the pickings are generous. Love life continues to be intense. Domestic life smoulders like a smorgasbord of Indian spice. Ganesha watches.

26 November: First Quarter in Pisces

The moon is in Pisces and you are occupied with domestic chores. Charity begins at home. You spend time helping the kids with studies and babysitting them. Gender roles are mixed now, with both partners working. There are odd jobs at home which demand your time, including caring for elders. You also take time off and pore through spiritual texts and meet with gurus and god-men. There is nothing specifically amiss in your world but you find solace in rituals and places of worship; they just give you inner peace. 'Ask the question, what is responsible for existence? The answer is Divinity. Without faith in the Divine, nothing can be achieved,' said Sai Baba. This is also a creative phase and you showcase your artistic skills. Ganesha is happy for you.

3 December: Full Moon in Gemini

The full moon is in Gemini and as the year leaps to an end, you allow your monkey mind full freedom. You want to spill your plans to the world and use every technological marvel to broadcast them. The world is indeed small now and you squeeze it further into your palm thanks to all the gadgetry available. This is also a creative phase replete with many breathtaking moments. As Thich Nhat Hanh says, 'Feelings come and go like clouds in a windy sky. Conscious breathing is my anchor.' You tweak your life and take to yoga, meditation and alternative healing. You also opt for a sartorial makeover. You are looking at a new you; so is the world. You want to enter 2018 in a different avatar. Ganesha smiles.

10 December: Last Quarter in Virgo

The moon is in Virgo and, despite the distractions of the season, you get down to hard work. The practical streak runs very deep in you and you don't need more than even a faint whiff of money or power in the distance to goad you on. I am not calling you corrupt, but metaphorically it is the ultimate bribe. Of course, I insist that you stick to the straight and narrow. I believe in the old-fashioned concept of hard work; it is as true and eternal as ageing. 'There is no agony like bearing an untold story inside of you,' said Maya Angelou, the poet. If you are an author, your best-seller is just moments away from being printed. You make a stirring orator in this phase. More power to you, says Ganesha.

18 December: New Moon in Sagittarius

You have been ending the last few years in style. The trend doesn't change. Venus is in your sign from 23 to 31 December, and life is more than just a bed of roses. You are in action mode and there are fun times too. Probably, you simply enjoy what you do, which is really the key ingredient of success. I am reminded of the famous lines of General George Patton, the US Army general during WWII. He said: 'A good plan, violently executed now, is better than a perfect plan next week.' Yes, you go for the jugular. Your timing is exquisite. You are the right person at the right place. Success cannot elude you. As I always do, let me pen a few lines on Venus. Venus is the planet for love, romance, sex, beauty and the good life. This is the planet of attraction, love, wealth, knowledge and prosperity. The compatibility of partners and the type of life the individual will lead are also judged from the placement of Venus in the horoscope. As a planet, Venus is considered to be beneficial, feminine and gentle. Venus symbolizes the force of attraction in the universe. In human beings this attractive force manifests as love and beauty. When Venus is well placed in the chart, there are love, art, beauty and all the goodies of life that make life worth living. Venus rules Libra and Taurus, though its role in every sign is important. Like other planets, it also has its transits. In Libra, Venus is aesthetic and cultured. In Taurus, it is more earthy, materialistic and sensual. Venus rules the venous system, kidneys, urinary tract, throat, larynx, and is responsible for good looks. In short, Venus in Western astrology stands for comforts, arts, wealth, relationships, sex, decorations, luxuries and wealth. Life bestows on you all that you craved for. Windfalls, love and lucky breaks seek you out. Of course, astrology never compels. But, in this case, I wish it does! I shall end with a quote from Danielle LaPorte which is so relevant here: 'Guilt and joy are not part of the same equation.' Enjoy, says Ganesha. It is your time in the sun.

26 December: First Quarter in Aries

The moon is in Aries and there is fire in your belly. Nothing can stop you or get in the way. Soon, a new year will dawn. You have done the hard work and been through the drill. You have spent time in the sun and rain. You have seen life in all its colours. Now you reap the whirlwind. 'We pervert reason when we humiliate life ... man stopped respecting himself when he lost the respect due to his fellow creatures,' said José Saramago. You ensure that you live in gratitude. You are filled with love, generosity and kindness. What more is needed? Ganesha blesses you.

AQUARIUS

23 January–22 February

Ganesha's Master Key: Inventor, humanitarian and eccentric

'We must become bigger than we have been; more courageous, greater in spirit, larger in outlook. We must become members of a new race, overcoming petty prejudice, owing our ultimate allegiance not to nations but to our fellow men within the human community.'
— Haile Selassie

The important traits: Eccentric, erratic, rebellious; Shocking others to prove one's individuality; Breaking rules to assert one's independence; Having elitist attitudes; Seeking relief from boredom through socializing; Overly socializing at the expense of home life; Snobbish towards other groups; Gaining an understanding of group consciousness; Altruistic, humanitarian; Opening the heart through impersonal love and activity; Learning to give one's energy to the group instead of draining the group energy; Having a cooperative attitude towards other groups; Becoming dedicated to the ideals of impersonal love, universal brotherhood and world peace; Seeing all humanitarian groups as loosely connected; Working within a group towards a transpersonal ideal; Working with others to help bring in the New Age; Aligning one's personal will towards group goals; Motivated by the highest good of the group and the greatest good for the greatest number; Working to help build and maintain networks which bring people and groups together loosely; Lovingly accepting what each group member has to offer.

Your Beauty-scope: The Aquarius colour is aquamarine. Wear any dress/sari/apparel you like, but as far as possible stick to this colour for both charm and luck. I am afraid you will be unconventional in attire/make-up. Ash as a colour is also highly recommended. Apart from being rather unusual, it is not frequently used. It goes with your mobile features. And mobile features are your single, greatest asset. It gives you scope, to chop and change your hairstyle and make-up! Generally, you are tall. But you do suffer from the middle-age spread! The texture of the hair is good and fine. Hair combs and clips may be used to turn your rivals green with envy; and the smile is radiant, wry, mischievous. The eyes are wide open and laughing – a very positive personality, a huge plus point.

CENTRAL IDEA

Creative, Erratic, Unconventional, Honest, Open-minded

Albert Einstein said, 'The most beautiful experience we can have is the mysterious. It is the fundamental emotion which stands at the cradle of true art and true science.' Ganesha affirms that this Einstein quotation sums up 2017 for you impulsive, energetic, go-ahead Aquarians. Remember that the quote is from a scientist. Yet, it talks of the vision and mystery needed for true research. Einstein talks of the 'mysterious'. It could also mean genuine spirituality and intuition. The reason I have emphasized these aspects is that Jupiter, planet of wisdom (different from intelligence and cleverness), will be in your ninth angle of evolution. This is the crucible, the melting pot, the turning point, for you. Science will be wedding religion! Stupendous! The beginning of a new era! Happiness will be tricking in!

Just as the modern 'smart bombs' seek out targets before the release – and here I must hand it to technology and weaponry – so also Jupiter will seek out material comforts. Ganesha willing, my words will be prophetic. Jupiter will be with you in marriage, journey, collaborations, ceremony, social and financial advancement, property and land value, and anything with a foreign slant to it, which can include studies, business, immigration, know-how, crash sources, visits, holidaying or having a home away from home.

Astrological advice? Even if you are called a 'quark', which is now used to mean eccentric, oddball, strange, it would pay to follow your ideas, intuition. As said at the outset, this year God is with you! Also, absolutely top-drawer time for the five Ts: travel, trade, ties, telecommunication and transport. A few of you could have glimpses of God, a feeling that He is by your side, or He could come in a dream and manifest Himself to you. I mean, these are possibilities. I understand that people can also have delusions in this matter and mistake them for the real thing. The possibilities suggested by this placing of Jupiter are endless. Yup, Aquarians represent the New Age of technology and humanity. Technology + Humanity = Aquarius.

Poets, writers, researchers, teachers, doctors, healers, psychiatrists and health buffs, scientists and statisticians, cost accountants and librarians, philosophers and policemen, will all be truly inspired. It will be as if they are carried forward on a huge tidal wave of progress and action.

In 2017, Saturn will be in fine and friendly relationship with Jupiter. By old astrology your main planet is Saturn. By modern astrology your main planet is Uranus. Saturn will be the friend of both Uranus and Jupiter. Therefore, it will be a win-win situation or a double whammy for you. Result? You will be both successful and happy. My father says success and happiness may or may not go together. But in your case they will join hands in 2017.

You Aquarians have broad human sympathy and empathy. The strange part is that you can also be detached, impersonal and objective, and therefore research-minded. So you have much going for you. You are the spearhead of our New Age. I request you very humbly, but very strongly, to help and guide all those who need you. My father says this is the real reason for your very birth. This is your real mission in life.

For you Venus has a great impact on house, home, office, land, building, construction, parents, journey, religion, ceremony, spirituality. Venus will help you from 4 February to 2 April, 21 April to 21 May, 7 to 30 November, 14 October to 6 November and, finally, 6 June to 4 July. You Aquarians are lucky in property matters.

Mercury represents children, hobbies, entertainment, education, loans, funds, joint finance, perks and promotions for you. Mercury will be in your own sign from 7 to 25 February, favourable from 21 April to 15 May, 7 to 20 June, 30 September to 16 October, and 6 November 2017 to 10 January 2018.

Mars gives you position, power, pelf, prestige, trips and ties. Mars will be working for you from 20 July to 4 September, 23 October to 8 December (important), 21 April to 4 June (lucky), 29 January to 9 March (be ready to carry out your ideas and plans).

MONTHLY ROUND-UP

January: Despite expenses and interferences, property matters and family conditions do give some satisfaction, buying/selling, journeying are emphasized. **February:** Go all out for the kill, roaring like a lion, and emerge victorious in whatever you do. **March:** Finances and funds will be augmented. **April:** Contacts, contracts, socializing, friendship, good news, and you will make your presence felt. **May:** Home, house, family, parents, property, renovation/decoration, buying/selling, leasing, shopping. **June:** Plenty of fun and frolic; children add joy to your life, hobbies give deep satisfaction, sports and creativity fulfil you – a great ending to a busy beginning, concludes Ganesha. **July:** Work and projects could tell on your health unless you learn to relax. **August:** Love/hate, attachments/separations, journeys, a home away from home, marriage/divorce. **September:** Funds for work/home, hurts, buying/selling/investing, capital formation. **October:** Journeys, publicity, exaltation and execution, collaboration, a grand reaching out to people and places. **November:** Work is worship could well be your motto; for good measure, add duty and beauty. **December:** Love life, laughter and the law of chances operate in your favour. So if you feel like it, take a few chances.

Money: As said earlier, Aquarius, Leo, Scorpio and Taurus are the four great money signs by Western astrology. Ganesha and Amba Mata both say you will make good money.

Happiness Quota: I give you 87 per cent. Help the needy, say Ganesha and Allah. You can go up to 89 per cent then. My father says that happiness is in sharing.

MONTH BY MONTH

January: It is a great start to the year. Make the most of it. You are charged and powered. There are fun times with loved ones and a general rise in prestige and acclaim. You could start the year with an engagement or marriage, or even have an addition to the family. Mid-month sees you busy with domestic concerns. There are also indulgences and erratic behaviour. As the month ends, there is new intensity in your life. Those in the creative arts hog the limelight. Applause, love, passion, energy and enthusiasm garland you.

February: This is a wonderful period and you have the Midas touch. Love and longing stroke your heart. There is also sustained hard work. You sizzle with passion and your life takes on an ethereal hue. Mid-month sees overseas travel and many celebrations. You may cross continents. You are blessed with the spark of genius. As the month ends, you seek out new vistas, new directions, new dreams and new people. You also take to philanthropy and give yourself without a care. There are maudlin moments too.

March: Your monkey mind continues to be at play. There are also home fires that need fighting. You also need to settle business accounts. Mid-month sees more stability. You decide to hack the past from your life and move ahead with direction. If an old illness recurs, resort to immediate medical attention. As the month ends, you eye money and hope. There is new work that keeps you on your toes. You discard maudlin moments and walk the straight and narrow. There could be overseas holidays, immigration, renovation, redevelopment of property, new hobbies and interests, even a complete rejuvenation of body and soul.

April: There are many domestic engagements that crowd you. Love also embroils you in a tight game of hide-and-seek. You open yourself to different experiences as a new breeze seeps into every crevice of your heart and soul. New vistas open. Mid-month sees you get down to the hard slog. Money and honey beckon. Awards and rewards, accolades and applause crowd you. There is a rise in prestige and status. As the month ends, you have grand visions and the stamina and temperament to make miracles happen. Your heartstrings are also tugged. Your ideas are futuristic and your genius shines through.

May: There are powerful drives goading you on. There are expenses, love and longing, money and honey, and an upward surge in your affairs. Mid-month sees you continue on the drive of rapid personal advancement. You also seek answers that your soul needs. You want to evolve and grow as you seek out a higher consciousness. As the month ends, you reach out to people and places. There could be travel, at the very least a family holiday. There are thrilling times.

June: You make progress. New vistas open. Your fantasies have a rich twinge. You anticipate the future. As an inventor you are without parallel. Mid-month sees inflated expectations, excessive idealism and several disappointments. There are transformation, expansion, spiritual awakening and several new realizations. You grow as a person. As the month ends, you are busy tidying up. There are many domestic chores to attend to. Love also calls. You may attempt to break free from rules and regulations.

July: The monkey mind is flirting with demons. There could be travel and many purchases. You spend money recklessly. Your life is a kaleidoscope of colours running riot. Mid-month sees you back on terra firma. You have energy, zest and enthusiasm propelling you. This is also a period when you go in for a complete sartorial makeover. You could also change your habits. You look at yoga, meditation and natural healing. As the month ends, there is an upswing to life. You make clever investments as you prepare a nest egg. You dazzle with the brilliance of your genius. If you have been working on an invention there are eureka moments. Love life sizzles.

August: This is also a powerfully creative phase and those in the fine arts receive awards and rewards. There are several domestic chores also tugging at your time. Mid-month sees windfall gains. You also get involved in neighbourhood support groups and win kudos. As the month ends, there are expenses, travel, love and longing, purchases, investments, passions and ego drives. The energies are powerful. You aim for the stars. You send the right messages to the universe and it responds.

September: There are tantrums, mood swings, indulgences, escapist tendencies, and a web of lies that engulf you. Your world is in a tizzy. Mid-month sees you networking with the world as though it was coming to an end. There are parties and fun times too. Love succumbs to your charms. As the month ends, you are back on terra firma. This is a period packed with energy and you get down to good, old-fashioned hard work. You check out new horizons and take the tide at the flood. Dame Fortune favours the brave.

October: There could also be adventure, risk and gambling inherent in your manoeuvres. Your passions are stirred. Ego drives are huge. Mid-month, domestic calls get you down. The health of elders, siblings and children are your prime concern. There are trying moments. A range of fiscal affairs also call out to you. There is no dull moment. Mid-month sees new energy goading you on. This is a powerful period. Optimize it. As the month ends, your core strengths are accentuated.

November: There may not be flashes of brilliance but there is sustained hard work. You are hopeful and positive. The monkey mind is tethered and you are filled with courage, conviction and confidence. Mid-month sees you on a business expansion spree. This is a power-packed period. Love also engages you. As the month ends, you are well and truly on the path of realizing your dreams. Your creative instincts are at play. Media folk and those in the fine arts receive kudos. Accolades and applause drown you.

December: You connect with people from all over the world. You are filled with new realizations. Mid-month sees you go on a long journey, even a pilgrimage. You seek out spiritual masters, there is new learning and you evolve. You are also networking in frenzy and connecting with peoples from all over the world. As the month and year end, you are filled with many dreams for the future. Besides, you put your money where your mouth is. You mean business.

WEEKLY REVIEW (BY PHASES OF THE MOON)

5 January: First Quarter in Aries

Venus is in Aquarius from the first day of the year for just two days. It is here for a very short sojourn in your sign. It is a great start to the year. Make the most of it. Aquarians are among my favourite people, with their eccentricities, oddities, offbeat behaviour and remarkable vision. They are also kind-hearted and filled with compassion for humanity. It is in this context that the lines of the historian A.J.P. Taylor make sense: 'Conformity may give you a quiet life; it may even bring you to a university chair. But all change in history, all advance, comes from the nonconformists. If there had been no troublemakers, no dissenters, we should still be living in caves.' You are charged and powered. You have the moon in Aries and the beneficial influences of Venus. There are fun times with loved ones and a general rise in prestige and acclaim. As often discussed, Venus is the planet for love, romance, sex, beauty and good life. This is the planet of attraction, love, wealth, knowledge and prosperity. The compatibility of partners and the type of life the individual will lead are also judged from the placement of Venus in the horoscope. As a planet, Venus is considered to be beneficial, feminine and gentle. Venus symbolizes the force of attraction in the universe. In human beings, this attractive force manifests as love and beauty. When Venus is well placed in the chart, there are love, art, beauty and all the goodies of life that make life worth living. Venus rules Libra and

Taurus, though its role in every sign is important. Like other planets, it also has its transits. In Libra, Venus is aesthetic and cultured. In Taurus it is more earthy, materialistic and sensual. Venus rules the venous system, kidneys, urinary tract, throat, larynx, and is responsible for good looks. In short, Venus, in Western astrology, stands for comforts, arts, wealth, relationships, sex, decorations, luxuries and wealth. The simple rule is that when Venus is in your own sign you will get comforts and luxuries, ornaments and money. You could start the year with an engagement or marriage, or even have an addition to the family. The indications are strong. Ganesha blesses you.

12 January: Full Moon in Cancer

Let me quote Eckhart Tolle here, 'Acknowledging the good that you already have in your life is the foundation of all goodness.' There are many domestic concerns that take hold of your life. Children, the spouse, elders at home, near and dear ones, all call for your time and attention. It grates, but you make room for everyone. This is a wonderful time for educationists, counsellors and caregivers. You network furiously and connect with the wide world as though it were your backyard. There are also indulgences and erratic behaviour. Children are difficult to contain and you could be prone to depression. Manic and panic attacks may not be uncommon. Ganesha holds your hand. I have always maintained that Aquarians can have different personalities. Their ruling planet is Uranus. They can be shy, sensitive, gentle and patient, and also quite the opposite – exuberant, lively and exhibitionist. They are humane, sometimes ethereal, intuitive, imaginative and idealistic. What a heady mix! The mind boggles.

19 January: Last Quarter in Scorpio

There is new intensity in your life. Success garlands you. The moon is in Scorpio and your blind spots and underbelly are exposed. You don't care, but to near and dear ones it can be shocking. Your creativity and eccentric streaks win kudos. You are like Messi beguiling the opposition with deft feints and Quixotic sprints. You curve the ball into an empty net from an acute angle when you can hit it straight and with ease. There is deception and guile. You are the master of it all. If you are a spinner you rock the wickets with a teesra! The ball bounces and then decides where to turn, leaving the batsman in a trance. Ganesha watches.

28 January: New Moon in Aquarius

The new moon is in your sign and you come into your own. Those in the creative arts hog the limelight. There are applause, love, passion, energy and enthusiasm for all that you want to do. Money wanders in without much purpose and wanders off just as carelessly. You are in the throes of fantasy. Dreamland cuddles you in your waking hours. In love, you surprise the object of your desires with unconventional behaviour. You are now the master of the ambush. The special forces would love to have you in their ranks. Ganesha is flummoxed too.

4 February: First Quarter in Taurus

'When you realize that nothing is lacking, the whole world belongs to you,' said Lao-tzu. The moon is in Taurus, bringing you much-needed stability. You work out your finances and get down to balance sheet management. Mercury is also in your sign from 7 to 25 February. This is a wonderful period and you have the Midas touch. Like I always do, let me explain the significance of Mercury, as it helps enrich the context. Mercury, the mighty, all-powerful planet, favours travels, meetings, conferences, interviews, trips, more brainpower, contacts, communication, correspondence and contracts. Mercury has a special connection with the circuits of the brain. Chess, crossword and other such games belong to Mercury. Also, short-distance runners and spin bowlers are controlled by Mercury. Mercury, in short, is the ambassador and salesman of the zodiac. Mercury is the symbol of news, views, messages, interviews, contacts, communications, travel and transport. Mercury gives an impetus to all of the above in the sun sign where it is located. Messages and trips are the special characteristics of Mercury. To paraphrase the Bard, take the tide at the flood and it will lead to fortune. Use your free will and optimize the largesse of the cards being delivered to you. Remember, astrology never compels. But these are the strong indicators. Ganesha is happy for you. Love and longing stroke your heart. As I always do, let me tell you about the international celebrities that you share your birthday with. They include game changers like Federico Fellini, Christian Dior, Jack Nicklaus, Humphrey Bogart, W.S. Maugham, Virginia Woolf, Wolfgang Mozart, Lewis Carroll, Anton Chekov, Ramakrishna, Charles Darwin, Abraham Lincoln, Mark Spitz, Boris Pasternak, Jules Verne, James Dean, Ronald Reagan, Norman Mailer, Sir Francis Bacon, James Joyce, Anna Pavlova and Yoko Ono, among others. As you can see, you are in excellent company. Chin up!

11 February: Full Moon in Leo

The full moon is in Leo and you are consumed by a new zest. There is a lot on your plate. There is sustained hard work calling out to you. You are also consumed in the throes of amour. You roast in its gravy like well-marinated Mughlai cuisine. You sizzle with passion and your life takes on an ethereal hue. The object of your desire is flummoxed by your passion. Money flows in and flows out but you are not perturbed. Right now, nothing makes sense as you play the field. You are lost in the vicious coil of the green anaconda in the Amazon jungles. In simple language, you are in love. I haven't lived so long to not know what love does to people! Ganesha watches. He knows that this too shall pass.

18 February: Last Quarter in Sagittarius

There is a lot of movement in your life. There could be overseas travel and many celebrations. You may cross continents to meet with loved ones. This is also your birth period and the signs are propitious. You meet up with old friends and lovers. You wander down memory lane and shed a quiet tear. It's like rain on parched land; these softer emotions on display nourish and water your soul. You look for more meaning to your life and meet up with enlightened masters. There is growth and progress on all fronts. Genius has lapses proportionate to its triumphs, while mediocrity is always at its best. You are blessed with the spark of genius now. Ganesha is impressed.

26 February: New Moon in Pisces

'Understanding a person does not mean condoning; it only means that one does not accuse him as if one were God or a judge placed above him,' said Erich Fromm, psychoanalyst and author. The new moon is in Pisces and you seek out new vistas, new directions, new dreams and new people. Someone from another culture influences you deeply. You take to philanthropy and give yourself without a care as you spend quality time and money with the less fortunate. Like Mother Teresa, you want to give until it hurts. There are maudlin moments and many regrets. You have to shake it off like a puppy doused in the rain, and move on. That is the only way. Spilt milk can never be recovered. Ganesha agrees and urges you to step on the gas. Remember, we have many influences working on us, from biorhythms to circumstances to even events and people who crowd our minds. The drunken monkey on a tripwire, or the mind, influences every cell.

5 March: First Quarter in Gemini

Often the influences of one week coalesce into another and this can happen for weeks on end. Your monkey mind continues to be at play. There are home fires that need fighting and fences made to keep out prying neighbours. You also need to settle business accounts. But your mind is on the wings of poesy, in fantasy land, eagerly eyeing drama, histrionics and a gamut of complicated emotions. You enter altercations and disputes with loved ones because you erroneously believe that the world owes you a living. You make it a point to cut your nose to spite your face; you slice the very branch that you are seated on. Some of you may even believe that your families have failed you and let you down when it mattered most. Use your free will and eject immediately from the state you are in. It does you no good. The only moment in your hands is right now. Grab it and nurture it. Do not wallow in yesterday, says Ganesha.

12 March: Full Moon in Virgo

The full moon is in Virgo and there is more stability in your life now. You decide to hack the past from the present and move ahead with direction and ferocity. You decide to count pennies; at least it is not wasted effort. You look at work with more seriousness and attempt to come out of the victim syndrome that has engulfed you so treacherously. Some of you may take to counselling. If an old illness recurs, resort to immediate medical attention. Ganesha watches.

20 March: Last Quarter in Capricorn

'Life doesn't have to be hard work, driving ambition, and exacting plans. If our inner nature is the nature of the universe, why do we have to struggle?' says Deepak Chopra. The moon is in Capricorn and you eye money and hope. There is new work that keeps you on your toes. If nothing else, hard work, at the very least, keeps the mind and soul occupied. Plus, more money in the bank need not be scoffed at. If you have been bad with accounts, this is the time to sort it out. You discard maudlin moments and walk the straight and narrow. You make every effort to straighten your boat and it works. Remember, there is no one to blame for your situation but yourself. You are the centre of the universe. You dwell in your mind. Change the perspective and your life gets a heave-ho. You also take a conscious decision not to have social intercourse with emotional vultures. You are on firm ground now and Ganesha is happy.

28 March: New Moon in Aries

The new moon is in Aries and you pummel away. This is a powerful period and you can make miracles happen. There could be overseas holidays, immigration, renovation, redevelopment of property, new hobbies and interests, even a complete rejuvenation of body and soul. Your plate is full and overflowing like Hyderabadi dum biryani. You de-clutter, wipe away the cobwebs, do a spring cleaning and optimize your life. You realize that you have been moping for too long. Now you decide to strike. The iron is hot and the sun is shining. Like Genghis Khan, you go for the kill. Ganesha blesses you.

3 April: First Quarter in Cancer

'The mystery of human existence lies not in just staying alive, but in finding something to live for,' said Fyodor Dostoyevsky. The moon is in Cancer and there are many domestic engagements that crowd you. If a child has left home for higher studies you feel lost and lonely. This is a passing phase and you will soon get over it. You cling to straws in the hope that you will be somewhat salvaged. Aquarians are the eccentrics of the zodiac. They are inventive geniuses, mavericks who don't fit in. This is the rub. Once you open up and get aware of your enormous potential, even the stars will kowtow to you. Love embroils you in a tight game of hide-and-seek. You have been on this path before and it has given you nothing but sorrow. You know what will happen but you enter the arena of amour with eyes open. Ganesha watches.

11 April: Full Moon in Libra

You continue with your love tryst. There may be several players, certainly more than one. You are unconventional, unorthodox and offbeat. There is no predicting what you will do next, though, as your favourite astrologer, I do my best. You are faced with several choices. Money slips through your fingers as you go with the flow. You open yourself to different experiences as a new breeze seeps into every crevice of your heart and soul. New vistas open and you realize that the world is indeed a complicated place, much more bizarre than you could aspire to be or imagined. That is a laugh, says Ganesha. I agree.

19 April: Last Quarter in Capricorn

Finally, you roll up your sleeves and get down to the hard slog. You are like Chris Gayle after a series of debacles. Now you straighten your bat and show the world what a cricketing onslaught really means as every ball ricochets from the boundary walls and the world's best bowlers scurry for cover. You are at your destructive best. I am reminded of Friedrich Nietzsche who said, 'He who has a why to live for can bear almost any how.' According to Nietzsche, the first step to finding sustainable happiness is to find something that is essential in our lives that will not only support us emotionally but will also help us overcome whatever struggles we encounter along the way. You are in that mode now and are propelled by powerful energy. Money and honey beckon. Awards and rewards, accolades and applause crowd you. There is a rise in prestige and status. You are now a person of renown. Your eccentricities are accepted as genius and you are the toast of the peer group. Emboldened by it all, you plunge into more work and attract more rewards. Ganesha is speechless.

26 April: New Moon in Taurus

The new moon is in Taurus and you continue batting on the front foot on an easy-paced wicket. You have grand visions and the stamina and temperament to make miracles happen. Though you have an infallible feeling for the fine, unnoticed sensitivities of others, and your heart strings are easily tugged, you don't lose track of your goal. Your philanthropic zeal is suitably camouflaged for the moment. Ego drives and passions are in check and you are amiable. You are a great team player and win brownie points. Your ideas are futuristic and out of this world as your genius shines through. Professors, scientists, IT professionals and those working with new ideas and designs are in great demand. Ganesha wishes you well.

3 May: First Quarter in Leo

You are pushing ahead on all cylinders. You don't spare the horses. There are powerful drives goading you on as the moon in Leo becomes your ally without quarrel. There are expenses, love and longing, money and honey, and an upward surge in your affairs. There are multiple influences at play as you burn the candle at both ends. Life is calling out to you and you are ready for the dance. Ganesha is pleased.

10 May: Full Moon in Scorpio

The full moon is in Scorpio as you continue on the drive of rapid personal advancement. You are seeking answers that your soul needs. They are profound and difficult. There are no ready-made solutions for your quick-fire or deliberate queries. You go looking for a guru and pore over the classical texts. Tanta, mantra and yantra fascinate you. There are also powerful sexual desires that tear at you. Use your free will with wisdom, suggests Ganesha. Tread carefully lest you commit some unpardonable folly in your haste and carelessness. Ganesha watches.

19 May: Last Quarter in Aquarius

I love this quote from Henry D. Thoreau and wish to share it with my readers. 'There is a subtle magnetism in nature, which, if we unconsciously yield to it, will direct us aright.' This is not only powerful but is a truism that is relevant to you in the mood you are in now. The moon is in your sign and you want to evolve and grow. You are seeking out a higher consciousness. You are in a tearing hurry and want all the answers as of yesterday. But, remember, you will be answered only when the time is ripe. You will have to be patient and await your turn in the giant cosmic pattern of life. To paraphrase a doha of the great poet Kabir, the plant will only flower in season and not when you pour buckets of water to nourish it. On the flip side are fun times with the family. Ganesha blesses you.

25 May: New Moon in Gemini

The new moon is in Gemini and you are reaching out to people and places. There could be travel, at the very least a family holiday. You could be fed up with the status quo and the routine and are waiting to burst forth like pollen from its pod. You use every marvel of technology to broadcast your views. You want to be heard and also taken seriously. You look at the world and what is becoming of it with gravitas. There are profitable personal and professional transactions as you meet up with people from different cultures, even if it is just a virtual exchange. There are thrilling times as your mind wanders through outer space like a UFO. Ganesha smiles.

1 June: First Quarter in Virgo

You clamp down on the monkey mind and get down to hard work. You make progress. New vistas open up and a person from another culture plays a significant role in your life. You flirt with different shades of success as though you were sampling what is on offer like a tea taster attached to plantations. David Schwartz says in his book, 'Success is determined not so much by the size of one's brain as it is by the size of one's thinking.' Your fantasies have a rich twinge. You anticipate the future, you beckon trends. As an inventor you are without parallel. You send the right messages to the universe and it responds with abundance. Ganesha is thrilled.

9 June: Full Moon in Sagittarius

The full moon is in Sagittarius and money runs out of your pocket like a rusty Mumbai municipal tap that has sprung a leak. 'Crave for a thing, you will get it. Renounce the craving, the object will follow you by itself,' said Swami Sivananda. My readers may notice that I pepper my predictions with quotes. You have been following me for years and I want you to absorb not only the astrological forecast but also my knowledge and learning. As long as I am able to, let me share my knowledge with you gracefully, expecting nothing but your love in return. In this period there are inflated expectations, excessive idealism and several disappointments. As Swami Sivananda said, renounce the craving and you will get what you want, if you really need it. Your plate is overflowing with goodies of all kinds. There is transformation, expansion, spiritual awakening and several new realizations. New vistas open, old doors shut. You grow as a person. Ganesha watches. That is more than enough. I am a Ganesha devotee and know what I am saying!

17 June: Last Quarter in Pisces

You are not one to suck in your tears, but in this period you may shed them copiously. It may be a chance meeting with someone or a movie or play, or even a book that you read that takes you down memory lane. You travel fast over a bumpy road as though the brakes have failed. There are maudlin moments of regret. You wish you had worked your past out better. Of course, spilt milk remains just that and no amount of moping will get it back into the tetrapack all pasteurised and ready to drink. Your intrinsic idealism is aroused and you take to allocating time and resource for the less fortunate. You take a break from routine and hit the hills for 'me' time. Life will unveil its plans for you in due course. You have to be ready for the startling changes in store. Brace yourself. Ganesha holds your hand.

24 June: New Moon in Cancer

The new moon is in Cancer and you are busy tidying up. There are many domestic chores to attend to. Love calls, and you have to apportion time for that too. 'Let your inner sunshine overcome the passing haze of discontent,' said Dodinsky. You may also attempt to break free from rules and regulations. You could get moody, irritable and neurotic. Your shadow side and blind spots are highly inflammable. There are temper tantrums and altercations and scuffles. You brook no opposition and flare up at the slightest provocation. Count to ten, as they say in all the yoga books, and think a million times before retaliating. You don't want to be scurrying for cover from the law. Ganesha leads you away from the danger zone. You are in safe hands.

1 July: First Quarter in Libra

'The most terrifying thing is to accept oneself absolutely,' said Dr Carl Jung, the renowned psychotherapist. The moon is in Libra and you are spoilt for choice. The monkey mind is flirting with demons. There could be travel and many purchases. You spend money recklessly. Love storms your bastion and you succumb. There could be fun times at home, including an addition to the family. Children bring joy but they may also be leaving home for greener pastures and the joy is tinged with sadness. Your life is a kaleidoscope of colours running riot. Ganesha watches.

9 July: Full Moon in Capricorn

You are back on terra firma and there is balance. The full moon is in Capricorn and you have energy, zest and enthusiasm propelling you. You get down to the hard slog. There is business expansion on foreign shores if you are dealing in any produce that can be marketed globally. Freelancers grab blue chip accounts and there is a general upswing in life. Money and power are the new demigods. Love consorts with you but it is nothing of consequence. You play the field without a care in the world. You are unable to tread the status quo and may look at alternative arrangements that buck it. Ganesha holds your hand as you steer a new path.

16 July: Last Quarter in Aries

'Art is the elimination of the unnecessary,' said Pablo Picasso. The moon is in Aries and you are moving ahead with the speed of a gazelle escaping a predator in the Serengeti National Park. In the process, you junk all that is not necessary and cut the flab to the bone. This is also a period when you go in for a complete sartorial makeover. You could also change your habits and trim your waist size before the doctor does it for you. You look at yoga, meditation and natural healing. You give self-discipline and a better body image a hard and serious look. You want to better yourself at all costs. The man in the ring is your shadow and you don't like it. Ganesha inspires you as you inch towards inner and outer evolution.

23 July: New Moon in Leo

The new moon is in Leo and you continue on the upswing in life. You go about making radical changes. There are clever investments as you prepare a nest egg. You could also be taking the family on a much-needed holiday. On the flip side, you could also join a charitable organization, take it to new heights and stake a claim to be embalmed for posterity. Please remember that we all have different personalities and differ from one another, like our fingerprints. So astrological predictions can influence different people differently based on circumstances, biorhythms and a host of other factors. Free will, which I will never discount, also plays a part, along with religious beliefs, etc. Astrology never compels, but it does provide the general idea. In this period you are receptive to new breeze. You rein in ego drives and passions and accommodate disparate and divergent opinions. As a result, you hoard brownie points. Ganesha smiles.

30 July: First Quarter in Scorpio

'Sometimes I go about in great pity for myself, and all the while a great wind is bearing me across the sky,' is an Ojibwa saying that I love. It is so simple and yet so profound. Its profundity lies squarely in its simplicity. The moon is in Scorpio and you are sizzling with intensity and charm. Your hormones could also be jumping all over the landscape and there could be indiscreet alliances that wreck your stability. Your reputation may come in for discussion. Ganesha urges you to hold your horses lest you run into trouble which can easily be avoided. You dazzle with the brilliance of your genius. If you have been working on an invention, there are eureka moments, and accolades are heaped on you. Love life sizzles; success is also a great aphrodisiac. Those in committed relationships take intimacy to delirious heights.

7 August: Full Moon in Aquarius

The full moon is in your sign and you are filled with philanthropic intent. 'If we have no peace, it is because we have forgotten that we belong to each other,' said Mother Teresa. You realize that very well and give of yourself without quarrel, to causes that enrich mankind. This is also a powerfully creative phase and those in the fine arts receive awards and rewards, my favourite phrase. There are several domestic chores tugging at your time. Family members may complain of ill health and you are pushed to the wall. Children may also be leaving home for higher studies. There are also strains of marital discord swallowing your peace. Your plate is overflowing. The caterpillar has to break through the cocoon to become a butterfly. In the process, it also strengthens its wings. You are on the path of evolution. With each challenge, you get to know yourself better. Ganesha walks with you.

15 August: Last Quarter in Taurus

There are stability and rapid growth in all areas of your life. There are windfall gains; you could win the lottery. If you are a gambling man, there are lucky breaks. Of course, I don't encourage you to gamble. These are just the indicators. This is a period when you are in tune with your feelings. Financially you are on solid ground, and emotionally you feel secure and loved. Jung, the psychoanalyst, always maintained that the inner life is as important as the outer, and if the inner life is unexplored it could show up in different ways. He is bang on. Your inner life is humming nicely and you are filled with good feelings for others. You get involved in neighbourhood support groups and win kudos. 'Love until it hurts,' said Mother Teresa. You listen to her words with the devotion of a dog to its master. Ganesha is impressed.

21 August: New Moon in Leo

The new moon is in Leo and there are expenses, travel, love and longing, purchases, investments, passions and ego drives, and some curry that slips off the plate and soils your clothes. This is a time for growth. The energies are powerful. Use it well, urges Ganesha. The monkey mind pushes you to think and act large. You aim for the stars. If in love, you will stop at nothing. Just ensure that you don't go overboard and cause harm. Violence in passion is not uncommon these days. Do not cause harm to the object of your desire or to yourself. This is also a passing phase and when you are done with it, hindsight will teach you many lessons. It is all a part of the mosaic of life. Rein in your mind and you rein in your life. We live in the mind. Try it. Change your thoughts, change your perspective, and notice how dramatically your life changes.

29 August: First Quarter in Sagittarius

The moon is in Sagittarius and you are in a zillion time zones all at once. You want to be Superman and Spiderman combined. 'I think and think and think, I've thought myself out of happiness one million times, but never once into it,' said the writer Jonathan Safran Foer. Time flies and waits for no one; it simply doesn't have the time! You are moving ahead fast and furious like a panther using the cover of darkness to cull its prey. There is stealth and cunning in your movements. There is also success. You give it a hundred per cent. You are like Virat Kohli. You induce success to be your handmaiden with your earnestness. You send the right messages to the universe and it responds. You could well be the new improved incarnation of Superman! Ganesha is thrilled.

6 September: Full Moon in Pisces

'I would rather follow a dream than wallow in regret,' said Nancy Fursetzer. The full moon is in Pisces and your imagination gets kindled like a forest fire. There are tantrums, mood swings, indulgences, escapist tendencies, and a web of lies that engulf you. Others may set a trap for you or you may just set a trap for yourself. For some reason, you are not able to come to terms with your inner being. It frightens you as much as it frightens your loved ones. You may need professional help. You walk down the thorny road to maudlin times and it does your mood no good. Youngsters have a particularly harrowing time. Love life screeches to a halt as though the traffic light just changed to red without a notice period and you are pounding the speed limit. Your world is in a tizzy. On the plus side is creative genius. Which side are you on? Ganesha holds your hand.

13 September: Last Quarter in Gemini

You are networking with the world as though it was coming to an end. You get on to all the social networking sites and scream for all that you are worth. Eventually, you are heard above the din. 'Be selfish, be generous,' said the Dalai Lama. You don't need prodding. You unselfishly give of yourself. There are parties and fun times. Those in creative careers sparkle. If you can rein in the monkey mind, miracles will storm your being as your creativity unfolds with spectacular flamboyance. You play the field as love succumbs to your charms with the ease of a rat being lured into a trap. Ganesha watches with excitement. He knows the script in advance but will not let on.

20 September: New Moon in Virgo

'If you can dream it, you can do it,' said Walt Disney. The new moon is in Virgo and you are touched by balance. You are back on terra firma and are faced with all the ups and downs of everyday living. You have to get on with life and the challenges it throws your way with regularity. You have to get up from the count and eyeball your opponent in the ring, even if you are bleeding from a wounded eyelid. It is the only way out for us mortals. There is no escape from the drudgery of existence. We have to sweat it out in the summer and shovel the snow aside in the winter. This is a period packed with energy. Swing it your way like the legendary Babe Ruth in the baseball league. Go for the home run as there is no other choice. You realize all this and get down to good, old-fashioned hard work. I don't have to add here that you come out trumps. Ganesha applauds.

28 September: First Quarter in Capricorn

You are moving ahead with both eyes on the goal. No quarter given, no quarter asked. That seems to be your motto as you engage in a ruthless, emotionless assault on the title. If this were the Olympic Games, you would have won the gold. But sport and life have a lot in common; both have winners and losers and also-rans and, at times, a mere nanosecond can subvert victory into defeat. 'Everyone can be great, because everyone can serve,' said Dr Martin Luther King Jr. You check out new horizons and take the tide at the flood. Dame Fortune favours the brave. You strike when the iron is hot and romp home smiling. You wear the laurels of victory with aplomb. Ganesha is happy for you.

5 October: Full Moon in Aries

The full moon is in Aries and you continue on the ascent. There could also be adventure, risk and gambling inherent in your manoeuvres. There are love and longing. Your passions are stirred. Ego drives are huge. If you are tolerant of others it is because of a powerfully imposed self-discipline. You could easily flip in the mood you are in now. New vistas open and you indulge the new breeze. Someone from another culture, maybe even of the same gender, may play an important role in your life. Genders are blurred now and the new world gives expression to different forms of longing. So I leave it open. I must also allow new ideas to invade the crevices of my mind. We all have to be open to change. It is the law of life. Ganesha holds your hand. In the backdrop, the church bells pound away, and your soul chimes in rhythm.

12 October: Last Quarter in Cancer

The moon is in Cancer and you are in several places at once. In simple words, you are feeling unsettled. Domestic calls get you down. Like a novice pitted against Olympian Sushil Kumar, you try hard to wrestle the issues to the ground, but it's a lost cause. The health of elders, siblings and children are your prime concern. You do your best and finally leave it in the hands of a higher call. There are trying moments and you feel like giving up. Finally, you just accept your fate; it doesn't hurt as bad now. Acceptance is a form of deliverance. 'Being willing to be a fool is one of the first wisdoms,' says Chögyam Trungpa. This is a learning period and you decide to be flexible. It helps. Along with this are a range of fiscal affairs that call out to you. Investments, stocks, realty, loans, inheritance, buying, selling, financial and legal issues grab your eyeballs. You are on your toes. There is no dull moment. Ganesha journeys with you.

19 October: New Moon in Libra

'Breathe in the joy and let it imprint on your cells,' says Danielle LaPorte. The new moon is in Libra and there is new energy goading you on. This is a powerful period. Optimize it. You are ambitious and look at business expansion seriously. There are expenses and travel. The domestic scene is more settled, but you want to move on, even if there is disquiet. The waters may be muddy and there is no point hanging around a stagnant pond. As I write this, even the great Ganga is going to be cleaned up in one of the most ambitious projects of the government. Yes, the water must flow and so should you. Movement is the master key to life. It is the only education. Ganesha blesses you.

27 October: First Quarter in Aquarius

The moon is in your sign and your core strengths are accentuated. You are in evolution mode. You look for greater meaning to your life and want to get out of the rut. You want to eject people in your life who have become emotional vampires. Anyone who usurps your time and wastes it is given the heave-ho. If you have given of yourself and your resources freely in the past, you put a full stop to it. You realize that time is running out and you will have to change direction if you expect to keep the momentum going till the very end. To paraphrase Charles Darwin, it is the species that adapts to change that survives. It has been the secret of the human race. Family life rambles along without sparks. Monogamy touches peaks of boredom. Of course, like I always say, astrology never compels. Ganesha empowers you.

4 November: Full Moon in Taurus

The full moon is in Taurus and there is balance. This is a period of profit and value. Use it well. You plug the leaks and get down to the hard slog. There may not be flashes of brilliance but there is sustained hard work for sure. It is perspiration that accounts for genius. You are hopeful and positive. The monkey mind is tethered and you are filled with courage, conviction and confidence. You are also aggressive and adaptable. Ganesha is impressed. You are charming and diplomatic. You are selfish enough to know how to get what you want. You take short cuts and, possibly, throw ethics to the bin. Ambition is a virtue but avarice certainly isn't. Need I say more?

10 November: Last Quarter in Leo

The moon is in Leo and you are on a money-making and business expansion spree. You want to be a person of consequence and you know that money talks the loudest in the circles that you currently inhabit. 'Never start a business just to "make money". Start a business to make a difference,' said Marie Forleo, the marketing leader. This is a good cue. This is a power-packed period. Love also engages you in a deadly hold. You are choked by amour. Your heart leaps to the skies and its thud reverberates and echoes in magnified Dolby sound. You are transported to new realms of ecstasy and fantasy. You paint gossamer baubles in the sky. Your entire being is revamped, rejuvenated, renovated and refurbished by a combine of hormones and emotions. I have lived long and know the enormous power of love. It can heal and give birth with the same potency with which it can destroy. Go for it, I say. Take the risk. Give it all that you have got. There is just one life. If your heart sings like a nightingale you are blessed; believe me, it doesn't happen often. In a world of terror, despair and subterfuge, it is better to be choked by the invisible chords of amour. Ganesha agrees wholeheartedly.

18 November: New Moon in Scorpio

'In order that people may be happy in their work, these three things are needed: they must be fit for it; they must not do too much of it; and they must have a sense of success in it,' said John Ruskin, author, art critic, and social reformer. Nothing succeeds like success and you are well and truly on the path of realizing your dreams. The new moon is in Scorpio and you are packed with a rare intensity. There is drive and ambition and you are able to give life to your dreams. You may also take the object of your desires to the next level. There could be engagements, marriages, additions to the family and many anniversary celebrations. There are money and honey. Ganesha is happy for you.

26 November: First Quarter in Pisces

The moon is in Pisces and your sensitivities are aroused. Your creative instincts are at play. Media folk and those in the fine arts receive kudos. Accolades and applause drown you in their whispers. On the flip side, you could also feel lost and without direction. If, somewhere along the way, you haven't updated your preferences, you could be losing out on big game. There is some inner disquiet that is bothering you. Worse, you cannot put a finger on it. You may need to revamp your life and recall the mojo. You want to be like the cheetah in the Serengeti Nation Park, and not an ageing sloth. Ganesha holds your hand.

3 December: Full Moon in Gemini

The full moon is in Gemini and you are connecting with people from all over the world as the year is slowly coming to an end. You have been through a lot. If you engage in 'me' time, and mindfully recall the events of the year, you will realize that you have been very blessed. The cosmos has conspired to elevate your life and it is necessary to be grateful for all the goodies showered on you with such generosity. If you have walked down maudlin corridors and camped there for prolonged periods, you realize that it has been mere indulgence and escapism. You have actually been given much more than you had bargained for. This realisation is good enough, says Ganesha. I agree.

10 December: Last Quarter in Virgo

As I have often mentioned, the tendencies of one week often slip into another. This is a more stable period and you are back on terra firma, not only planning for the year ahead but also getting down to action mode. Sa'di says, 'The sun and moon, and the rain and clouds, all are busy to prepare your food for you, and it is unfair indeed if you do not appreciate it in thanksgiving.' You have worked this over in your head and heart many times over, and fully agree. This is party time but you are introspective. You may go on a long journey, even a pilgrimage. You seek out spiritual masters and grow as a person. There is new learning and you evolve as you allow new breeze into your soul. Ganesha blesses you.

18 December: New Moon in Sagittarius

The new moon is in Sagittarius and there is sustained travel. You are some kind of modern-day Marco Polo. You are also networking in a frenzy and connecting with peoples from all over the world. But you also realize that the world is round and every human being is intrinsically the same. You have been on a learning curve and there is new knowledge; that is consolation enough. I am reminded of Homer's Odyssey. After his wild adventures, all Odysseus wants is to come home and bounce his grandson on his knee. You feel more settled now and your life purrs along happily. Ganesha is delighted.

26 December: First Quarter in Aries

This is the last week of the year and I want to end it with a quote from a person I greatly admire. 'Let us remember: one book, one pen, one child, one teacher can change the world,' said Nobel Prize winner Malala Yousafzai. The moon is in Aries and you are filled with many dreams for the future. Besides, you put your money where your mouth is. You mean business. The party boys and girls also call out to you. You have also got new dancing shoes. Yes, you hit the floor with abandon. Ganesha joins you in the festivities.

PISCES

23 February–22 March

Ganesha's Master Key: Dreamer, escape artist, spiritualist

The great Albert Einstein and Steve Jobs were both mighty Pisceans. They set the world on fire and changed the course of history. To Einstein life was sacred, mysterious and beautiful. Let it be so to you also, sensitive and shy Pisceans.

The important traits are: Ungrounded, 'spaced out'; Lacking direction, vague; Feeling guilty; Having difficulty saying 'no'; Depressed, self-pitying; Desiring to escape; Gullible, overly sensitive; Non-committal, non-aggressive, subservient; Having fanatical beliefs, addicted; Compassionate, flexible, perceptive; Loving wisely; Understanding things in a metaphysical way; Understanding that we can create our own realities; Discriminating between self-initiated energies and those initiated by others; Being able to release unwanted energies which are absorbed from outside oneself; Discriminating between what is conducive to spiritual self-growth and what is not; Being aware of the limitations of ingrained belief systems and seeking to destroy them; Destroying outworn beliefs which are inhibiting growth and expansion; Helping people rise, and destroying old thought systems; Abandoning useless conventions to create a wider reality; Breaking up crystallized cultural attitudes and philosophies; Replacing absolute faith with intuitive wisdom; Getting rid of that which is blocking deeper and wider perception.

Your Beauty-scope: Mind over matter could cause actual physical changes in you, making you look beautiful one day and absolutely a drag the very next. So learn to be cheerful even if it means extra effort. In Pisceans, there are two distinct types. The first has a wishy-washy look. The second has character. Environmental incompatibility affects you, and no make-up in the wide world can hide it ever! The features have a fish-like outline, and the upper lip is generally slightly pouting and sensitive. Play it up! As the complexion is pallid, the skin soft, I personally suggest either very bright and fun make-up or a very subtle one, depending on the mood you are in! The hands are usually soft, sensitive, conical. They should never be without a pearl, a bloodstone, even an emerald, or at least a coral, preferably violet or mauve. The feet are often splayed, and as they give physical trouble too, good care should be taken of them. The face is large, extremely quick in reflecting moods; the eyes bright and steady.

CENTRAL IDEA

Moody, Hypersensitive, Loving, Creative, Secretive

Ganesha says there will be a tremendous push for getting on in life, getting desired results! It will work for you in the following ways: better health, more money, an opportunity to job switch; transact business or try your luck games of chance; religious rites and pujas for the living and the dead will need to be performed.

The details which I need to spell out are: Finances, money and legal matters, whether dealing with wills and legacies, real estate and codicil, insurance, joint finances, transits and inheritance, will be of utmost importance and occupy centre stage in your activities and preoccupy you. That is not to say that you do not indulge in power plays, passionate encounters, a bit of a speculation – in short, spills and thrills. Raising capital, buying and selling stocks and shares, or just making canny investments, shopping for long-term gains, will all thrill and interest you this month. Ganesha sums it all up: money, vitamin M, filthy lucre, as the ancients called it, will excite you and more importantly befriend you. Jupiter, the money planet, is responsible for bonding with money. That is my own expression! Like it? Matters pertaining to insurance, finance, buying/selling/representation could be important and successful. You could even start a new venture. The theme is opportunities for business – tenders, contracts, hypothecation. Loans can go in your favour. Taxes may need to be paid and expenses met. Joint finances, securities, shares, debentures, instruments of negotiation, wills, codicil, moving home, pujas, tantra and mantra, pilgrimages, havans and offerings are all included in the orbit.

The main purpose is to help you use the money of others. Examples are joint finance, inheritance, gratuity, provident fund, funds, trusts, loans, taxes, chit funds, lotteries, gambling and casinos, trading and commission, buying and selling. Jupiter is a planet of expansion and generosity.

Therefore, you must learn two things: 1) to save money and 2) finding new ways and outlets for gain.

By Western astrology, Saturn will be in Sagittarius till 20 December 2017. Saturn will help you to perform very well and execute your plans to perfection. In simple words, Saturn will make you a doer, a man of action. Saturn will stimulate you and motivate you into a flurry of energy and activity.

By the old school of astrology, Jupiter is your main planet. By the new school of astrology, Neptune is your main planet. Saturn will not be in a good relationship with Neptune, but Saturn will be in a wonderful relationship with Jupiter and Uranus. Therefore, this year you will have a chance or opportunity for a job hop or change or promotion or perks. Also, thanks to Uranus, you may get into sudden money. I am sure you know very well that money is always welcome because money helps you to help yourself and others too. Money is a double header. Be happy about it. But there is a downward side or slide to Saturn. If you become greedy and power-hungry and trample over others, you will be finally knocked out, suffer a great defeat or fall. Ganesha therefore suggests, and suggests very strongly, use your power wisely and well. That is the real secret of joy and happiness. Yes, this is what my father has told me a thousand times and, therefore, it has sunk into my brain, as we say in our Indian English. All of us have a right to laugh at our own self. It really clears the air and balances our life. Pride, prejudice and pomposity are the three Ps which will destroy us.

Venus has control over your trips and ties, communication and contacts, loans, funds and investments, capital raising, buying and selling. Venus will be favourable from 3 January to 3 February, 3 to 27 April, 5 July to 25 August, 14 October to 6 November, 25 December 2017 to 17 January 2018.

Mercury has sway and power over your marriage, collaborations, house, home, office, godown, parents and in-laws. Mercury helps you in every possible way from 26 February to 13 March, 11 January to 6 February; 21 June to 5 July, 13 September to 18 October, and finally, 17 October to 5 November. Be sharp. Be bold. Kick and kiss your way to greatness and glory, as my father would say.

Food, finance, family, journeys and ceremonies, advertisements and publicity, preparing blueprints for future action; yes, all these come under the direct influence of Mars. 1 to 27 January is action time. Money time is from 28 January to 9 March. The period from 5 June to 19 July is for romance, finance, hobbies, children, entertainment and the good life. From 21 April to 4 June the period is for renovation, decoration, buying and selling of property, be it office, house or warehouse. Let me, however, make it absolutely clear that I am not God. Astrology is not perfect and quite a few events may or may not really happen. My father always says honesty and integrity gives honey and money.

MONTHLY ROUND-UP

January: A golden harvest for the trouble taken and the seeds planted, and that says it all. **February**: Expenses, work, contracts, secret affairs, heart illuminations, though there could be inflammation of your (foot) sole. **March**: Wishes granted, rewards realized, wish-fulfilment is possible; you will feel wonderful and strong, ready to take on all comers. **April**: Finance, food, family, and that does mean entertainment, amusement, doing the social rounds. **May**: Gains, friends, children, creativity, group activity, joy and delight in life. **June**: House, home, parents, in-laws, a home away from home, travel, get-togethers and separations. **July:** 'Open sesame' to fame, fortune, children, romance, hobbies, creativity. **August:** Health, work, colleagues, irritations over pets, projects, and other trifles. **September:** Collaborations, partnerships at all levels, a journey with a stopover, reaching out to people, places. **October:** Joint finances, insurance, loans, public trusts, low vitality, sex and love in strange mix. **November:** The luck of the draw, knowledge, evolution, wisdom, ancestors and rites, genuine spirituality, long-distance connections, pilgrimages. **December:** A high-powered month for work and play, prestige and promotion, parents, in-laws, boss and life mate.

Money: I have written about money earlier in the Saturn piece. Read it carefully please.

Happiness Quota: I give you 86.5 per cent.

MONTH BY MONTH

January: You begin the year with contrasting influences working on you. There could be shifting of residence or office, many new purchases and a complete break from the past. You are moving fast and furious. Mid-month sees you busy with domestic calls. Work pressures mount too, and you are fighting fire on all fronts. As the month ends, you are intense and forthright. This is a propitious period. Make the most of it. The bull run continues. You are bubbling with creative genius. There is change and new vistas open.

February: There is increased stability. Work calls and you roll up your sleeves and hit the shop floor. You are ambitious, and sometimes even ruthless. There are many expenses along with business expansion. You are busy with fiscal instruments, taxes, mutual funds and other avenues of monetary expansion. Mid-month could see travel and philanthropy. Towards the end of the month there are money and honey. The stars are in your favour.

March: You are busy networking with the world. You want to cavort with fantasy and danger. Love walks in and out of your life. This is a good period for media folk. Writers strike pay dirt. Mid-month sees you get about expanding your business with serious intent. You sidestep the opposition with charm and dexterity. As the month ends, you are moving fast and furious towards your destination. As the month ends, you go for the jugular. Love and longing call out to you.

April: The focus shifts to the family and several domestic calls that have got more strident by the minute. There are new acquisitions and you prepare a nest egg. Add exotic travel to the mix and you are truly blessed. Money runs through your fingers mid-month. You love the good life and will not stop at half measures. You are grace and charm personified. As the month ends, your sights are honed. Success garlands you. Love courts you. The gods serenade you. Whatever you embark on leads to success.

May: There is business expansion and a rise in earnings. This is also a good time for serious study. You delve into the esoteric sciences to learn more about the world and your role in it. Mid-month sees you fuelled by a rare intensity. You are impatient and in a hurry to get things done. You want your writ to reign and do not entertain divergent views. As the month ends, there are indulgences and escapist tendencies. This is also a creative phase.

June: There is relative stability. You examine your life and look at plugging the leaks. You look at change and catching up with the times. There could be international travel. At the very least, you connect with people from different vistas and contexts and grow as a person. Mid-month can see intellectual withdrawal. You step back and reflect, rethink and recharge. As the month ends, you spend time at home, sorting out issues. Your health may come under the scanner.

July: You are eyeballing an array of choices. You want to move on but that entails getting out of the comfort zone. You are highly motivated, charged and restless. You want it all. Money and power beckon. Mid-month sees you on a bull run. There is peer group applause. There could be foreign travel. There are many possibilities. As the month ends, you are seized with burning ambition. There are many desires that need to be met and you go all out. There is success.

August: Your creative urges are on a high and this can be a great time for writers and actors. Applause and accolades serenade you. Mid-month sees you push ahead. There is success on all fronts. You make money by the bushels. You sign important business deals. Family life is stable and children bring joy. As the month ends, there is international travel. The mood is buoyant. You are in demand and love the limelight.

September: You are in a formidable space. There are money and honey and your world is merrily humming along. You are busy ideating and making plans for future business expansion. You are creative and filled with hope and optimism. Mid-month sees maudlin moods. As the month ends, you seem to have emerged from the inner battles with new learning. You are disciplined and determined and your critical faculties are sharp. You excel at business negotiations. You are reaching for the stars.

October: You continue on your power run. The energies of the last few weeks have snowballed into a vortex of decisive action. This is a profitable period. Mid-month sees many domestic distractions. Love catches you off guard. There are medical expenses, home renovations and business expansion. There are indulgences and escapist tendencies. As the month ends, there are windfall gains and possibly international travel. Your ideas are futuristic and you receive kudos for your forthrightness, vision and brilliance.

November: This is a powerful phase. There is balance in whatever you do and you make mature decisions. Logic and rationale equip you to forge ahead. Mid-month you could get carried away and overstep your brief. As the month ends, you are buoyed by a powerful intensity. This is a good time to get out of the rut and embark on a new and exciting venture. New vistas await you. Ego drives and passions slay you. You are vibrant, pulsating, throbbing and alive.

December: You take to social networking and journaling. You are filled with zest, enthusiasm and creativity. Money rushes through your fingers. There are creative outbursts and you play the field with abandon. Mid-month sees some stability. You see the rewards of sustained hard work and slog harder. As the month ends, there could be travel. There could be a job change and even a change in marital status. There is determination in your actions as you wipe the slate clean and embark on new beginnings.

WEEKLY REVIEW (BY PHASES OF THE MOON)

5 January: First Quarter in Aries

'That which binds you in life can also free you. The door that imprisons you is also the door to liberation,' says Sadguru, the contemporary mystic. You begin the year with contrasting influences working on you. Mars is in Pisces from 1 to 27 January. Venus is also in your sign from 3 January to 3 February. The moon is in Aries and you begin the year action-packed. There could be shifting of residence or office, many new purchases and a complete break from the past. There will be the usual niggles that accompany change, but in the long run it will be for your good. You have to empty the cup for new wine to be poured into it. If you have already moved you will be settling in well into the new environs. Let me tell you a bit about Mars here before I get to Venus in the third week. This will help you understand the influences working on you at the start of the year. Mars is like the volcano of vitality inside you and influences endurance, persistence and discipline. Mars was named for the Roman god of war, and is also known as 'the bright and burning one'. Red is the colour of Mars, and it stimulates the dynamic, potent and fertile drives that power our lives. Mars rules physical energy and action and governs energy, strength, courage, life force and expansion. Well-placed Mars endows powerful energy and an indomitable will to succeed. Mars propels us like an ignited rocket. It is an important energy, since it determines how we pursue what we want to achieve in life. In short, Mars represents energy, force, violence, aggression, sports, combat, wars, battles, accidents and operations. Mars in your own sign gives energy, courage and a very positive attitude. You are moving fast and furious, obliterating everything in your path, like a hurricane that has arrived in the neighbourhood without ringing the doorbell. Ganesha watches nonplussed.

12 January: Full Moon in Cancer

'Each morning we are born again. What we do today is what matters most,' said the Buddha. The full moon is in Cancer and you busy yourself with domestic calls. Children have their issues and you have to be around. Elders and the spouse also need your presence. You are like a balm in an area of conflict and are in great demand. Work pressures mount too, and you are fighting fire on all fronts. As you move from one challenge to another you grow as a person. Your heart is filled with love and compassion for the less fortunate. You give of yourself easily. It is a marvellous space that you are in. Ganesha is happy for you.

January 19: Last Quarter in Scorpio

'Joy is the best make-up,' says Anne Lamott. The moon is in Scorpio and you are intense and forthright and need little prodding to look and feel your best. As I mentioned at the start, you are also under the influence of Venus for a month. This is a propitious phase. Make the most of it. There could be fancy purchases and travel. You could be in the throes of a windfall and preparing a nest egg with glee. The bull run continues and if you use your free will well, nothing can come between you and success. Money and the power it wields is the theme song for this period. Money has many uses. It also provides emotional succour and you just adore that feeling of comfort it provides. As often discussed, Venus is the planet for love, romance, sex, beauty and good life. This is the planet of attraction, love, wealth, knowledge and prosperity. The compatibility of partners and the type of life the individual will lead are also judged from the placement of Venus in the horoscope. As a planet, Venus is considered to be beneficial, feminine and gentle. Venus symbolizes the force of attraction in the universe. In human beings, this attractive force manifests as love and beauty. When Venus is well placed in the chart there are love, art, beauty and all the goodies of life that make life worth living. Venus rules Libra and Taurus, though its role in every sign is important. Like other planets, it also has its transits. In Libra, Venus is aesthetic and cultured. In Taurus, it is more earthy, materialistic and sensual. Venus rules the venous system, kidneys, urinary tract, throat, larynx, and is responsible for good looks. In short, Venus, in Western astrology, stands for comforts, arts, wealth, relationships, sex, decorations, luxuries and wealth. The simple rule is that when Venus is in your own sign you will get comforts and luxuries, ornaments and money. There is love and longing in this period along with intense, ethereal bonding. You could get married or move in together, depending on the situation. But you most certainly take the object of your affections to another level. Ganesha blesses you.

28 January: New Moon in Aquarius

The new moon is in Aquarius and you are bubbling with creative genius. Writers and playwrights strike pay dirt. You live and love out of the box. You break the rules and listen to your own drummer. This can work both ways; you are either crowned by success or you loiter along the highway without direction like a rambling brook or a toxic weed that strikes root wherever it can. But there is change and new vistas open. You emerge from it a different person altogether. Times have changed and the real world beckons now, but in the mood that you are, you could have been a hit in the post-war Hippie movement. You may join a mass movement and take to activism, depending on the circumstances and demands of the time. As I always do, let me tell you about the great company you keep. This helps broaden the perspective of a prediction and also makes interesting reading. You share your birthday with Anais Nin, Gabriel Garcia Marquez, Henrik Ibsen, George Washington, Albert Einstein, Constantine The Great, Cindy Crawford, Alexander Graham Bell, Gloria Vanderbilt, Rupert Murdoch, Steve Jobs, Bruce Willis, Farrah Fawcett and several other celebrities. You are indeed in esteemed company. Ganesha wishes you well.

4 February: First Quarter in Taurus

With the moon in Taurus, there is increased stability. Your monkey mind is quelled for the moment. You get down to the hard slog. Work calls and you roll up your sleeves and hit the shop floor. You are ambitious, and sometimes even ruthless. Under that kind and sensitive demeanour can rest a tyrant ensnared by the delusions of a restive mind. Like they say, never judge a book by its cover. Of course, this is a general reading and a lot depends on your personal horoscope. I must also tell you a bit about Pisces here. Pisces is a water sign and can be careless, indecisive, melancholy, impractical, indolent, compassionate, charming, romantic, emotional, intuitive and artistic. They generally hate altercations and disagreements. They don't like hurting others, so they suffer fools and get into relationships from which an exit is difficult. They are masters of disguise and have an amazing capacity to slip into anyone's shoes. They are filled with empathy and sympathy. They don't mean to lie and deceive, but often live in faraway fantasy lands and can be difficult to fathom. They are all about emotion, and generally their hearts rule over their heads. They also have brilliant minds and are extremely talented. They can be movers and shakers in their domains of activity. Ganesha is impressed.

11 February: Full Moon in Leo

You are moving ahead fast and furious and with great enthusiasm like the new monorails in the developing world. The full moon is in Leo and you live and love large. There are many expenses, and business expansion too. If you have been gifted a substantial inheritance you go about securing ways to multiply it. You are busy with fiscal instruments, taxes, mutual funds and other avenues of monetary expansion. Love serenades you and you eyeball it without murmur. The possibilities are endless. Ganesha agrees.

18 February: Last Quarter in Sagittarius

This is a good time to take the family for a holiday. There could also be solo travel but you prefer company, even if it is a compromise of sorts. You are also filled with compassion for the less fortunate and donate generously to causes that you believe in. If you are religious, you could get ritualistic and engage in yajnas and pujas. There could be an addition to the family and many fun times with loved ones. Ganesha blesses you.

26 February: New Moon in Pisces

Mercury is in Pisces from today to 13 March. The new moon is also in your sign and this is your birth period too. This can be a fantastic period. There are money and honey, awards and rewards, accolades and applause. You have the Midas touch. To paraphrase the Bard, take the tide at the flood and it will lead to fortune. Strike while the iron is hot. In simple words, strike now. Need I say more? Mercury, the mighty, all-powerful planet is in your sign now. It favours travels, meetings, conferences, interviews, trips, more brainpower, contacts, communication, correspondence and contracts. Mercury has a special connection with the circuits of the brain. Chess, crossword and other such games belong to Mercury. Also, short-distance runners and spin bowlers are controlled by Mercury. Mercury, in short, is the ambassador and salesman of the zodiac. Mercury is the symbol of news, views, messages, interviews, contacts, communications, travel and transport. Mercury gives an impetus to all of the above in the sun sign where it is located. Messages and trips are the special characteristics of Mercury. The year has begun with a flourish and now, for close to a fortnight, you can reap the largesse of Mercury. Astrology never compels but the indications are very strong. You cannot go wrong in this period. Let me recount a real-life anecdote concerning Michelangelo, the famous sculptor. A passer-by once asked him, 'Why are you working so hard, chiselling this large piece of rock? Why don't you go home and take some rest?' Michelangelo replied: 'I am trying to release the Divine that is in the rock. I wish to bring out of this lifeless stone the living Divinity that is embedded in it.' That is the mood you are in. The stars are in your favour too. Go for it. Ganesha is at your side.

5 March: First Quarter in Gemini

The moon is in Gemini and you are busy networking with the world. You use every modern marvel at your disposal and make your presence felt. You are looking for a cause, and if you find one you are pitchforked into the stratosphere.

You want to cavort with fantasy and danger. Remember, it is your birth month and the energies are powerful. Tweak it well. Love walks in and out of your life like a fashion parade at the Lakme fashion week. You play the field but no one torches your heart. Instead, you could take an exotic pet home. This is a good period for media folk. Writers strike pay dirt. Ganesha is happy for you.

12 March: Full Moon in Virgo

Your mind has wandered long enough. Now it is time to be tethered. You have given it a long lease and allowed it to strangle all reason and logic from your heart. The tide turns now and you get down to hard work. There are bills to be paid and the business of living calls out like the koel in summer. The full moon is in Virgo and you get about expanding your business with serious intent. You are powered with a rare intensity. Besides, there are direction and purpose in your dealings and you run through every detail with a comb. You sidestep the opposition with charm and dexterity. You are level-headed and husband your resources with aplomb. Success garlands you. Ganesha applauds.

20 March: Last Quarter in Capricorn

'Action is eloquence,' said William Shakespeare. The moon is in Capricorn and you are moving fast and furious towards your destination. There are money and honey, rewards and awards, accolades and applause. You know what it takes to butter your bread, and make no bones about it. There is a fragrance to crisp greenbacks that send your senses tingling. Even if the notes are crumpled or soiled, they pass muster. In the developing world where I live, they win every argument; they could be the difference between life and death. You are aware of all that and don't rein in the horses. Ganesha cautions you to stick to the straight and narrow. Ambition is wonderful but avarice is a terrible sauce.

28 March: New Moon in Aries

As the month ends and the moon settles into Aries there is no letting up. You go for the jugular. The subcontinent is heating up and so are you. With the alacrity of a mongoose sizing up a cobra, you strike. You could well be a commando baulking a terrorist attack single-handedly. Love and longing call out to you with some desperation. Your hormones are all fired up. You make no bones about playing the field. Beauty entraps you and you are lost in its vicious coil. Those in committed relationships don't even allow the wandering breeze to snip at their togetherness. Even Ganesha is kept away.

3 April: First Quarter in Cancer

'Have no fear of perfection. You will never reach it,' said Salvador Dali. He probably wasn't talking about you in this phase. Venus is in Pisces once again from 3 to 27 April. In the mood that you are in you don't need an excuse to welcome Venus. The moon is in Cancer and the focus shifts to the family and several domestic calls that have got more strident by the minute. Elders need attention and children may be leaving home. The spouse too has several demands. You attend to it all with responsibility and maturity. You win brownie points in family circles. I have written about Venus at the start of the predictions and so will not repeat it. There are new acquisitions and you prepare a nest egg. Add exotic travel to the mix and you are truly blessed. Ganesha is impressed.

11 April: Full Moon in Libra

The full moon is in Libra and you are on a shopping spree. You love the good life and will not stop at half measures. Money runs through your fingers with ease, probably faster than it enters your wallet. But you want to buy your loved ones only the very best. You are in an indulgent mood and feel that expensive gifting is an expression of caring. So be it. You also go about clearing misunderstandings. If there has been a problem with a neighbour or colleague you eschew pride and ego and any false sense of importance. You are grace and charm personified. This helps. You are moving ahead with dexterity like Dhyan Chand, the hockey wizard, who mesmerized the Germans in the epochal Berlin Olympic Games. So magical was he that Hitler, who was watching the match, gave him a standing ovation and an offer to join the German army as a general. Of course, Dhyan Chand declined. The good times roll and Ganesha journeys with you. That is an added bonus.

19 April: Last Quarter in Capricorn

The moon is in Capricorn and your sights are honed. You are like a sharpshooter with his target in sight. All you have to do is pull the trigger; you have the precision of Forsyth's Jackal. You are propelled by zeal, power, energy and drive. Nothing fazes you. Hard work and a goal to achieve are a fabled combination. Success garlands you. Love courts you. The gods serenade you. You cavort with the good times. Need I say more? Ganesha is also impressed.

26 April: New Moon in Taurus

'We are what we think. We make the world with our thoughts,' said the Buddha. The new moon is in Taurus and the energies are powerful. Whatever you embark on leads to success. You also have a steady head on your shoulders and your business acumen is bereft of emotion; your decisions are cold-blooded, based on hard facts. You have the knack of minting and milking the moment. You roll up your sleeves, dirty your elbows and scrape your knees; you lead by example. You believe that nothing is impossible. There is peer group applause. The opposition is stumped and you love the hurrahs like Chris Gayle after a blitzkrieg. Ganesha is thrilled.

3 May: First Quarter in Leo

'The character of our life is based upon how we perceive it,' says Bruce Lipton, in *The Biology of Belief*. The subcontinent is roasting and you are on a bull run. The moon is in Leo and you live and love large. 'Make your life large,' prompts an advertisement doing the rounds these days. You don't need prodding of any kind. You go for the jugular instinctively. There is business expansion with a rise in earnings. This is also a good time for serious study. You delve into the esoteric sciences to learn more about the world and your role in it. Love follows you everywhere but the time you devote to it is dependent on how you husband your free will. Your plate is garnished with goodies and grandeur. There are also snafus and subterfuge. Tread carefully, says Ganesha.

10 May: Full Moon in Scorpio

'Modern man is too impatient and wants to master the art of meditation immediately,' says Swami Rama. The full moon is in Scorpio and you are fuelled by a rare intensity. You are like van Gogh's palette with the colours spilling all over in psychedelic formations. Like Swami Rama mentioned, you are impatient and in a hurry to get things done. You want your writ to reign and do not entertain divergent views. The colours on your palette bleed and coalesce into new forms. Love enters your life and runs riot. You are in the coil of the anaconda and nothing makes sense. You are consumed by lust and longing. This too shall pass but, until then, the world can take a walk! Youngsters are difficult to contain and family life goes for a toss. Ganesha watches.

19 May: Last Quarter in Aquarius

Your monkey mind takes over your being. You hang out with people below your standing in life or with those whose views are vastly divergent from yours. In normal circumstances, you wouldn't even share subsoil with them in the same cemetery. But this is the mood you are in. There are indulgences and escapist tendencies and you flaunt your offbeat plumage with unabashed flair. This is also a creative phase and writers, musicians, actors and fashion designers excel. 'Reality is merely an illusion, albeit a very persistent one,' said Albert Einstein. Your concepts of reality go for a toss. It is coloured in many hues. This is the time for ideating and taking time off. This is not the phase for hard, sustained work. Love life is psychedelic, and the less said about monogamous relationships the better. Ganesha has nothing to add.

25 May: New Moon in Gemini

The new moon is in Gemini and you continue with the scattered run of the previous week. Sometimes trends continue for weeks on end, like a ball that has been set in motion. You are going nowhere. Life events baulk you at every twist and turn. It is not your fault. The cards are not in your favour. However hard you try, your boat refuses to straighten up, despite your earnest efforts. You just have to give yourself to a higher power and wait for better times to float by as they will. 'If you are obsessing, distract yourself with gratitude,' says Danielle LaPorte, the life coach. This is probably the time to do just that. I must add here that astrology never compels and this is a general reading as I do not have your personal chart. Use your free will to advantage. Ganesha holds your hand.

1 June: First Quarter in Virgo

The moon is in Virgo and there is relative stability. You examine your life and look at plugging the leaks. You have lost a sense of direction and it is time to get on track. It is possible that your methods are antiquated and you have to change from within. You realize that you cannot be resistant to change and insist on the status quo for ever. The world is passing you by and time and tide wait for no one. There is a new technology knocking at the doors of evolution and progress and it is imperative that you change. There is a new generation too, smarter and more 'with it'. You will be left behind to fossilize in no time. George Bernard Shaw, the Irish playwright, said: 'Progress is impossible without change, and those who cannot change their minds cannot change anything.' Ganesha urges you to make the necessary changes and move on. I agree. I have even changed the format of my predictions!

9 June: Full Moon in Sagittarius

The full moon is in Sagittarius and this is movement time. There could be international travel. At the very least, you connect with people from different vistas and contexts and grow as a person. A new breeze blows into your life and you realize that your comfort zone has now become obsolete. 'I have been and still am a seeker, but I have ceased to question stars and books; I have begun to listen to the teaching my blood whispers to me,' said Hermann Hesse, the German Indologist and author. You look to raise your consciousness. You also look at new ways of working and living. You realize that you need to adapt or perish. You mix pragmatism with idealism and reassess your goals. You begin the ascent to more relevant realities. Ganesha journeys with you.

17 June: Last Quarter in Pisces

'Learning and wisdom are superfluities, the surface glitter merely, but it is the heart that is the seat of all power,' said Swami Vivekananda. The moon is in your sign and your sensitivities are at a high point. You could get moody and irritable. Like the fish, you are difficult to catch; the moment an attempt is made you slip out. Friends and loved ones cannot fathom you. This could be a time of intellectual withdrawal when you use 'me' time to step back and reflect, rethink and recharge. You examine your priorities and tweak personal and work needs. You look at optimizing your life. You want your life to be of some consequence, and not a wasted one. Ganesha blesses you.

24 June: New Moon in Cancer

A Zen proverb says: 'If you realize that all things change, there is nothing you will try to hold on to.' The new moon is in Cancer and you are busy with domestic demands. You spend time at home, sorting out issues. Your health may come under the scanner. There are also renovations and repairs to attend to. There are inheritance issues to work out and you pore over papers with diligence and deliberation. There could be an addition to the family and children may also be leaving home for higher studies. There is a lot on your plate and you run from pillar to post looking for solutions. There could be moody, maudlin times and disagreements with partners. You may also be prone to avarice and deceit. Ganesha cautions you against breaking the law of karma. Additionally, there is also the law of the land to contend with!

1 July: First Quarter in Libra

'You can reshape your mind according to the discipline of mindfulness,' says Chögyam Trungpa, the Tibetan master. 'If you want to make your mind into a horse, an elephant, a giraffe, a square, a triangle, or just a round ball, you are free to do so.' Of course, I must add here that whatever you do now should be within the ambit of propriety. These days, under the guise of freedom of expression, a lot of political propaganda is strewn around. I do not advocate that. Mindfulness is about living in the moment with a deep and powerful connection, honest to yourself and to your intentions, without causing any harm to anyone, including yourself. The moon is in Libra and you are eyeballing an array of choices. Life is posting many posers. You want to move on but that entails getting out of the comfort zone. You also have to be practical, as reality often knocks hard and you don't want to be out for the count. You weigh the pros and cons, even in your sleep, and come up with no conclusion. You then decide to leave it all to a higher power. It is passing the buck in a sense but you have no option, or at least you think you don't. Ganesha helps you out of this mess. Love and longing make their presence felt, but you have other more challenging pursuits to attend to.

9 July: Full Moon in Capricorn

'Stand aside and watch the working of the divine power in you,' said Sri Aurobindo. The full moon is in Capricorn and you are powered and moving ahead without a pause, possibly even without a cause. You are highly motivated, charged and restless. You want it all. Money and power beckon and you cannot resist its allure. If you believe that the end justifies the means you may stoop to anything. Sri Aurobindo's words ring a bell here; it may be worth your while to heed it. Like I have stated earlier, Pisces is an enigmatic sign. Calm and composed on the surface, you could actually be torn apart by a million thoughts. You are the master of disguise and the prisoner of your mind. Like your symbol: two fishes swimming in opposite directions: one part of you may never know or even acknowledge the other. Every sign has its shadow side and blind spots, and you are no exception. I am not singling you out. This is also a general reading. Having said that, you are out to conquer the world with your charm, cunning and charisma. Ganesha watches.

16 July: Last Quarter in Aries

The moon is in Aries and you are on a bull run. 'Be like water making its way through cracks. Do not be assertive, but adjust to the object, and you shall find a way,' said the legendary martial artist Bruce Lee. You do just that. You charm your way through tough situations and engage with your pot of gold. There is peer group applause, money and honey. There could be foreign travel, possibly even international trade. You may even look at emigration seriously. The whole family may be planning to move, lock, stock and barrel. There are many possibilities as you push the envelope. This is a period of rapid growth. Ganesha is happy for you.

23 July: New Moon in Leo

The new moon is in Leo and you continue on the path of progress with renewed vigour and zest. The immortal lines of Robert H. Schuller, retired American pastor and author, come to mind: 'What great thing would you attempt if you knew you could not fail?' You are seized with intensity, burning ambition, lust and love. Passions and ego drives are strong. Money slips through your fingers. You live and love large. Plus, there is business expansion and you make huge monetary outlays for that. There could also be altercations and court cases. Family life betrays ruffled feathers as you insist on playing the field. You may even be caught out during one of your more indiscreet escapades. Of course, astrology never compels and I do not have your personal chart. Ganesha holds your hand.

30 July: First Quarter in Scorpio

You are working and living at peak intensity. There are many desires that need to be met and you go all out. There is success too. You indulge in jugaad and take short cuts. In the developing world this is inevitable if you are in a hurry to get where you want to go, with the least inconvenience. On the flip side, there is also an inner journey at play. You want to know more about the purpose of your life. Is it all about just making money, or is there more to it? What happens to the body when it is finally laid to rest? These and innumerable other related questions plague you. According to Shankara, Turiya is the fourth, or superconscious state, which is beyond the three ordinary states of consciousness

– waking, dreaming and dreamless sleep. It is the state of unitary consciousness and pure bliss. This, he says, is not a state, but the Atman. You are in that state now. You step out of line, new vistas open and you are enriched by the encounters. There is a search for guru, pilgrimages and an earnest plunge into the esoteric sciences. Tantra, mantra, yantra and rudraksha fascinate you. There is new learning and you grow. Ganesha blesses you.

7 August: Full Moon in Aquarius

The full moon is in Aquarius and your shadow side is on display. 'Ego interrupts intuition,' says Danielle LaPorte, the life coach. That doesn't bother you. Your ego is safely tucked away like a child's teddy bear. Your creative urges are on a high and this can be a great time for writers and actors. You participate in art shows, concerts, book readings and film festivals, and hobnob with the literati and glitterati. Applause and accolades serenade you. The media spotlights your achievements. Love is offered to you on a platter; what you do with it is your free will. This is most certainly an eventful week. Ganesha is impressed.

15 August: Last Quarter in Taurus

Carlos Castaneda said, 'Things don't change, only the way you look at them.' You are pushing ahead, hard and true. There is success on all fronts. You make money by the bushels and love the feeling. It goads you on to rake in the moolah. There could be business expansion, and a promotion and better perks for the employed. Freelancers net in blue chip accounts. You are in balance and are clear-headed about what you want. You take your time and sign important business deals, leaving the opposition flat-footed.

Family life is stable and children bring joy. The home fires burn merrily. Ganesha is happy for you.

21 August: New Moon in Leo

The new moon is in Leo and this is a propitious period. Use the power of the waxing moon well. Optimize the energies that so happily fall on your lap. 'Peace of mind comes from not wanting to change others,' said Gerald Jampolsky. This is advice that you should heed now as you want to hoist your will on everyone you meet and it is not well taken. The key is to give others space or at least to be seen to be doing that. You may be investing in a new office space or residence. You have made money and it is time to invest wisely. Lovers experience show-jumping hormones as they take their ecstasy to ethereal heights. Life is good. You have no complaints. It is all going according to plan. Ganesha blesses you.

29 August: First Quarter in Sagittarius

'Live in the sunshine, swim the sea, drink the wild air,' said Ralph Waldo Emerson. You are moving in every direction possible. If there is international travel you could strike gold. There could be an exotic holiday with the family. You could be cruising through the French Riviera or examining the pyramids of Egypt from handshaking distance. The mood is buoyant. You have worked hard and earned well. It is now time to spend. Money slips through your hands like grains of sand in the hands of a Bedouin. But you are not perturbed. Those in academic circles could be invited to chair important meetings. You are in demand and love every moment in the limelight. Musicians and painters usher genius at will. The power is with you. Ganesha is happy.

6 September: Full Moon in Pisces

The full moon is in Pisces and you have come into your own. 'Don't compare yourself to anyone in the world. If you do so, you are insulting yourself,' said Bill Gates. You are in a formidable space. There are money and honey and your world is merrily humming along like a purring feline. There is a lot to be done, and a lot of water has flowed under the bridge too. But you are not unduly perturbed. The monkey mind is harnessed and you are filled with gratitude for all that the Lord has provided. If you hunger for more it is pure avarice – which is listed as one of the seven deadly sins. You are busy ideating and making plans for future business expansion. You are creative and filled with hope and optimism. You network and shout out your plans to others. Love comes calling. Ganesha hears you too.

13 September: Last Quarter in Gemini

'The clearest path to happiness emerges when what you think, what you say, and what you do are in harmony,' said Mahatma Gandhi. This is a powerful creative phase. Along with it are mood swings. You could get morbid, morose and maudlin. You feel that you have a bigger share of the world's problems on your shoulders and it is blatantly unfair. These feelings are misplaced, but that is the mood you are in. There are insecurities and sensitivities that are exaggerated. There could be sibling rivalry and misunderstandings about inheritance and profits from family-run businesses. Friends and loved ones, employees and colleagues, find it hard to fathom you. You are on your own trip. You take time off from various social interactions, get to know yourself better and then claw back. This is a significant period. Once you know the real you, most of the battle is won. Ganesha agrees.

20 September: New Moon in Virgo

You have emerged from all the inner battles with new learning. This is a stable phase. The monkey mind is suitably quelled. There is balance and you are aware of your role in life. Now, you roll up your sleeves and get down to the hard task of making a living, without all the shrieks, frills and fanfare. 'In stillness the world is restored,' said Lao-tzu. Your world is restored for sure. It has been rescued, to put it more appropriately. You are assertive and your energies are high. Your passions are well directed. You spend long hours at the workplace and long to catch a whiff of the fragrance of greenbacks. You are more enthusiastic about money than meeting your loved ones. You put all the energy into getting ahead in life and you do just that, with aplomb. Ganesha is impressed.

28 September: First Quarter in Capricorn

'There is no such thing as work-life balance: it is all life. The balance has to be with you,' says Sadguru. You have found your mojo and the meaning to your life. You are on a bull run. You don't shirk from hard work. You are disciplined and determined and your critical faculties are sharp. More importantly, you count pennies. You realize that money saved is money earned and you plug all leaks. You excel at business negotiations and sign big deals. Those who are self-employed cast the net wide and get lucky breaks. You may hire an image consultant, which is in vogue these days, and market yourself assiduously. You are reaching for the stars. The moon is in Capricorn and you are like the mountain goat ascending the peak. Ganesha applauds. There is little time for family life. It plods along.

5 October: Full Moon in Aries

The full moon is in Aries and you continue on your power run. The energies of the last few weeks have snowballed into a vortex of decisive action. This is a profitable period. If you make the right choices, they carry you over long distances. You raise the bar and keep the opposition out of the race. Like Usain Bolt, you breast the tape, leaving the competition nowhere in sight. 'I want to stay as close to the edge as I can without going over. Out on the edge you see all kinds of things you can't see from the centre,' said Kurt Vonnegut Jr. You do just that. You take risks, gamble and even win the lottery. If you are a betting man, this is a good period. Luck favours you. Of course, I am not suggesting anything. Astrology never compels; these are mere indicators. Love swallows you in its inferno. There is little time for anything else. Ganesha watches.

12 October: Last Quarter in Cancer

The moon is in Cancer. The bull run continues but there are also many domestic distractions. Love catches you off guard and delivers a telling blow like Vijender Singh in his new avatar as a professional boxer; it could well be a first round knockout. While you are still reeling from it there are medical expenses, home renovations and business expansion. Money runs through your fingers like water in the Thar. 'Don't look for the right one. Be the right one,' says Deepak Chopra. You are fighting fire with every ounce of energy at your disposal. You need to get a handle on domestic issues before you can move on. You don't want bad blood and so your negotiating skills are at their best; they are sharp and finely honed. You also give in strategically. You lace it all with dollops of charm. You emerge the winner in the end, and have it your way. Kudos, says Ganesha.

19 October: New Moon in Libra

The new moon is in Libra and your plate is bubbling over like an overactive volcano. You are on overdrive. Money continues to slip out of your fingers. There are many indulgences and escapist tendencies. To add to the discomfiture created by circumstances, you go on a comfort shopping spree. You buy things that you will probably never use. But you feel good about lugging huge shopping carts around and no one can reason you out of it. I do not want to be gender-unfriendly, but women could be particularly prone to theatrics. These are the indicators. Youngsters could also be difficult to handle and the household is set for a steamy session, quite like the Indian parliament. 'Show me a sane man and I will cure him,' said Jung, emphatically. Right on! We all have so many shades to us and there is no telling which one gets flamboyantly expressed and when. Ganesha knows it only too well.

27 October: First Quarter in Aquarius

'Dancing, singing, storytelling and silence are the four universal healing salves,' says Gabrielle Roth. You share your opinion with all and sundry. You network with a rare frenzy. There are windfall gains and you could be eyeing international travel. This is also a creative phase and you are acknowledged by your peer group for strokes of genius. Perspiration and inspiration in a good marriage leads to miracles. There are applause and rewards for your breathtaking efforts. While your idiosyncrasies are in plumage mode, you are also amiable and charming. Your offbeat traits attract an audience. You could be a hit at literary meets. Your ideas are futuristic and mind-blowing. You are far ahead of your times and receive kudos for your forthrightness, vision and brilliance. Mediocre minds are unable to fathom you and critique you. But it is their problem and not yours; you refuse to play to the gallery. Ganesha is suitably impressed.

4 November: Full Moon in Taurus

The full moon is in Taurus and you get down to hard work. There are goals to be met and many ambitions to be realized. You also live and love large. Lust leaves its calling card behind and you don't need much prodding to be on time. There are no half measures or compromises. You don't encourage passengers either. It is all or nothing. There are expenses that accompany business expansion. This is a powerful phase. There is balance in whatever you do and you make mature decisions. Logic and rationale equip you to forge ahead. In love too, you view the pros and cons and then take the leap. You can be accused of being bereft of feeling but you can live with that. What you cannot live with is emotion bleeding sanity out of you. You have been through that and it is worse than being on the banks of the Brahmaputra when it floods. Ganesha agrees wholeheartedly. He can see that good sense has finally prevailed.

10 November: Last Quarter in Leo

'By having a reverence for life, we enter into a spiritual relation with the world. By practising reverence for life we become good, deep, and alive,' said Albert Schweitzer. The moon is in Leo and you are moving ahead, fast and true, like an arrow seeking the bullseye and the gold medal at the archery events of the Olympics. You look for big gains in all your dealings. You love large and overstep. There could be brushes with the law. You get carried away and overstep your brief. You are tempted by big gains and could take to unethical routes to achieve your ends. The rush of money does strange things to people and you are no exception. After all, you are human too. There could be serious domestic disharmony if you dip untidy fingers into joint accounts. Avarice takes hold of you. Allow your free will to steer your path. Give yourself to a higher power. Give yourself to Ganesha before you commit errors from which there is no redemption.

18 November: New Moon in Scorpio

The new moon is in Scorpio and you are buoyed by a powerful intensity. This is a good phase and you could use its energies well. But before that, you must sort out your priorities. There is a lot on your schedule and you are multitasking like a beehive. This is also a good time to get out of the rut and embark on a new and exciting venture. You may have lingered and languished in your comfort zone far too long. Life is calling from the horizons. New vistas await you. It is your insecurity that makes you drag your feet. Get into dynamic mode and make your day, like Clint Eastwood used to urge his adversaries. Circumstances and situations change and our lives bob around like seaweed in the well of life. Ganesha wishes you well.

26 November: First Quarter in Pisces

'Liberation is not about banishing the ego: it's about integrating it,' says Danielle LaPorte. The moon is in your sign and you take a step back and work out options to make the best of the situation. You realize that you want money and will do anything for it. You also realize that wrongdoing will not be pardoned by the laws of life. You are confused and do not know what to do. You meet up with gurus and god-men and spend time with charities in an attempt to assuage your troubled soul. You mean no harm and yet uncontrolled desires take hold of your being and they have to be exorcised before they consume you in a brutal inferno. Ego drives and passions slay you. You are vibrant, pulsating, throbbing and alive. You sense that something has to give. The problem is that you don't know what or when. You are like the prisoner of Zenda and there is no great escape in sight. Ganesha holds your hand.

3 December: Full Moon in Gemini

'Anyone who possesses consciousness, anyone who possesses mind, or the unconscious mind – all are candidates for attaining bodhisattva. Anyone can become an awakened person,' says Chögyam Trungpa. This is some consolation, considering the infernal demons that you have been battling in recent times. The full moon is in Gemini and the monkey mind is in awesome form as it pirouettes flamboyantly, with designer intent, on a tiny reed. You decide to tame it and take to social networking and journaling. Work can calm a besieged mind and you decide to do just that. The year is slowly ending and it had a buoyant start. You want it to also end in a flourish. You are filled with zest, enthusiasm and creativity. There are indulgences and escapism. Money rushes through your fingers without permission. You are at your wit's end. Whatever you earn disappears; you have to plug the leak. There are creative outbursts and you play the field with abandon. Ganesha watches. He knows what you are going through.

10 December: Last Quarter in Virgo

With the moon in Virgo there is some stability. You are back in balance and on terra firma. You roll up your sleeves and get to work. You burn the midnight oil. This tough schedule straightens you out somewhat. It secures you from a mind that insists on playing games with you. 'And to love life through labour is to be intimate with life's innermost secret,' said Kahlil Gibran. Work has always been your balm, your succour, your escape. You take to it with a vengeance. Additionally, it has paid your bills and met your ambitions head on. You realize that it has been your closest ally. For the moment at least, all other distractions are laid to rest. You see the rewards of sustained hard work and slog harder. Ganesha is happy for you.

18 December: New Moon in Sagittarius

'That sorrow which is the harbinger of joy is preferable to the joy which is followed by sorrow,' said Sa'di, the great poet. The new moon is in Sagittarius and you decide to make a move. There could be travel, in several senses of the word. You may also be relocating or even emigrating. These are difficult moves, done after great thought, possibly only after being pushed against the wall. If personal and professional life is a mess it is time to sort it out. You take concrete steps and move on. There could be a job change and even a change in marital status. Later, on hindsight, you realize that you should have moved on a long time ago. Ganesha agrees. Time and tide wait for no one and one has to strike at the right time or the water in the well gets sullied and muddied. These are crucial life lessons.

26 December: First Quarter in Aries

You are moving ahead with purpose. There is determination in your actions as you wipe the slate clean and embark on new beginnings. A new journey begins when one ends. It is all a continuum. You manage to spend the last days of the year with family and loved ones. There is a semblance of stability but your ambitions have not been fully realized and there is an inherent disquiet. Of course, let me add that astrology never compels and I do not have your personal chart. The Mother of Pondicherry said, 'We must aspire to conquer all mistakes, all obscurities, all ignorance.' This could well be the signature tune of 2018 that you carry forward so fervently in your bosom. Ganesha wishes you well. I add here, like I did last year too, that Neptune will be in Pisces till 30 March 2025. (Yes, this is a long time). Neptune in your own sign gives you imagination, inspiration and intuition. But all your dreams and visions may not be real. You can be cheated. Hallucinations and illusions often go with Neptune. Neptune is a sword which cuts both ways. But there is an important point I mustn't fail to mention: Please remember, dear readers, that Neptune, Pluto and Uranus influence countries more than people. They are marathon runners. They stay in one sign for a number of years. I am sure this will help you know yourself a little better. That's what astrology and life are all about.

Achievements

The biggest blessing was that our Ganesha devotee Bejan Daruwalla went to the Iranshah fire festival in Udvada on 26 December 2015 and received blessings from the Holy Fire, the High Priest Khurshedji Kekobar Dastoor, and all the mighty energies of Udvada, the mighty focal point of the Zoroastrians, who are known as Parsees. Ratan Tata was the chief guest. Cyrus Poonawalla, the famous racing king, sponsored the mighty Iranshah Udvada Utsav. Actually, Iranshah refers to the great and original Fire which the Parsees brought from Iran to India. Parsees are fire and nature worshippers. Bejan's son, Nastur had the good fortune of meeting Ratan Tata at the very entrance of the Parsee Fire Temple in Udvada. The best part of it was that the Parsee High Priest Khurshedji Kekobar Dastoor was also present. Bejan calls it a shower of blessings.

On 31 October 2015, our Bejan inaugurated and blessed Anand Jewels, Indore. Bejan said, 'The young, able, very modern owners, Gautam and Arzoo, represent and symbolize our new India.'

On 31 January 2016, Behram Mehta, a real estate dealer and owner of well-known Aava Waters, invited Bejan to bless his son Shiroy and fiancée Megha at a resplendent ceremony. Behram's father, Rusy, and Bejan were college mates.

On 22 November 2015, Chandni, the daughter of chartered accountant Ashok Gupta, married Pankaj. Bejan blessed them and gave the welcome speech. He says Ashok is unique.

On 23 September 2015, the divine saint Pramukh Swami Maharaj of BAPS Swaminarayan blessed the 2016 yearly horoscopic book of Bejan. Thus, I am sure the blessings will come to me and also my son, Nastur. Bejan bows his head once again in reverence to this living saint. He says this is our Indian way and I am proud to be an Indian. The world knows that Dr A.P.J Abdul Kalam, the late president of India, wrote a book of glowing tributes to Pramukh Swamiji.

On 29 January 2016, Bejan blessed and also spoke lovingly of Shilpa and Pravin, who tied the knot. Manoj Soni, the brother of the bride, is an old friend of Bejan's son, Nastur.

On 27 September 2015, Gujarat chief minister Anandiben Patel launched Nastur, the son of Bejan, as an independent astrologer in his 2016 yearly horoscope. Yes, the powerful Parsee weekly *Jam-e-Jamshed* was gracious enough to publish the photo of Nastur and the chief minister of Gujarat, Anandiben Patel, launching the book officially.

Bejan was thrilled to be interviewed on the first page of the *Speaking Tree*, a sister newspaper of the world famous *The Times of India*. Later on, Narayani Ganesh, the editor of the *Speaking Tree*, along with Mona, Ranjan Singh and five other staff members met Bejan at the Parsee Dharamshala in Delhi, and Bejan blessed them repeatedly. We believe the vibrations and frequencies of the blessings went right through the roof and hit the skies. Bejan loves to dramatize, laugh at himself and spread good cheer. He resembles Santa Claus and Ganesha. Dadi Mistry, his old friend and the government-recognized spearhead of the Parsees, was there too and had a merry good time.

Believe it or not, at the ritual of the religious Navratri (nine nights) of Amba Mata, the cardinal female principle that rules and rides over the world, Bejan tried his hand at writing the Garba in Gujarati. It was sung by the famous musician Pancholi in Ahmedabad. It was Jaimin Oza who organized it all.

Once again, Bejan says it was his good luck to be the brand ambassador of India of the world-famous charitable institution, the Round Table.

On 31 December 2015 and 1 January 2016, five TV channels, namely, Business India, IBN7, CNBC Gujarati, CNBC English and CNBC Hindi descended on poor Bejan. As if all this was not enough, India News took a shot at Bejan on 3 February 2016. Bejan is both tired and happy.

Bejan is named as one of the 100 great astrologers in the last 1,000 years in the great *Millennium Book of Prophecy*, published by HarperCollins, USA.

But Bejan happily acknowledges that there are quite a few astrologers superior to him, for example, Vashishth Mehta, Liz Green, Robert Hood, Mohan Patel and a few others. Bejan is happy to be just himself. He loves to love and to laugh.

Eminent neurologist Sudhir Shah of Ahmedabad was awarded the Padma Shri on 25 January 2016. He is the appointed doctor to the governor of Gujarat. He admits very happily that Bejan predicted the recent award many years ago and he thanked Bejan for it too.

Ganesha says Byram Avari wears many hats: Asia's sailing champion, mighty successful hotelier, leader of the Parsee community, philanthropist and more importantly, a perfect gentleman. The name Byram comes from the Parsee angel Behram Yazade, referring to purity, good luck, wealth and wisdom. The world expects great things from him. His brilliant and beautiful wife, Goshpi, is his anchor and inspiration.

Brijendra Singh Parmar, owner of Daman Ganga Valley Resort in Silvassa, requested Bejan to bless and inaugurate his conference hall. Bejan gave it the title 'Victory' by both astrology and numerology. Brijendra is a fine man with a brilliant future.

Bejan says, 'I was proud and thrilled to bless Maninder Singh Bitta, the chairman of the All India Anti-Terrorist Front. So spick and span, powerful and a real lion. Yes, I bestowed a picture of the Panchmukhi Vishnu Ganesha, which I had the privilege to help to install at Shirdi. I salute him.'

My darling son, Sattejit, married his love, Kritika. He deserves my heart and blessings. He has earned it because of his humility, intelligence and, above all, integrity.

Once again, my adopted son Prince Lakshyaraj Singh Mewar from City Palace, Udaipur, has my blessings for the simple reason that he has added a life force to his mission for public welfare.

We Indians cannot do without special messages. The message of Bejan is this: 'Goodness is its own reward. Cleanliness is the sister of purity. Purity is the greatest energy in the world.' Bejan calls purity 'Ganga Maiya'. But Bejan also admits that you readers have a right to your own opinion. Keep an open mind.

Ganesha devotee Bejan was awarded the Lifetime Achievement Award by Chief Minister Harish Rawat of Uttarakhand. Bejan predicted most emphatically his victory in front of 500 people in Uttarakhand. Bejan says purity, goodness and Ganga Maiya make a handsome spiritual trio.

Our Ganesha devotee Bejan Daruwalla was the official astrologer on Star TV for the Olympics in August 2016.

World Horoscope 2017

To the spirit who rules by his might
we have joyfully sung praises.
His blessings flow a thousandfold
and ever more abundantly.

Ganesha says that the nightingale sings breast to thorn. He says that Bejan Daruwalla predicts to ease the world's pain. Finally, Ganesha says one could doubt his intelligence, but never his intuition or integrity.

I am writing this piece on 27 October 2015. The year 2017 is a long way off, which makes predicting difficult. But I am not afraid of going wrong. In the name of Ganesha I can say to my readers that there is a fine chance of peace and understanding for the entire world from 10 September 2016 to 10 October 2017.

Human Nature: Modern astrology is all about human behaviour. We are so magnificent and yet, we can be so cruel; so great yet so small; giving yet unforgiving; selfless yet self-centred – yes, we are a bundle of contradictions.

No discipline can explain it entirely and astrology is no exception. But this is what I have observed again and again in my sixty-five years of practice: if a person has Jupiter in Cancer he is likely to be generous, charitable, emotional. If that same person has Saturn in Aries it could make him cold, sadistic and uncompromising. Therefore, he has all these positive and negative qualities. When a quality becomes active depends on the other planets and the movements of each planet at a given time. In other words, sometimes we are angelic, sometimes we are devils. But that is the beauty and paradox and irony and greatness of human nature.

What is my conclusion? For whatever it is worth, I see a mighty evolution between 2017 and 2023. I have finally taken a stand on 24 November 2015 at the age of eighty-five. Now I can breathe easily. Astrophysicists tell us that the sun and the Milky Way anchor our very existence. After billions of years our sun will die, become a mere ember, and finally disappear – as will we. By that time, we will all be on another planet. If we are on this earth our doom will come through an asteroid. It will be sudden and final. I could be hopelessly wrong. But I am sure of one thing. We will die with a smile.

Special Features: Space travel; messages for aliens; new inventions and discoveries in aviation, drones, biology; open minds; increased tolerance; more people willing to listen to others. We are all a family of man, but also unique, resourceful and adaptable, driven by the will to survive and finally prevail. So 2017 will yield rewards for the human spirit and our past endeavours. The mystery of the black hole will become clearer, receive more attention; the purification of mother Ganga seems likely; the marriage of technology and humanity will show interesting results. The year will also see progress in the fields of health care, climate change, agriculture and genetics. Human behaviour will also evolve.

Yes, 2017 will bring peace and progress. The year 2018 will go down in history as a period for the realization of dreams and the practical application of technology, surgery, farming, medicine, and spirituality for the whole world. The year 2018, especially after May, will see our dreams, our principles, our ideals work their way into actions. The possibility of a World Constitution starts from 2018. It is a defining year for use of ideas to help humanity. The year 2020 will reveal the key to managing good, productive and happy lives – a year of prosperity, progress, peace. The year 2021 goes beyond progress and peace. Ganesha, the energies, talk in unison of a mighty thrust towards evolution. It is fascinating to imagine a combination of intellectual brilliance, new technology and humanity on such a scale. Your Ganesha devotee says that this year actually represents the focal point of the Aquarian age, which has to do with inventions, science, genes and the coming together of all the nations of the world in a whole new way. The actual way right now escapes me because I am writing this piece on 19 November 2015. One thing I do know: the secret of life and astrology lies in the timing.

On Numbers: When I was seventeen, I met a gentleman who combined astrology, numerology, palmistry and physiognomy. It was he who pointed out to me that the sign Capricorn represents Saturn and by the Hebrew Kabbala of numbers, Capricorn's number is eight. I first used it in my book *Star Signs and Numerology* published in 1991 by Jaico Publishing House. There are different interpretations of numbers by numerologists. To each his own. But my experience of over sixty-five years leads me to believe that the number eight stands for solidity, spirituality, striving and succeeding against all odds. Finally, the number eight represents salvation through duty and responsibility. Of course, you are free to come to your own conclusion. Two great examples of number eight are our Republic Day, 26 January, and our Air Force Day, 8 October. I am writing this piece on 20 November 2015. The Constitution of India came into effect on 26 November: $2 + 6 = 8$. This example tells it all.

The Formula: I could be wrong, but I believe that we human beings can do amazing things which once seemed to be beyond our capabilities. It is this ability to adjust to change that makes me predict: we human beings will finally prevail, have peace, and use technology brilliantly, effectively, but above all very humanely for the good of us all. My new world formula is: technology + evolution + communication + purity + love + intelligence + pure goodness = transformation of all of us into good human beings.

Ganga: To me the purification of Mother Ganga is perhaps the single most important factor for the development and happiness of India. I am aware of Modi's five Ts (talent, tradition, tourism, trade, technology). I have met Narendra Modi thrice and know it is in his destiny to purify the Ganga. Narendra is a Virgo. The keyword for Virgos is purity. Secondly, Narendra was born on 17 September. The number seventeen in the tarot cards depicts a lady pouring water on to the earth. Water signifies the Ganga. Therefore, I predict that Narendra will purify the Ganga.

Your Ganesha devotee believes in personal observation and verification. For example, as I write today on 19 November 2015, Jupiter, by Western astrology, is in Virgo. Virgo is the recognized sign of cleanliness and purity. Narendra Modi also called for Swachh Bharat Abhiyan from 2015 itself. Bill Gates stressed the importance of clean energy in December 2015.

The Secret: Ganesha says that timing is the secret of astrology. It means that the right person at the right place and time will succeed. But time goes on changing forever and this presents variables in predicting success. On the chessboard of life all the planets are the energies. Each planet has a different energy and significance. Therefore, it is in the relationship of all the planets to one another that the accuracy of prediction depends. This requires skill and knowledge. Add to it keen observation of previous incidents under similar circumstances and the process is further complicated. The astrologer requires flashes of intuition and inspiration to predict correctly. Intuition is a strange thing. You cannot control it. It is like poetry. Not even the greatest poet is uniformly wonderful. I believe it must be in the fate of the astrologer to predict the fate of others.

It is said, 'Time and tide wait for no man.' As we say, 'Your time is up.' To me, time is the mask of God. We are all mortals and therefore vulnerable to chance, circumstances, pain, pleasure and situations out of our control. Therefore, to me at least, life is an adventure and astrology gives us a few signposts to guide us along the way. But astrology is not perfect. Therefore, finally, it still remains an adventure. If you ask me, I like it that way. Surety and certainty are the two great enemies of creativity. Creativity leads to development, progress and final evolution.

Today, 19 November 2015, I will tell you the real secret of astrology as I see it. Time alone is king. Even the greatest of us has a time limit for achievements and greatness. Finally, all of us disappear from the earth. I understand that we human beings are resourceful, capable, intelligent and do have a cosmic connection. Therefore, I am not underestimating the human race. Yes, the entire cosmos will shut down one day. But we will brave it with laughter on our lips and a challenge in our eyes.

Merkel and Germany: Ganesha asks us to give a standing ovation to Cancerian Angela Merkel of Germany. With her humanity and economic skills, she has won many hearts.

For Germany, I take the signs Scorpio, Aries and Taurus. Germany stands for technology and accuracy (example: the launch of GTS sports car, Mercedes Benz India, which sells at Rs 2.4 crore as of 25 November 2015). Merkel will face opposition in Germany during the next three years. In her personal chart she has the combination of Jupiter (good luck) and the Sun (power). In 2019 Germany will showcase its prowess in technology, science, chemistry and weapons of war. Germany is power plus. Germany is perhaps the only country which is called the Fatherland. It is ruled by Merkel, the mother of economics and humanity. A fascinating contradiction.

Obama and America: Obama is a Leo. He will go down in history for uplifting the low, the weak, and the downtrodden. Obama was born on 4 August 1961. The date, four, vibrates with the planet Uranus. Uranus means originality and innovation. The month August signifies the sun and the number one. The number one is the most powerful in the world. Therefore, Obama has both the power of number one and the innovation of number four. America will help the world in 2017. It will knock out China. But, for America the months to watch out for are March, June, September and December.

Modi and India: I have said a thousand times that India will be the superpower of the twenty-first century. By Western astrology, India comes under the sign Capricorn and is greatly influenced by Libra and Scorpio.

Narendra Modi is the right person at the right time and place for India. Capricorn is an earth sign. Narendra Modi is a Virgo (17 September) and Virgo is also an earth sign. You may not agree, but intuition, emotion and spirituality may not always sound rational. To me the mighty Ganga does not mean mere prosperity and development. To me the Ganga is a life force and represents great creativity, the core of motherhood and divinity itself. It is in the destiny of Narendra Modi to cleanse and purify the Ganga. Therefore, to me at least, Narendra is great. Certain things are above reason and logic. But you, my dear readers, have the right to not believe in them.

In 2017 the power of the terrorists will start to wane and with this, India will definitely gain. The only thing that can stop India is tunnel vision, dogmatism, rigid religious opinions, caste and creed and the deep conviction that only certain groups are right and all the other Indians wrong when it comes to a difference of opinion. The key is in the amalgamation, the coming together, of all Indians.

Jupiter, the planet of good luck and prosperity, will be in Libra, the sign of harmony, balance and coming together, in 2017. Secondly, Jupiter will be in a fine relationship with Saturn in Sagittarius. Sagittarius is the sign of religion. Saturn symbolizes India. So, in simple terms, it means Jupiter in Libra will shake hands with Saturn in Sagittarius. Therefore, there will be harmony and peace. I may be right or wrong. But at least I have given you my astrological reasons for peace and harmony.

Putin and Russia: Putin, the boss of Russia, is a Libran. Let me clarify a misunderstanding. Most readers think that Libra is the sign of peace, balance and harmony. I agree with it. But this is only half the story. The real story is that Libra is all about relationships. Relationships can be both harmonious and discordant, even hateful. Therefore, Libra stands for both love and war.

This explains the hostility between Putin and Ukraine. Both are tough. Both mean well. But they are at loggerheads. It is a no-win situation. But in 2017 Jupiter will be in Libra and as Putin is a Libran he will be liberal and therefore peace is possible. Putin has both the Sun (glory) and Saturn (strange moods, strong likes and dislikes, stubbornness) in the sign Libra. Even for me it becomes difficult to find out the real Putin. The best part of it is that he can turn on great charm when he wants it. This man is very complex, self-contradictory, at times very liberal and at times rigid and immovable like a mountain. Of all the leaders, he is the most mysterious. The period 2018–19 will not be happy for Putin.

Bashar al-Assad, Putin and the World: The entire Middle East comes under the influence of Taurus, Scorpio and, to a certain extent, Sagittarius. This is my personal observation after sixty years of astrological predictions.

Bashar al-Assad is a Virgo with the master number eleven. There are only two master numbers, eleven and twenty-two. You cannot be born on the thirty-third or forty-fourth day of a month and so on. Born on a Saturday, the day of Saturn, he is tough, determined and responsible. His idea of taking responsibility may not be our idea of it. That, dear readers, is a different matter. That is the source of all the conflicts of the world. Secondly, Assad has Mercury, the sign of sharpness, craftiness, selfishness and wisdom (yes craftiness and wisdom very surprisingly can go together) in the sign Virgo, the sign of service. In other words, he is tough and intelligent. I believe that despite tremendous opposition, he will survive. There will be an end to the conflict by late 2017.

I must explain that sometimes I use different methods for prediction. Astrology comes down to self-analysis. Once you have analysed yourself, you find the courage and conviction to analyse others. Of course, it is impossible to analyse anybody completely. Something always slips away from you. That is the X factor. This X factor can only be revealed by poets and sages.

China: Ganesha says that his devotee Bejan finds China under the influence of Libra and Cancer. There may be a touch of Capricorn to it as well. The leader Xi Jinping was born on 15 June 1953. He is certainly smart, flexible, a good politician and very nimble. I believe that in 2017 China will be able to contribute to world peace. There may be a compromise with Tibet.

Japan: By mundane astrology Japan comes under Virgo, Cancer and Libra. There is a certain contradiction, dichotomy or separation in the mindset of Japan. The leader Shinzo Abe was born on 21 September 1954. Like Modi he is a Virgo, with Jupiter in the noble sign Cancer. This man is worth his weight in gold. Good for Japan and good for the world.

Pakistan: Pakistan comes under the sign Sagittarius, Aries and Capricorn. Sharif, the Capricorn leader, may have a tough time. But if he is in the saddle in 2017 (I am writing this piece on 13 December 2015) he will certainly contribute towards a happy relationship with India and the world. This man is practical and, therefore, reasonable and open to dialogue. Dialogue is the key to happy relationships anywhere and in all situations.

A Confession: I have with me the horoscope of Einstein, one of the greatest geniuses the world has seen. He was born on 14 March 1879. I must make it clear that it is impossible to identify the cause of his genius, but the sun in the intuitive sign Pisces, the moon (the mind) in the sign Sagittarius, signifying space and travel, and Jupiter in Aquarius, the sign of technology, may help explain his genius. Strictly speaking, genius defies complete explanation. Surprisingly enough, Steve Jobs, the founder of Apple, was also a Piscean.

Finally, for all my predictions and good wishes, there has been no compromise between India and Pakistan so far; the Arabs and Israel are also in conflict. Perhaps 2017 is the answer. But it certainly proves that while astrology can help us make accurate predictions, it also fails from time to time and falls flat.

I openly admit that I have gone wrong on India–Pakistan and Arab–Israel relationships. I am sure that my feelings and love for peace have come in the way of my astrological analysis. Luckily, I am sure that in the course of time, technology and spirituality will combine and change the very fabric of our personality and being. All this will have an extra thrust between 2017 and 2022.

Key Dates for 2017

ARIES

January: 3–5, 8–9, 13–15, 18–19, 22–23, 31; **February:** 1, 4–6, 14–15, 19–20, 23–24, 27–28; **March:** 4–5, 9–10, 14–15, 18–19, 26–28, 31; **April:** 1–4, 10–11, 14–15, 23–24, 27–29; **May:** 6–9, 12–13, 20–21, 25–26, 30–31; **June:** 4–5, 8–9, 12–13, 16–18, 21–22, 27; **July:** 1–2, 5–7, 10–11, 14–15, 18–20, 29–30; **August:** 2–3, 10–11, 15–16, 24–26, 29–30; **September:** 2–3, 6–9, 11–12, 16–17, 25–26; **October:** 1, 4–5, 8–10, 13–15, 18–19, 23–24, 31; **November:** 1, 4–6, 14–16, 19–20, 24–26, 27–28; **December:** 2–3, 12–13, 17–18, 21–22, 25–26, 29–30.

Special Note: October is for trips and ties. For Aries, this is perhaps the best month to meet and interact with people, advises Ganesha.

TAURUS

January: 1–2, 11–12, 16–17, 24–26, 29–30; **February:** 2–3, 7–8, 12–13, 16, 21–22, 26; **March:** 1–3, 6–8, 13–15, 20–21, 29–30; **April:** 3–4, 8–10, 15–17, 24–26, 30–31; **May:** 1, 6–8, 13–15, 18–19, 24–24, 27–28; **June:** 1–3, 11–12, 14–15, 19–20, 23–25, 28–30; **July:** 3–4, 8–10, 12, 13, 16–17, 21–22, 26–27, 21–31; **August:** 1, 4–5, 8–9, 12–14, 17–18, 22–23, 27–28, 31; **September:** 1, 4–5, 9–10, 13–15, 17, 18–20, 23–24, 27–28; **October:** 2–3, 6–7, 11–12, 16–17, 21–22, 25–26, 29–30; **November:** 2–3, 7–8, 12–13, 16–17, 20–22, 26–27, 29–30; **December:** 1, 4–6, 14–15, 19–20, 23–24, 27–28, 31.

Special Note: May is very important for contacts and communications. July is for feeling the pulse of the masses, a key month for emotional tidal waves. September is an outstanding month for children, romance, entertainment, meeting people en masse. November is for love, marriage, partnerships and journeys. People will seek you out, even if you hide in a cave!

GEMINI

January: 2–4, 8–10, 13–15, 22–23, 27–28; February: 1, 4–6, 9–11, 14–15, 19–20, 23–24, 27–28; March: 4–5, 9–10, 14–15, 18–19, 22–23, 31; April: 1–2, 5–8, 14–15, 18–19, 23–24, 27–29; May: 2–4, 12–13, 16–17, 20–21, 25–26, 30–31; June: 4–5, 8–9, 12–13, 16–17, 21–22, 26–27; July: 1–2, 5–6, 10–12, 18–20, 23–25, 28–29; August: 2–3, 6–7, 15–16, 19–21, 24–26, 29–30; September: 2–3, 6–8, 11–12, 16–17, 21–22, 29–30; October: 1, 8–10, 13–15, 18–19, 27–28, 31; November: 1, 4–6, 9–11, 14–16, 23–24, 27–28; December: 2–3, 6–9, 17–18, 21–22, 26, 29–30.

Special Note: In February, trust people to inspire you to give your best shot. June is your launch pad to people and places. October is for loving and being cherished. Partnerships range from passionate to platonic. In December you are loved and hated in equal measure.

CANCER

January: 1–2, 6–7, 11–12, 16–18, 20–21, 24–26, 29–30; February: 2–3, 7–8, 12–13, 16–17, 21–22, 25–26; March: 1–3, 6–8, 11–12, 16–17, 20–21, 23–25, 29–30; April: 3–4, 8–9, 14–15, 16–17, 20–22, 30; May: 1, 5–6, 10–11, 14–15, 17–19, 22–24, 27–29; June: 1–3, 10–11, 14–15, 19–20, 24–25, 28–30; July: 3–4, 8–9, 11–13, 16–17, 21–22, 26–28, 30–31; August: 1, 4–5, 8–9, 12–14, 17–18, 22–23, 27–28, 31; September: 1, 4–6, 9–10, 13–15, 18–20, 23–24, 27–28; October: 2–4, 6–9, 11–12, 16–17, 21–22, 25–26, 28–30; November: 2–3, 7–8, 12–13, 17–18, 21–22, 25–26, 29–30; December: 1, 4–6, 8–10, 11, 14–16, 19–20, 23–25, 27–28, 31.

Special Note: In January, be brave, be valiant, be demonstrative. Strangers and foreigners may walk into your life in March. May is for group activities and social gatherings. July, your birth month, is excellent for sensations and sensibilities. November is for bonding and mating.

LEO

January: 3–5, 8–10, 18–19, 27–28, 31; **February:** 1–2, 5–7, 9–11, 14–15, 23–24, 27–28; **March:** 4–5, 9–10, 14–15, 23–24, 27–28; **April:** 1–2, 11–13, 19–20, 23–25, 28–29; **May:** 3–4, 8–10, 16–17, 20–21, 25–26, 30–31; **June:** 4–6, 8–9, 16–18, 21–22, 26–27; **July:** 1–2, 5–6, 10–11, 14–15, 18–20, 28–29; **August:** 2–3, 6–7, 9–12, 15–16, 19–21, 23–26, 29–30; **September:** 1–3, 6–8, 11–12, 16–17, 21–22, 25–26, 29–30; **October:** 1–2, 4–5, 8–10, 18–20, 23–24, 27–28, 31; **November:** 1–2, 7–8, 14–16, 21–22, 27–28; **December:** 2–3, 7–9, 12–14, 17–18, 21–22, 25–26, 30–31.

Special Note: Group activities and social circles in June are where you make eye contact with people and study sign language.

VIRGO

January: 1–2, 6–7, 11–12, 16–17, 21–22, 24–26, 29–30; **February:** 1–3, 7–8, 12–13, 16–17, 21–22, 25–27; **March:** 1–3, 6–8, 12–13, 16–18, 21–22, 25–26, 29–31; **April:** 3–4, 8–10, 13–14, 17–18, 21–22, 25–27, 30; **May:** 1, 5–6, 10–11, 14–15, 18–19, 22–24, 28–29; **June:** 1–3, 6–7, 10–11, 14–15, 19–20, 23–25, 28–30; **July:** 4–5, 8–9, 12–13, 16–18, 21–23, 26–28, 31; **August:** 1, 4–5, 8–10, 12–14, 17–18, 22–23, 27–28, 31; **September:** 1, 4–5, 9–11, 14–15, 19–20, 24–25, 28–29; **October:** 2–3, 6–7, 11–12, 16–17, 21–22, 25–26, 29–30; **November:** 2–3, 7–8, 12–13, 17–18, 21–22, 25–26, 29–30; **December:** 1, 6–7, 10–11, 15–16, 20–21, 23–24, 27–29.

Special Note: January will set the pace for the whole year for contacts, partnerships and travel. The doors of relationships hinge on the month of March. In May, claim your heart and money. The home and the outside world meet in July. September is for renewing old ties, forming new attachments. September means relationships. Remember that correspondence, trips and calls are important ways for meeting people.

LIBRA

January: 2–4, 8–10, 13–14, 18–19, 22–23, 27–28, 31; February: 1, 4–6, 9–11, 14–15, 19–20, 23–24, 27–28; March: 4–5, 9–10, 14–15, 18–19, 22–23, 26–28, 31; April: 1, 5–6, 10–11, 14–15, 18–19, 23–24, 27–29; May: 2–4, 7–8, 12–14, 17–18, 20–21, 25–26, 30–31; June: 4–5, 8–9, 12–13, 16–17, 21–22, 26–27; July: 1–2, 5–7, 14–15, 18–20, 23–25, 28–30; August: 1–3, 6–7, 10–11, 15–17, 19–21, 24–26, 29–30; September: 2–3, 6–8, 11–12, 16–17, 21–22, 25–26, 29–30; October: 1, 4–5, 9–10, 14–15, 19–20, 23–24, 27–28, 31; November: 1–2, 5–6, 9–11, 14–16, 19–20, 23–24, 27–28; December: 2–3, 7–8, 12–14, 17–18, 21–22, 25–26, 29–30.

Special Note: In the second half of February, you sway to love's magic. In April, there is a chance to remarry and enjoy life to the full. In June you will be reaching out in different ways to an assorted multitude and paradoxically find yourself. August is a month of acceptance and rejection, love and hate, likes and dislikes, gatherings and meets. In October your tentacles will reach far and wide, and money will speak its universal language. December is definitely the crowning glory for love, luck and laughter.

SCORPIO

January: 1–2, 6–7, 11–12, 16–17, 20–21, 24–26, 29–30; February: 2–3, 7–8, 12–13, 16–18, 21–22, 25–26; March: 1–3, 6–8, 11–13, 16–17, 20–21, 24–25, 29–30; April: 3–4, 8–9, 12–13, 16–17, 20–21, 25–26, 30; May: 1, 5–6, 9–12, 14–15, 18–19, 22–24, 27–29; June: 1–3, 5–6, 10–11, 14–15, 19–20, 23–25, 28–30; July: 3–4, 8–9, 12–13, 16–17, 21–22, 26–27, 30–31; August: 1, 4–5, 8–9,

12–14, 17–18, 22–23, 27–28, 31; **September:** 1, 4–5, 9–10, 13–15, 18–20, 23–24, 27–29; **October:** 2–3, 6–7, 11–12, 16–17, 20–22, 25–26, 29–30; **November:** 2–3, 7–8, 12–13, 17–18, 21–22, 25–26, 29–30; **December:** 1, 3–5, 9–11, 14–16, 19–20, 23–24, 27–28, 31.

Special Note: January is the month for marriage to martial arts; from love to fight is your range. May is for beauty and blossom, but alas, bubbles could burst. In July the domestic scene becomes part of a much wider universe. A collage of relationships is yours. September is excellent for interacting with people and yet maintaining privacy. November is a fast-paced, action-packed month; therefore, relationships will keep on changing.

SAGITTARIUS

January: 3–5, 8–10, 14–16, 18–19, 23–24 ,27–28, 31; **February:** 1, 4–5, 9–11, 14–15, 19–20, 23–24, 27–28; **March:** 4–5, 9–10, 14–15, 18–19, 22–23, 26–28, 31; **April:** 1, 5–7, 10–11, 14–15, 18–19, 23–24, 27–29; **May:** 2–4, 7–9, 12–13, 16–17, 20–22, 25–27, 30–31; **June:** 3–5, 8–9, 12–13, 16–18, 21–22, 26–27; **July:** 1–2, 5–7, 10–11, 14–15, 18–19, 23–25, 28–29; **August:** 2–3, 6–7, 10–11, 15–16, 19–21, 24–25, 29–30; **September:** 2–3, 6–8, 11–12, 16–17, 21–22, 25–26, 29–30; **October:** 1, 4–5, 8–10, 13–15, 18–20, 27–28, 31; **November:** 1, 4–6, 9–11, 14–16, 19–20, 23–24, 27–28; **December:** 2–3, 7–8, 12–13 ,17–18, 21–22, 25–26, 29–30.

Special Note: In January people just start coming into your life, like late arrivals at a party. In April the cannons of hate and love start booming. June is actually a halfway house for both romance and friendship. Marriage or official engagement cannot be ruled out. In August even your boss or superior could be bowled over! In December, everything comes together for you – a month of wish-fulfilment.

CAPRICORN

January: 1–2, 6–7, 16–17, 20–21, 24–26, 29–30; **February:** 2–3, 7–8, 12–13, 16–18, 20–21, 25–26; **March:** 1–3, 6–8, 11–13, 16–17, 20–21, 24–25, 29–30; **April:** 3–4, 8–9, 12–13, 16–17, 20–22, 25–26, 30; **May:** 1, 5–6, 10–11, 14–15, 18–19, 22–24, 27–29; **June:** 1–3, 6–7, 10–11, 14–15, 19–20, 23–25, 28–30; **July:** 4–5, 8–9, 12–13, 16–18, 21–23, 26–28, 31; **August:** 1, 4–5, 8–9, 12–14, 17–18, 22–23, 27–28, 31; **September:** 1, 4–5, 9–10, 13–15, 18–20, 23–24, 27–28; **October:** 2–4, 6–7, 11–12, 16–17, 21–22, 25–26, 29–30; **November:** 2–3, 7–8, 12–13, 17–18, 21–22, 25–26, 29–30; **December:** 1, 4–6, 9–11, 14–16, 19–20, 23–24, 27–28, 31.

Special Note: In January, through contacts and communication, you could meet your fair lady or your knight in shining armour. March is for personal matters. May is for old flames and new fires! July is both the meeting point and the melting point. In September everything at a long distance will be a close-up for your heart and imagination. Style and substance have a marriage this month.

AQUARIUS

January: 3–5, 8–10, 13–15, 18–19, 22–23, 27–29, 31; **February:** 1, 4–6, 9–11, 14–15, 19–20, 23–24, 27–28; **March:** 4–5, 9–10, 14–15, 8–19, 22–23, 26–28, 31; **April:** 1–2, 10–11, 14–15, 18–19, 23–24, 27–29; **May:** 2–4, 7–8, 12–13, 16–17, 20–21, 25–26, 30–31; **June:** 4–5, 9–10, 13–14, 17–18, 21–22, 26–27; **July:** 1–2, 5–7, 10–11, 14–15, 18–20, 23–25, 28–29; **August:** 2, 6–7, 10–11, 15–16, 20–22, 24–26, 29–30; **September:** 2–3, 6–8, 11–12, 16–17, 20–21, 25–26, 29–30; **October:** 1, 4–5, 8–10, 13–15, 18–20, 23–24, 27–28, 31; **November:** 1, 4–6, 9–11, 14–16, 19–20, 23–24, 27–28; **December:** 2–3, 7–8, 12–13, 17–18, 21–22, 25–26, 29–30.

Special Note: Expect the strange, the bizarre, and the unusual to bind you with others in February. April is not the cruellest, but one of the happiest months for you. In June the cornucopia of love and exuberance will be yours to overflowing. Your ability to fan out to others will literally decide your heartbeats in August. In October sweet companionship will lead to genuine happiness, rare and ever so ennobling. In December the rainbow of relationships shines ever so sweetly for you. Pick any colour.

PISCES

January: 1–2, 6–7, 11–12, 16–17, 20–21, 24–26, 29–30; **February:** 2–3, 7–8, 12–13, 16–18, 21–22, 25–26; **March:** 1–3, 6–8, 11–13, 16–17, 20–22, 24–25, 29–30; **April:** 3–4, 8–9, 12–13, 16–17, 20–21, 25–26, 30; **May:** 1, 5–6, 10–11, 14–15, 18–19, 22–24, 27–29; **June:** 1–3, 6–7, 10–11, 14–15, 19–20, 23–25, 28–30; **July:** 3–4, 8–9, 12–13, 16–17, 21–22, 26–27, 30–31; **August:** 1, 4–5, 8–9, 12–14, 17–18, 22–23, 27–28, 31; **September:** 1, 4–5, 7–10, 13–15, 18–20, 23–24, 27–28; **October:** 2–3, 6–7, 11–12, 16–17, 21–22, 25–26, 29–30; **November:** 2–3, 7–8, 12–13, 17–18, 21–22, 25–26, 29–30; **December:** 1, 4–6, 9–11, 14–16, 19–20, 23–24, 27–28, 31.

Special Note: January makes your heart flutter with the first gentle breeze of romance. You could even develop wings! March, for you, is not the ides of March but the merry madness of March. You could be a Mad Hatter! In May your love may very well come in a car/a scooter/a bicycle made for two. You will hum a song, thrum a guitar, sing of love in July. September is for love at first sight, or at full flight! In November you will be the hunter with a supersonic, telescopic-sight rifle. Target will be blown away or brought home.

Your Birth Time Reveals You

(By Western astrology only)

(Sunrise will naturally change with the seasons. Therefore, slight adjustments will have to be made in the time.)

Birth time – 4.00 a.m. to 6.00 a.m.: Your sign is in the first house, giving you a good constitution and self-confidence. You will be assertive and will have sudden good fortune. It also assures success.

Birth time – 6.00 a.m. to 8.00 a.m.: Your sign is in the twelfth house, which makes for many mysterious happenings that cannot be explained away easily. It would be best, therefore, to work on a tight schedule and keep a cool head. Expenses could outrun income.

Birth time – 8.00 a.m. to 10.00 a.m.: Your sign is in the eleventh house, which means plenty of friends, social life and the money necessary for it. Your bread, butter and jam will come from knowing your well-wishers and retaining your friends. Many times, you'll find that you earn a little more than you deserve, or get into money without sweating it out.

Birth time – 10.00 a.m. to 12.00 noon: Your sign is in the tenth house, a very strong place to be in according to both Western and Indian astrology. This assures a good position in your chosen work. It also means the successful completion of projects and plans. It would prove best to be on your own. The misuse of power and a bossy attitude could get you into trouble.

Birth time – 12.00 noon to 2.00 p.m.: Your sign is in the ninth house, or the house which indicates journeys, philosophy, religion, higher mind, philanthropy and publicity by all the different media. You should be popular, famous and rich. It is the house of good fortune, and so you may expect lady luck to smile on you. You will become benevolent.

Birth time – 2.00 p.m. to 4.00 p.m.: Your sign is in the eighth house, which shows a tendency to get involved or tangled in money matters, say, loans, legacies, trusts, public funds, banks and so on. Many astrologers also connect it with sex and accidents. Therefore, a degree of self-control and caution is advisable in your case. Legal matters will crop up from time to time.

Birth time – 4.00 p.m. to 6.00 p.m.: Your sign is in the seventh house, commonly called the house of partnerships (all kinds). Evidently, marriage affects you more than it does others. So do try to make it a success, even if it means working hard for it. Also, you will find that you will have to deal directly with the general public. Choose a profession or business which leads you on to direct contact or dealing with people. Since the seventh house is also the house of your enemy or enemies in life, legal issues might give you sleepless nights. However, it is a strong placing for the sun. You will make news.

Birth time – 6.00 p.m. to 8.00 p.m.: Your sign is in the sixth house, which means all will depend upon the cooperation you get from colleagues and subordinates. It is also an indication of social service and you will have much to do with the health and hygiene of people. This position of the sun favours work in which you have to attend to details. You will be meticulous and painstaking, qualities which make for success and respect in the long run.

Birth time – 8.00 p.m. to 10.00 p.m.: Your sign is in the fifth house, giving you innate artistic ability and talent. It also gives you an optimistic outlook on life and a willingness to take chances. Your hobby can be made into a profession or a vocation. Also, your heart will reach out to people easily and spontaneously, and this could make you responsive to all outside influences. You could play the great lover both on stage and in real life. But try not to overdo it.

Birth time – 10.00 p.m. to 12.00 midnight: Your sign is in the fourth house, which is a splendid placing for home and property. You could gain through any work tied up with land, real estate, farms and so on. Since home signifies parents, they will affect life for better or for worse to a remarkable extent. Be more outgoing.

Birth time – 12.00 midnight to 2.00 a.m.: Your sign is in the third house and it foretells marked intellectual ability and a love of travel and high adventure. In fact, it favours all media of transport and communication, say, journalism, TV and so on. Also, your brothers, sisters and neighbours will either make you or mar you. But it is certain that you will have much to do with them. This position of the sun makes you fond of company, though you will not be very choosy about it. It is also excellent for stimulating social life.

Birth time – 2.00 a.m. to 4.00 a.m.: Your sign is in the second house or the house of finance and family. Naturally, it means that you'll be able to make money, if not keep it. In Indian astrology, the second house stands for speech and food. You could be an ideal host, a great orator. Yes, you should be in money too; other planets aspect your Sun favourably.

The Aquarian Age

Ganesha says we are in the Aquarian age. It stands for humanity as a whole. In other words, it stands for all of us coming together, becoming united, seeking unity through the mighty power of technology and spirituality. Technology will marry spirituality. Therefore, it is very obvious that all the religions of the world will finally find a single golden thread running through them. That golden thread will be made of unanimity, tolerance, peace, and finally, evolution. If this is the final fate of all of us, it stands to reason that we will have to be open-minded and tolerant. Equality will be the guiding principle for all of us. We are reasonably intelligent and forward-looking. We know very well that change is in the very nature and fabric of society and the world. If we do not change with the times and open the doors of our heart, mind and spirit, we will certainly perish. The simple universal truth is: adapt and adopt or be extinct or die. Our choice.

Jupiter in Virgo

Today, as I am writing this piece (16 December 2015), Jupiter is in the sign Virgo, by Western astrology. What does it really mean?

The sign Virgo has an obvious reference to the Virgin. The Virgin is clean and pure. Jupiter, the heavyweight of the Zodiac, is the planet of all-round prosperity. Therefore, he is called the mighty protector of the entire cosmos. If we combine the good-luck planet Jupiter with the clean and pure sign Virgo it could well mean that climate change, personal hygiene and cleanliness will be activated and emphasized, and the results will be excellent. Perhaps, in a small way, this explains the mighty climate change deal in Paris, in December 2015. As *The New York Times* says, 'It represents the biggest shift we have ever seen on this global crisis.'

Jupiter will be in Virgo till 9 September 2016. By this time the real purification of Mother Ganga will come into active operation. That, to this Ganesha devotee, is the master key to the prosperity and greatness of Bharat that is India. I am now eighty-five years old. I stand or fall by this prediction.

Important Announcement

Our Ganesha devotee Bejan Daruwalla has moved from Mumbai to Ahmedabad. His Ahmedabad address is:

Bejan Daruwalla
Astrologer and Columnist
C/o Nastur Daruwalla
A-5, Spectrum Towers
Opposite Police Stadium
Shahibag
Ahmedabad 380004
India

Telephone
079-32954387
09825470377
08141234275

Email
info@bejandaruwalla.com
bejandaruwalla@rediffmail.com

Website: www.bejandaruwalla.com